Jew Among Jews

Jew Among Jews
Rehabilitating Paul

Kimberly Ambrose

WIPF & STOCK · Eugene, Oregon

JEW AMONG JEWS
Rehabilitating Paul

Copyright © 2015 Kimberly Ambrose. All rights reserved. Except for brief quotations in critical publications or reviews, no part of this book may be reproduced in any manner without prior written permission from the publisher. Write: Permissions. Wipf and Stock Publishers, 199 W. 8th Ave., Suite 3, Eugene, OR 97401.

Wipf & Stock
An Imprint of Wipf and Stock Publishers
199 W. 8th Ave., Suite 3
Eugene, OR 97401

www.wipfandstock.com

ISBN 13: 978-1-4982-1846-7

Manufactured in the U.S.A.   11/16/2015

Dedicated with gratitude to my supervisor,
Dr. William S. Campbell, who critically, patiently,
and gently taught me to accomplish this research.

Contents

Preface: My Journey | xi
Abbreviations | xiii

Chapter 1: Why Paul's Jewishness Matters | 1
    A Pharisee of Pharisees | 1
    Turning against Tradition | 4

Chapter 2: Paul and Hellenistic Thought | 6
    Baur: "A New Religion" | 6
    Contemporary Scholars' Views | 9
        • Boyarin: Platonic Paul | 9
        • Engberg-Pedersen: Neither Jew nor Greek | 11
        • Malherbe, Betz, and Stowers | 11
        • Barclay, Sampley, and Deming | 13
        • Hock, van Unnik, Longenecker, and Ehrensperger | 16
    To What Extent Was Paul Influenced by Hellenism? | 20

Chapter 3: More Recent Views of Paul | 23
    In Search of the Historical Paul | 24
    A Different Kind of Judaism | 26
    The Political Apostle | 28
    Views of Paul's Embeddedness in Judaism | 29
        • Beker: Apocalyptic | 30

Contents

- Tomson: Halakhah in Paul's Letters | 34
- Nanos: The Shema in Romans | 38

Paul's Thought and Jewish Roots | 41

Chapter 4: Divergent Perceptions of Paul's Theology | 44

The New Perspective | 45
- A Problem with Judaism | 48
- "Covenant Nomism" | 53
- Reaction and Differentiation | 55
- No Real Consensus | 57

The Center of Paul's Theology | 58
The Next Step | 62

Chapter 5: How Paul Uses Scripture | 63

Paul, Pharisees, and the Use of Midrash | 65
Paul's Form of Argumentation | 68
Two Examples in Romans | 74
- Romans 10:5–8 | 74
- Romans 2:24 | 81

The Consistency of Paul's Interpretation | 84

Chapter 6: Paul, Judaism, and Unbelieving Jews | 86

How Does Luke Portray Paul? | 86
Did Paul Turn His Back on Judaism? | 94
- Divergent Views on Galatians 1:13–17 | 95
- Evaluation | 102
- Paul's Focal Point | 106

Did Paul Advocate Exclusion of the Jews from Salvation? | 110
- Paul's Use of Scripture in Galatians 4:21–31 | 110
- Who Did Paul Refer to as "Cast Out"? | 113
- Views of the New Consensus | 115
  Excluding Both Jews and Jewish Christians | 115
  Excluding Only Jewish Christians | 116
- Not Exclusion but Restoration | 121
- Conclusion | 122

Did Paul Curse Jews Who Opposed the Gospel? | 122
- Paul's Use of Ἰουδαῖοι | 124

- Are All Jews "Christ-Killers"? | 125
- Are All Jews under God's Wrath Forever? | 126
- Did Paul Oppose Judaism and the Jewish People? | 129

The Controversy over the Mosaic Covenant | 130
Did Paul Consider Judaism Rubbish? | 134
Did Paul Deny the Election of Israel? | 136
- Identifying "All Israel" | 143

Did Paul Urge Believers to Separate? | 148
Did Paul Encourage Abandoning Jewish Identity? | 150
- The Antioch Incident | 154
- Scholars' Views on Galatians 2:11–14 | 154
- Evaluation | 161
- A Lesser Commandment | 163
- Did Paul Abandon His Jewish Identity? | 164

Gentile Believers' Identity | 166
A Faithful Jew | 168

Chapter 7: Paul and True Judaism | 169
Love beyond Purpose | 170
More Like Marriage | 172
Redemption Not Completed | 173
The Promise of Future Restoration | 174
Is the Church the "Israel" of Galatians 6:16? | 176
Equal in Christ | 180

Chapter 8: Paul, a Hebrew of Hebrews | 182
What We Know of Paul | 183
- Paul's Way of Thinking | 183
- Paul and Scripture | 183
- Paul and Covenant | 184
- Paul and Jewishness | 185

Paul, Defined | 186

Bibliography | 187
Author Index | 207
Ancient Document Index | 211

Preface

My Journey

SINCE I BECAME A student of the Bible, I have become aware of a problematic contradiction between the "Old Testament God" and the God of the New Testament. Especially when I started to study the Pauline epistles, I found that many pastors and scholars interpreted Paul as being opposed to the Old Testament in general. In other words, these thinkers believe that Paul abandoned the Mosaic Law (the Torah) and set aside the Jewish people, and further that Paul had breached from first-century Judaism because he saw Mosaic Law as legalistic, whereas the gospel is based on grace.

At that point I started to raise questions. Something didn't add up here. If God is the one God of the universe, how can his nature possibly differ from Old Testament to New Testament? This quest for clarification led me to research this subject at the University of Wales, Lampeter, UK, and I submitted the doctoral dissertation that would become the basis for this book in 2008 under the title of "The Portrayal of Paul as Jewish in the Light of Contemporary Scholarship." I could not have completed this research without the encouragement and support of many others.

I especially thank my supervisor, Dr. William S. Campbell. Without his critical guidance and encouragement, this book would not have been completed. I must also extend my gratitude to Dr. George Pierce. Without his help and encouragement, I could not have finished this book. I especially want to thank Dr. John Fischer, who taught me and gave me a foundation for my work. I also express gratitude to Dr. Wellington W. Whittlesey

Preface

and Dr. Myron M. Miller, who gave me motivation and encouragement to start this research project.

I would like to express appreciation to all the scholars who taught me to think critically. I could not list all their names here, but I am thankful to so many who gave me support and encouragement. I especially thank my husband, Gene, who has patiently supported and encouraged me all along. Also, this work would not have been possible without my mother's prayers and my brother's and sisters' love. I am especially thankful to my teacher Noh Peng-Gu, who never saw this work completed. He is the one who originally gave me a challenge and a motivation to begin the research that has culminated in the book before you.

Kimberly Ambrose

Abbreviations

AGJU	Arbeiten zur Geschichte des antiken Judentums und Des Urchristentums
AnBib	*Analecta biblica*
Bib	*Biblica*
BibInt	*Biblical Interpretation*
BTB	*Biblical Theology Bulletin*
CTR	*Criswell Theological Review*
HNT	Handbuch zum Neuen Testament
HUCA	*Hebrew Union College Annual*
IB	*Interpreter's Bible*
IBS	*Irish Biblical Studies*
ICC	International Critical Commentary
JBL	*Journal of Biblical Literature*
JBV	*Journal of Beliefs and Values*
JSNT	*Journal for the Study of the New Testament*
JSOT	*Journal for the Study of the Old Testament*
KJV	King James Version (of the Bible)
LXX	*Septuagiant* (the Old Testament in Greek)
NASB	New American Standard Bible

Abbreviations

NEB	New English Bible
NIV	New International Version (of the Bible)
NPNF	*Nicene and Post-Nicene Fathers*
NRSV	New Revised Standard Version (of the Bible)
NTS	*New Testament Studies*
PG	J. Migne, *Patrologia graeca*
RB	*Revue Biblique*
RSR	*Recherches de science religieuse*
RSV	Revised Standard Version (of the Bible)
SBL	Society of Biblical Literature
TS	*Theological Studies*
VT	*Vetus Testamentum*
WTJ	*Westminster Theological Journal*
WUNT	Wissenschaftliche Untersuchungen zum Neuen Testament

1

Why Paul's Jewishness Matters

MISUNDERSTANDING OF PAUL HAD already started in his lifetime—and his letters offer many examples of these misunderstandings. Through the centuries, Paul has continued to be misunderstood by both Jews and Gentiles, especially in relation to his view of the law and the covenant.

However, with the discovery of the Dead Sea Scrolls and other texts, many new sources now enable us to better understand Paul's first-century background. The outcome of this and other developments in scholarship offers potential for a new scholarly attempt at discovering the historical Paul.

A Pharisee of Pharisees

Paul's own self-understanding is crucial because he, as a Pharisee, struggled with the law and sought to comprehend it afresh in the light of Jesus the Messiah. In the epistle to the Romans, he used the term "law" more than seventy times, which demonstrates its significance in Paul's thought. As a Jewish scholar of Torah, Paul had formerly been a champion of law-keeping—and even as a Christ-follower, he was an expert commentator on giving midrashim of the law in the Pharisaic tradition. For this reason, when we try to understand Paul's conception of the law, we ought to understand him and his epistles in his own cultural milieu and in his own time, instead of in the light of later developments.

Paul's understanding of the law is important as a corrective to the tendency of Christians throughout the centuries to misinterpret the law. Christians, especially in the last two centuries, have sometimes equated the law with legalism and regarded the law as being totally abolished. Some more radical scholars believe that Paul set aside the law, the Jewish people, and the Old Testament. This sort of belief is not entirely new, but emerged as early as 144 CE with Marcion, who was condemned in Rome for denying the Old Testament and for proposing only one gospel, among other things. Despite this, even today some scholars continue to underestimate the place of the Old Testament and the Jewish people in God's covenant.

Paul understood that the consistency of God's grace is demonstrated through his people Israel and manifested most completely through Jesus the Messiah. Paul proclaimed God as faithful and Jesus as the one who was promised. When he preached against those who misused the law, Paul sought to demonstrate righteousness by faith from the old covenant and reapplied this to the new covenant. He certainly did not generalize and stereotype all first-century Judaism as legalistic. Nowhere does Paul say that Jews should not keep the Torah. Rather, he used the Old Testament (the law) to give guidance on how to walk with God, even when the Christ had come (e.g., Rom 13:8–10).

Although Paul was clearly a product of both Judaism and Hellenism, Paul's thinking is, in my perspective, more properly understood within the context of the Jewish thought of his time. In his theological thinking, Paul did not abandon his earlier Pharisaic training, but emerged and developed from it. This being the case, we would do well to ask how Paul's thought differed from that of other Jews. One key difference originates in Paul's calling—which in many essentials was like that of the prophet Jeremiah, but possibly also very similar to Ezekiel's.

In Paul's understanding, God had personally revealed himself and guided Paul to an understanding of the law's true meaning, which pointed to Jesus, the Messiah, as it's ultimate goal (Rom 10:4). If Paul was properly trained in Jerusalem in accordance with Luke's image of him, which scholars believe holds some historical foundation, then Paul had authority to interpret the Torah in relation to Christ. Paul made good use of his Pharisaic training by applying it to new contexts in the light of Christ. As a person brought up in the Diaspora, Paul read and used the Septuagint and communicated the gospel in Greek. However, the basis of his thought patterns appears to have been predominantly Jewish.

Why Paul's Jewishness Matters

Paul, as a Pharisee within first-century Judaism—a culture that held an expectation of the messianic age—transformed his theology after his encounter with Christ. In other words, he renewed his theological thought in the light of Jesus, the Messiah, rather than founding a new religion (e.g., Rom 3:31).

Paul used Pharisaic methods to exegete the law in the light of the actualization of the Messiah's presence in Jesus. In Jewish contexts, Paul followed the prescribed pattern of Jewish life, but he was adamant that Christ-following Gentiles should not become Jews (Gal 5:2). He believed that these Gentiles as well as Jewish Christians would be saved through Jesus Christ because of the covenant God made with Abraham.

The reinterpretation Paul achieved in light of Jesus the Messiah was that God made a covenant with Abraham for blessing all nations, both Jews and Gentiles (Gen 15:1–21), and that he demonstrated this covenant through his people—Israel—in history, thus fulfilling the promise he made to his servant Abraham. God faithfully worked out his covenant through Moses (Exod 19; Lev 27) and David (2 Sam 7:5–16; Ps 89:1–37). Finally, God renewed his covenant through Jesus the Messiah, thus affirming his promises to the Jewish people and enabling the Gentiles to enter the kingdom.

For Paul, after God accomplished his covenant through Jesus' sacrificial death and resurrection, the way to salvation was open to Gentiles as well. Though not the first to come to this new understanding, Paul became its most eminent proclaimer. He believed that Jesus called apostles to proclaim this good news first to Jews and then to Gentiles (Rom 1:16). In this sense, God had called Paul as his messenger to Jews but particularly to the Gentiles. God sought the restoration of Israel in a roundabout way via the "fullness" of the Gentiles in Christ (Rom 11:17–25).

Paul—as a Pharisee who had encountered Jesus—regarded himself as called by the resurrected Jesus, who had proved to him that was the Messiah, the promised one. Paul was a faithful Jew who served his Messiah with all his heart throughout his life. No breach occurred between Paul and Judaism or the Jewish people. Paul himself did not abandon the law, his own people, or a Jewish pattern of life, though he interpreted this more broadly than some of his contemporaries, many of whom were critical of his flexibility in eating with Gentiles.

Turning against Tradition

Today, the New Perspective[1] influencing the scholarly community has begun to turn the tide against some traditional interpretations of Paul, and divergent views on Paul's understanding of the law and covenant have emerged. The insight of this New Perspective is significant insofar as it helps us to understand more precisely the social context and cultural background of Paul's theology.

Ever since E. P. Sanders's study characterized first-century Judaism as "covenantal nomism," scholars have begun to discover (or rediscover) that Paul's understanding of first-century Judaism was not legalistic. Although Sanders demonstrated that first-century Judaism was not legalistic, Sanders still reads Paul's epistles in the traditional way, as though Paul had made a breach with Judaism. In the end, Sanders sets Judaism in antithesis to Christianity and holds that Paul created, or was instrumental in creating, a third entity that was neither Jewish nor Gentile.[2] Along with Sanders, contemporary scholars such as Heikki Räisänen,[3] Francis Watson[4] and N. T. Wright[5] hold that Paul left Judaism for various reasons. Taken together, these New Perspective scholars all collectively disagree with the conventional view of whether and why Paul left Judaism,

The New Perspective has gone some way toward redressing the balance in interpretations of the image of Judaism in the New Testament, especially in the area of Pauline scholarship. Yet even New Perspective adherents such as Sanders, Dunn, and Wright still tend to view Paul as somehow rising above or leaving behind his Jewishness. Even after the advent of the New Perspective, there is still a need for Paul to be interpreted from the perspective of his Jewish context, which is what this study seeks to accomplish.

Paul has often been misunderstood because his form of argument, his use of Scripture, his view of Jews and Gentiles in Christ (especially of those Jews who were not convinced that Jesus was Messiah), and his view of what constitutes true Judaism do not seem to conform to our expectations and perceptions of the apostle. We have been accustomed to read his letters as describing someone who was emancipating people from Judaism, as one

---

1. Dunn coined the phrase "the New Perspective," which came to consist of a combination of Sanders' work and Dunn's work. See Dunn, *Jesus, Paul and the Law*, 183–203.
2. Sanders, *Paul, the Law*, 178–210.
3. Räisänen, *Paul and the Law*, 160–202.
4. Watson, *Paul, Judaism*, 56–85, 168–72.
5. Wright, *Paul Really Said*, 38, 82–84.

who sought to obliterate all ethnic distinctions rather than maintain the identity of Jews and Gentiles even in Christ. By building on some New Perspective insights and by developing other more recent insights, this book aims to present a more consistent and credible Paul as a first-century Diaspora Jew organizing a mission to Gentiles.

By researching how scholars have interpreted Paul in various contexts in the past, then re-examining controversial passages from Pauline writings in light of contemporary interpretation, I will seek to demonstrate that Paul did not break with first-century Judaism.

I use Acts as an additional historical source of limited value, even though its historical reliability is still somewhat controversial. Despite the debate among scholars regarding Luke's portrayal of Paul and Paul's own testimony, some studies show significant elements of historical reliability in Acts. Therefore, we should allow some value in Luke's portrayal of Paul, even if some of Luke's views of Paul are disputed. (For example, some scholars dispute whether Luke deliberately portrays Paul as a Pharisee for his own ends: Overman even questions whether Paul is accurately depicted as a Pharisee or whether this image is merely convenient for Christian critiques of Judaism.[6])

Although I, myself, find it difficult to clearly distinguish my own assumptions about Paul from those of my Christian background, I will try to present Paul in his own Jewish context in a way that is fair, balanced, and in keeping with contemporary scholarship.

---

6. Overman, "Kata nomon Pharisaios," 180–93.

2

Paul and Hellenistic Thought

IN THE NINETEENTH CENTURY, Ferdinand Christian Baur[1] and other scholars emphasized Paul's Hellenistic context. Recently, a strong tendency to view Paul mainly from his Hellenistic background in Tarsus has again emerged.[2] This important development is only part of the story. We will first look at how and why some current scholars argue Paul's thought was strongly influenced by Hellenistic thought, even going so far as to consider him as no longer a Jew but a Greek and a proponent of a universal perspective.

Baur: "A New Religion"

"Christianity is the absolute religion, superior to all others because of its spirituality," Baur wrote. "The point of departure for understanding Christianity is Jesus, 'the founder of a new religion.'"[3]

Baur described Judaism as a monotheistic but narrow, racial, and anthropomorphic faith that had been outgrown: "The special superiority which distinguished the Hebrew religion from all the religions of the

---

1. Baur, *Paul the Apostle*, 1:321–81, 2:182–211; ibid., *Church History*. See a more detailed study on Baur in Tyson, *Luke, Judaism*; Baird, *Deism to Tübingen*, 258-68; Kelley, *Racializing Jesus*, 70-80.

2. E.g., Boyarin, *A Radical Jew*; Deming, "Paul and Indifferent Things," 384-97; Samply, *Paul in the Greco-Roman Word*, 4:5-6, 15. I will discuss this later in "Contemporary Scholars' View."

3. Baird, *Deism to Tübingen*, 262.

heathen world was the pure and refined monotheistic idea of God, which from the earliest times had been the essential foundation of the Old Testament faith."[4] Baur also argued that Christianity exhibits a higher consciousness than Judaism. He stressed:

> But on the other hand the Old Testament conceived God as the God, not of the human race, but of a particular nation. And the particularism, the limitation of the blessings and hopes of religion to the Jewish race, which was partly the cause and partly the effect of this conception of God, stood in the strongest contrast to the spirit of Christianity. If the Old Testament notion of God was ever to be a sufficient form for the consciousness of God which belonged to the universal and absolute nature of Christianity, it was necessary that it should first be freed from this national one-sidedness and defectiveness. It was necessary that it should discard all that belonged only to the narrow range of vision of the Jewish theocracy, and that it should no longer, in accordance with the conceptions of antiquity, ascribe to God a human form and human passions.[5]

Although Baur acknowledged that the Acts portrait concerning Paul (with the exception of Acts 13:39) was a Pharisaic Jew, he interpreted Paul only through Gal 2:11–14. In this "Antioch incident," Baur saw conflict between the two apostles over issues relating to Torah and Jewish practices in the early church. According to Baur, in Galatians Paul "emancipated Christianity from Judaism, by freeing it from circumcision, the outward sign of subjection which Judaism wished to impose on it as the necessary condition of salvation."[6] Baur believed that Paul thought the law (Judaism) and faith (Christianity) exist in opposition.

"Now this contrast, which is found deepest and most intense in the individual human consciousness, presents itself also as a great historical contrast in the relation of Judaism and Christianity," Baur asserted. "It was through a breach with Judaism that the apostle's Christian consciousness first took shape, and thus it came about that he regarded Christianity in the main as the opposite of Judaism."[7] In addition, Baur interpreted Acts' main theme as "the hatred that the two Christian groups have against one

---

4. Cf. Tyson, *Luke, Judaism*, 13.
5. Tyson, *Luke, Judaism*, 13–14.
6. Baur, *Paul the Apostle*, 322.
7. Ibid., 2:182.

another and directed toward unbelieving Jews."[8] Also, according to Baur, "Historically, the meeting [Acts 15] resulted in two gospels, two spheres of mission, and a continuing battle between Jewish particularity and Pauline universalism."[9] Paul was primarily moved by a vision of universalism; thus he rejected Jewish particularism.

Even though Baur himself had criticized the use of the Hegelian dialectic between Pauline universalism and Jewish particularism in the writing of history,[10] he eventually adopted this Hegelian view to interpret Paul's epistles as a thesis in contrast to its antithesis in Jewish Christianity such that a synthesis finally emerges in the universal Catholic Church. This perspective is well illustrated in Baur's comments: "That which is presented in its simplest elements in the Epistle to the Galatians, and which in the Epistle to the Romans passes over to the abstract sphere of dogmatic antithesis, widens out in the Epistles to the Corinthians into the full reality of concrete life, with all the complicated relations which must have existed in a Christian church of the earliest period."[11]

According to Shawn Kelley, for Baur, "both the historical and the cultural are informed by the specific views that he inherits from Herder and Hegel"[12]:

> There are three major spiritual principles/peoples who prepare the way for Christianity. The Oriental Jews lack spiritual inwardness and, therefore, their morality is rooted in fear and compulsion

8. Tyson, *Luke, Judaism*, 20.

9. Baird, *Deism to Tübingen*, 264.

10. Cf. Tyson, *Luke, Judaism*, 15. For more detail on Hegelian influence, see Kelley, *Racializing Jesus*, 33–62. According to Kelley's study, "Hegel's Judaism remains external, legalistic, ritualistic, and ceremonial. The honor rendered to God, the subjective side of religion, was still very limited and unspiritual in character, however spiritual the objective conception of Him may have been Judaism occupies a lower level of ethical consciousness than Western Christianity. Judaism's spiritual principle may be the precondition for the West, but the Jewish people remain fundamentally mired in the despotism and cultural atrophy of the East. Jewish monotheism and morality must be dialectically purged of its Jewish particularism and its Oriental despotism before it can become the foundation for Western culture and freedom. *Geist* will be able to simultaneously purge the Jewish principle of its particularism and appropriate this principle as it marches forward. The Jewish people, on the other hand, are not so pliable. Their bad habits and disagreeable temperament cannot be purged, even by *Geist* . . . In Hegel's Judaism, spirit, having separated itself from nature, is recognized as spirit . . . Greek religion is nothing but the concrete embodiment of the Greek spirit" (ibid., 8–9, 60).

11. Baur, *Paul the Apostle*, 1:268.

12. Kelley, *Racializing Jesus*, 79.

and their worship is the embodiment of empty ceremonialism. In a single moment of brilliance, they do provide the world with monotheism, which will form a significant aspect of the objective content of Christianity, but even this is tinged with nationalism, particularism, externality, and sensuality. The Western Greeks are the spiritual antithesis to the Oriental Jews. They are marked by spiritual freedom and subjectivity that is fitting for the Western free nature.[13]

For Baur, Paulinism is the triumph of a new and higher consciousness over Judaism, which he viewed as a "lower state of religious consciousness." It was, Baur concluded, "the narrowing influence of their Jewish standpoint, which naturally increased their inability to raise themselves from their low state of religious consciousness to a higher and a freer one."[14] Until the twentieth century, Baur's view of Paul was dominant among scholars, who continued to interpret Paul almost exclusively in this specific Hellenistic context. But even today recent New Testament studies are still indebted to Baur, not only for his useful emphasis on the historical context of Paul's letters, but also for some of his more extreme views, which still tend to detract from a full understanding Paul's indebtedness to Judaism.

Contemporary Scholars' Views

Boyarin: Platonic Paul

Although Baur's view of Paul was dominant among scholars until the twentieth century, since World War II there has been a growing tendency to look at Paul in his Jewish context. In particular, W. D. Davies and E. P. Sanders reacted against Baur's view because it produced a one-sided and anti-Jewish view of Paul that did not represent some scholars' divergent views on Paul. However, more recently, a strong tendency to view Paul mainly from his Hellenistic background in Tarsus has again emerged. Daniel Boyarin interprets Paul with a view somewhat similar to Baur's. Boyarin tends to read Paul in the context of universalism, i.e., Hellenism.[15] "Paul was motivated by a Hellenistic desire for the One, which among other things produced an ideal of a universal human essence, beyond difference and hierarchy,"

---

13. Ibid.
14. Baur, *Paul the Apostle*, 1:263.
15. Boyarin, *A Radical Jew*.

Boyarin states. "This universal humanity, however, was predicated (and still is) on the dualism of flesh and the spirit, such that while the body is particular, marked through practice as Jew or Greek, and through anatomy as male or female, the spirit is universal."[16]

Moreover, Boyarin regarded Paul's thought as strongly influenced by Platonic dualism. Unlike Baur, Boyarin did not see "Paulinism as the triumph of a new and higher consciousness over Judaism as a 'lower state a religious consciousness,'"[17] but rather considered Paul's dualistic thought to be a key to Paul's theology, as shown in the interpretation of Galatians. Boyarin stressed:

> Paul's anthropological dualism was matched by a hermeneutical dualism as well. Just as the human being is divided into a fleshy and a spiritual component, so also is language itself. It is composed of outer, material signs and inner, spiritual significations. When this is applied to the religious system that Paul inherited, the physical, fleshy signs of the Torah, of historical Judaism, are re-interpreted as symbols of that which Paul takes to be universal requirements and possibilities for humanity. Thus, to take the most central of all Paul's examples, literal circumcision, which is for Jews alone, and for male Jews at that, is re-read as signifying baptism in the spirit, which is for all.[18]

For Boyarin, Paul, influenced by Platonism, re-interpreted the Hebrew Scriptures for all humanity and thus must be considered a universalistic Hellenistic thinker. But, alternatively, Paul's universalism could also be found in Judaism, as Mark D. Nanos has recently asserted.[19] This form of universalism is expressed in the Shema (Deut 6:4). Unlike Baur and Boyarin, however, Nanos's view of Paul's universalism does not exclude Jewish particularism.

---

16. Ibid., 7.
17. Ibid., 11.
18. Ibid., 7.

19. Nanos, *Mystery of Romans*, 9–10. He says, "The purpose of Israel's special call was in the service of universal salvation, not triumphant exclusivism. Paul argued that failure to recognize the equal status of Gentiles among Jews as the people of God through their faith in Jesus Christ involved the misguided denial that the One God of Israel was the One God of the nations (Rom. 3:29–4:35; 10:12–13)" (ibid., 9).

Engberg-Pedersen: Neither Jew nor Greek

Some scholars do not deny that Paul was a Jew, yet believe that Paul was also influenced by his Hellenistic environment in terms of his language, style, literary genre, and philosophical ideas. Then the question now is, how and to what degree was Paul influenced by Hellenism? Troels Engberg-Pedersen introduces a perspective that differs from more traditional views. Engberg-Pedersen stresses that "Paul was neither specifically Jewish nor specifically Hellenistic."[20] His scholarly position is "to avoid falling back into the traditional traps of presupposing uniqueness for Paul and playing out Judaism and Hellenism against one another" and, hence, "one must look entirely open-mindedly at the facts."[21] Engberg-Pedersen claims that Paul is beyond Judaism and Hellenism—yet he still tends to interpret Paul somewhat similarly to Baur and Boyarin, at least with regard to universalism.

Engberg-Pedersen redefines Hellenistic culture more broadly than had previous scholars, seeing it as a mixture of original Greek cultural elements with non-Greek cultural elements added in. He insists that "the term 'Hellenistic' itself should not be understood as signifying those elements in the Hellenistic cultural melting-pot that were specifically and originally Greek."[22]

Engberg-Pedersen also interprets Paul's letters (Philippians, Galatians, and Romans) in the light of Stoicism. In his book *Paul and the Stoics*, Engberg-Pedersen shows how he uncovered the comprehensive pattern of Paul's thought by applying a Stoic lens to the literary structure of the letters. He says that "what appeared problematic and incoherent in Paul's letters falls into place and makes coherent sense once it is seen in the light of certain central ideas in Stoic ethics."[23] In other words, for Engberg-Pedersen, Paul's letters are perfectly coherent when read in the Stoic context.

Malherbe, Betz, and Stowers

Along with Engberg-Pedersen, other scholars interpret Paul specifically in relation to Hellenistic culture. Abraham J. Malherbe points out in his essay "Determinism and Free Will in Paul: The Argument of 1 Corinthians 8–9"

---

20. Engberg-Pedersen, *Paul in His Hellenistic Context*, xvii.
21. Ibid., *Paul Beyond the Judaism*, 3–4.
22. Ibid., *Paul in His Hellenistic Context*, xviii.
23. Engberg-Pedersen, *Paul and the Stoics*, 4.

that in 1 Cor 8–9, Paul used Stoic and Cynic reflection on determinism and free will.[24] Malherbe argues that Paul "is familiar with the philosophic slogans of the Corinthians, and with the assumptions underlying those slogans. He draws out the philosophical as well as practical consequence of the Corinthians' and his own philosophical claims."[25]

Indeed, "the philosophic traditions are for him not merely a pile of *topoi* or slogans from which he can draw in order to lay a pseudo-intellectual veneer over a wooden argument," Malherbe says. Instead, "Paul is rather to be seen as working within a milieu in which issues that engaged him and his converts were already widely discussed."[26] According to Malherbe, Paul's argument is not merely due to the exigencies of the moment.

"To think of Paul as either Jewish or Greek is not only superficial but wrong," Malherbe continues. "If one simply cannot work without labels, that of eclectic may be applied to him, but only if that label were not taken to describe him as though he indiscriminately collected thoughts from hither and yon."[27]

Hans Dieter Betz, in his essay "Transferring a Ritual: Paul's Interpretation of Baptism in Romans 6," indicates that "Judaism itself is a Hellenistic phenomenon, whereas 'Jewish context' refers to the specific conditions within Judaism at this time which had their roots in pre-Hellenistic Palestine,"[28] and "this Hellenistic perspective can to an extent explain in its own terms what Paul was doing as an apostle of Jesus Christ."[29] Betz goes on to say that the ritual of baptism was a transferal from Judaism. This transfer involved multi-recontextualization. In the epistle to the Romans, Paul "undertook the full recontextualization of baptism in terms of his theology. Interpreting baptism as the Christian initiation ritual then also explains why there are so many analogies to other Hellenistic initiations, especially those from the mystery religions."[30]

Stanley K. Stowers, in his essay "Romans 7:7–25 as Speech-in-Character" also shows that this Romans passage employs a widely used rhetorical technique in which the text represents not the speaker or writer himself but

---

24. Malherbe, "Determinism and Free Will," 231–55.
25. Ibid., 255.
26. Ibid.
27. Ibid., 243–44.
28. Betz, "Transferring a Ritual," 84.
29. Ibid., 84–85.
30. Ibid., 118.

another person or character. Stowers stresses that "Paul would have learned to recognize προσωποποιία in his elementary schooling and later have received instruction in its composition."[31] Therefore, naturally, Paul understood what the Greco-Roman rhetoricians and grammarians describe as προσωποποιία or ἠθοποιία. According to Stowers, the technique is apparent in Rom 7. Thus Stowers also interprets Paul to a certain extent in the light of his Hellenistic contextualization.

Barclay, Sampley, and Deming

John M.G. Barclay, on the other hand, does not deny that Paul was influenced by Hellenistic thought but asserts that the influence was very slight. Barclay argues that Paul was a highly assimilated Diaspora Jew in terms of his social behavior and his relationship with Gentiles, but that he has "little acculturation in the core of his theology, and he rarely attempts to effect any cultural synthesis with the Greco-Roman world he sought to evangelize."[32] Barclay compares Paul's letters with other Diaspora literature and concludes that Paul used Hellenistic theology, anthropology, and ethics minimally. Barclay insists that "Paul is considerably less acculturated than the author(s) of Wisdom, whose stylistic sophistication and dualistic anthropology bear much closer comparison with Philo."[33] He further elaborates that "the letter in which such parallels have been most diligently sought (1 Thess.) has as its theological core (1 Thess. 4.13–5.10) a depiction of salvation whose apocalyptic concepts are far removed from the main currents of Greco-Roman thought."[34]

Barclay also mentions in regard to Paul's education that Paul's "letters are written in good, but not polished, Greek prose, argumentatively effective but not stylistically grand."[35] He goes on to remark that Paul "does not give the impression of one who has undergone the literary and rhetorical training which was characteristic of the gymnasium. It seems he had no more than a rudimentary knowledge of Greek literature."[36]

---

31. Stowers, "Romans 7. 7–25," 202.
32. Barclay, *Jews in the Mediterranean*, 387.
33. Ibid., 392.
34. Ibid., 390.
35. Ibid., 383.
36. Ibid.

According to Barclay, Paul "shows little inclination to forge any form of synthesis with his cultural environment, yet he employs the language of a culturally antagonistic Judaism to establish a new social entity which transgresses the boundaries of the Diaspora synagogue."[37] For Barclay, although Paul was influenced by Hellenistic thought, that influence was very slight, and Paul nevertheless did discontinue with Judaism.

Recently, J. Paul Sampley, editor of the book *Paul in the Greco-Roman World*, has attempted to interpret Paul within the Greco-Roman background, even though he acknowledges Paul's Jewish roots. Sampley reasons in the introduction of this book that Judaism, at the time of Christian beginnings, had already been Hellenized. In other words, it was already to some degree influenced by the Greco-Roman world and its ethos.[38] According to Sampley, Paul is best characterized as a Roman Jew. Sampley stresses that "Paul's free and ready capacities to engage his predominantly Gentile auditors in their own terms and on their own grounds is not a rejection of Paul's Jewishness; rather, it is an attempt to develop the larger picture with care."[39] In other words, "Paul's 'co-option' or 'borrowing' of Hellenistic or Roman conceptions or conventions or practices was simply his creative way of packaging the gospel."[40]

Sampley argues "there is no such thing as a version of the gospel without culturally situated supposition and conventions."[41] Hence, "the only valid gospel expressions are the ones pertinent to and viable for the speaker and the auditors."[42] For Sampley, "the gospel is this filter, his [Paul's] lens through which he sees and evaluates all things. Paul is convinced that believers already live in the new creation, even while walking in the evil aeon."[43] Sampley asserts that we need to see Paul in the Greco-Roman world in order to understand the whole Paul. Perhaps it is more correct to say that we need to see Paul in the Greco-Roman world in order to properly understand how the Jewish Paul communicated with his Gentile audience.

---

37. Ibid., 393.
38. Sampley, *Paul in the Greco-Roman World*, 4–5.
39. Ibid., 5.
40. Ibid.
41. Ibid., 5–6.
42. Ibid., 6.
43. Ibid., 15.

In this line of thought, Will Deming[44] points out that the understanding of Stoic notions about "indifferent things" (ἀδιάφορον)[45] is important to the understanding of Paul even though the extent of Stoic influence on Paul is not Deming's primary concern. Deming is not claiming that Paul's ethics have to be understood in the light of Stoic "indifferent things," but he insists that "we must acknowledge that almost any system of ethics will distinguish between what is good, what is bad, and what is neither, or 'indifferent.'"[46] Moreover, the Stoic definition of "indifferent things" in the Greco-Roman context was preceded by and competed with Platonic and Aristotelian positions.[47]

Deming, however, suggests that Paul's treatment of "indifferents" in these selected passages (Phil 1:20–26; 1 Cor 7:25–38; and 1 Cor 7:20–23) is parallel to Stoicism.[48] He asserts that Paul did not intentionally borrow from or imitate Stoicism, but "Rather, either he or a Jewish, or Jewish-Christian contemporary has integrated basic elements of Stoic ethical theory into the very heart of Christian theology and applied them to issues facing the early church."[49]

For Deming, understanding Stoic thought is relevant to understanding Paul.[50] If this is the case, then the question arises: Does Paul make better sense in light of Stoic ethics? Deming left this question for scholars to debate further. However, recently William S. Campbell has argued that despite some parallels, by itself Paul's Stoic thought on indifferent things is not adequate to fully explain Paul's ethic.[51]

---

44. Deming, "Paul and Indifferent Things," 384–97.

45. Ibid., 384. According to Deming, "ἀδιάφορον is the Stoic term for an 'indifferent thing'... The Stoics held that everything in existence was either a 'good thing' (ἀγαθόν), a 'bad thing' (κακόν), or an 'indifferent thing' (ἀδιάφορον). Because they used 'good' as the equivalent of 'morally beautiful,' good things or simply 'goods,' for the Stoics consisted of virtue and all things that 'participated' in virtue... Everything else in the world was an 'indifferent.' Thus, indifferents were neither virtue nor vice, nor did they participate in virtue or vice. They included things like health and sickness, wealth and poverty." For more detail on this, see ibid., 384–86.

46. Ibid., 386.

47. Ibid., 387.

48. Ibid. 384–87.

49. Ibid., 396.

50. Ibid., 397.

51. Campbell, review of *Paul in the Greco-Roman World*, 294. Campbell says, "Whilst the Stoic parallels illuminate and indicate influence upon, Paul's thinking, these by themselves do not fully account for his stance in 1 Cor. 7 where he advises the Corinthians to

Hock, Unnik, Longenecker, and Ehrensperger

In contrast to Barclay, Ronald F. Hock argues in his essay "Paul and Greco-Roman Education" that Paul was educated beyond the secondary stage. In spite of Paul's humble claim, "His status as an aristocrat makes education a given, and the letters themselves betray such a command of the Greek language as well as a familiarity with the literary and rhetorical conventions of Greek education that only a full and thorough education in Greek on Paul's part makes sense of the evidence."[52]

Hock goes on to argue that "evidence of Paul's secondary education is also evident, although more obviously in his ability to cite and interpret literary texts—which were, in his case, the Greek Jewish scriptures, or Septuagint—than in the more technical study of grammar. Still, some signs of grammatical study appear, such as Paul's careful distinction between the singular and plural of a word in his understanding of the promise to Abraham (Gal. 3:16)."[53]

Hock gives more evidence that Paul's education went beyond the secondary stage. Paul's letters themselves, given their length, complexity, and power, "Clearly point to an author who had received sustained training in composition and rhetoric, and it was only during the tertiary curriculum that such instruction was given. Accordingly, a fuller discussion of Paul's awareness of the forms of progymnasmata as well as the forms and rules of rhetorical speech and argumentation is required."[54]

Hock provides the evidence to prove that Paul had received tertiary Greco-Roman education. Contrary to Hock's view of Paul's youthful education, however, Paul may have learned these skills from a Jewish education rather than a Greek one, though this training would also have been indebted to Greek thought.

---

remain in the state of circumcision or uncircumcision in which they received their call." Similarly, see ibid., *Unity and Diversity*, 106–123.

52. Ibid., 198.

53. Ibid., 208–209.

54. Hock, "Paul and Greco-Roman Education," 209. According to Hock, in Greco-Roman primary education the starting age was at about seven, and they were taught how to read, write, and compute (ibid., 199). When students had mastered this primary education, they start, at about age ten or eleven, secondary education to learn grammar and literature (ibid., 201). After the secondary curriculum, students moved on, at about age fifteen, to the tertiary stage of education. In this stage of the curriculum, "which typically meant study either with a philosopher or with an orator, and overwhelmingly with the latter. Accordingly, the focus here will be on the rhetorical curriculum" (ibid., 204).

Paul and Hellenistic Thought

Unlike Hock, W. C. van Unnik in his book, *Tarsus or Jerusalem*[55] insists that Paul received a fundamentally Jewish rather than Greek education. For van Unnik, Paul's home and the period of his youth was a fundamental and enduring aspect of his development. Van Unnik says, "Although Paul was born in Tarsus, it was in Jerusalem that he received his upbringing in the parental home just as it was in Jerusalem that he received his later schooling for the rabbinate."[56] Although we do not know exactly when Paul's parents moved back to Jerusalem, van Unnik argues that in Acts 22:3 and 26:4–5, the use of the word ἀνατεθραμμένος indicates that Paul moved back to Jerusalem quite early in life.[57] Van Unnik's view concerning Paul's education differs from others in that he does not deny Paul's knowledge of Hellenism but instead argues that Paul gained his knowledge of Hellenism during his second period, i.e., after his conversion.[58]

In other words, Paul's youthful education in Tarsus is improbable. His early education was also Jewish.[59] If Paul received Jewish education in his youth, as van Unnik has noted, then Richard N. Longenecker has the right to claim that Paul used Greek to explain his Pharisaic theology. As Longenecker observes, "All he [Paul] accepted from Hellenism was accepted because it could convey his meaning, and not with reference to what it really meant outside ... The elements in his thinking to which parallels have been found in non-Jewish literature, in Greek religion or in pagan mysteries, are obviously secondary. They belong to the surface rather than to the core of this thought and teaching."[60]

---

55. van Unnik, *Tarsus or Jerusalem*. See a contrary view to van Unnik in Murphy-O'Connor, *Paul*, 32–33, 46. He denies that Paul was actually educated in Jerusalem, taking the statement of Acts 22:3 as a fabrication by Luke to give Paul greater credibility. Therefore, van Unnik's mistake is to believe Luke's report on Acts 22:3.

56. van Unnik, 52.

57. Ibid., 52. The verb ἀνατρέφω, or "brought up," can mean either to nourish "physically" or "spiritually" or both.

58. For van Unnik, there are three periods of Paul's life: "(1) The period of Paul's youth, during which he studied and walked in the Jewish religion and which closed with his conversion. For lack of data the duration of this period of his life cannot be determined. (2) His first years as a Christian, which he spent partly in Arabia and partly in Tarsus (Cilicia) ... (3) The last period is that which Luke introduces with this special instruction of the Holy Spirit: 'Set apart for me Barnabas and Saul for the work to which I have called them' (Acts 13:2)" (ibid., 1–2).

59. van Unnik, *Tarsus or Jerusalem*, 57–58.

60. Longenecker, *Paul*, 58.

Most recently, Kathy Ehrensperger has asserted in her book *That We may be Mutually Encouraged* that "since Hellenism was the prevailing culture of the Mediterranean world, it could hardly be ignored, nor can its influence on Judaism in the Diaspora as well as in Palestine be dismissed."[61] But she raises many questions: "Was Paul enculturated in the Hellenistic world, and if so, to what extent? And/or did he maintain a particular Jewish identity that was based mainly on the Jewish Scriptures?"[62]

Ehrensperger does not have any doubt that Paul received some influence from Hellenistic culture, because he lived in an era dominated by Hellenistic culture. She acknowledges that Paul shows knowledge and skills valued in Hellenistic culture in both his rhetoric and in his use of the diatribe style.[63] Ehrensperger points out that first-century Judaism was influenced by a variety of different stages and aspects of Hellenism—and that even some methods of Jewish exegesis have their roots in Hellenism.[64] Her research illustrates how difficult it is to determine absolutely what may have come from Hellenism and what can be traced to Jewish roots, though this difficulty does not prevent Paul from having his preferences as a Hebrew of Hebrews.

Ehrensperger also reaffirms that Paul's upbringing was in Tarsus and that he received his education in Jerusalem, as van Unnik has indicated.[65] She stresses Paul's own word that he "advanced in Judaism beyond many among my people of the same age," being "far more zealous for the traditions of my ancestors" (Gal 1:14) rather than Paul emphasizing a Greek education. Moreover, Ehrensperger did not find that Paul expressed the gospel in the terms of Hellenistic culture: "His world map is based on the scriptural division between Jews and the nations/Gentiles (Gal 2:8-9; 1 Cor 1:23; Rom 3:29; 9:24; et al.)."[66] In contrast to many other scholars who see Paul mostly as enculturated in Hellenism, Ehrensperger points out that

---

61. Ehrensperger, *That We May*, 83–84.

62. Ibid., 125.

63. Ibid., 126. See also Ehrensperger's recent critical discussion of the concept of Hellenism in ibid., *Paul at the Crossroads*, 18–29.

64. Ehrensperger, *That We May*, 126. Boyarin also indicates that the Palestinian Judaism was Hellenized to some degree in Boyarin, *A Radical Jew*, 6–7.

65. Ehrensperger, *That We May*, 126. See more detail on Paul's education in ibid., 129–32. See also van Unnik, *Tarsus or Jerusalem*, 3–4; contra Du Toit, "Tale of Two Cities," 375–402.

66. Ehrensperger, *That We May*, 131–32.

Paul had the typical dual identity of his time. Paul, at the core of his identity, was still a Jew even though he was also a Roman citizen.[67]

Regarding Paul's core identity, my assessment is that Paul remained a Jew in spite of his Roman citizenship. I myself can identify as a person with a dual identity, as a Korean with an American citizenship and enculturation. I was educated and have lived in the United States for more than twenty years, during which time I have been thoroughly assimilated into American culture and language. And yet, when I write, I am thinking in Korean and then translating those thoughts into written English. Ehrensperger indicates in her article "Paul's Identity: 'A Hebrew of Hebrews' or a Hellenistic Confluence of Ideas?" that "Engberg-Pedersen's approach is idealistic in its 'universalistic' and 'open-minded' claim."[68] For Ehrensperger, "This approach somehow has to depict Paul as an 'empty vessel,' or 'a place of confluence of ideas,' a figure detached from any given context, a sponge soaking up whatever comes from outside without using, shaping, or integrating these influences according to his own roots or purposes."[69] She criticizes Engberg-Pedersen for misusing ideological criticism, even though it is necessary as a tool for clarification, and also for the view that it is possible to leave behind all presuppositions. She goes on to articulate that "in calling for a move beyond the Judaism/Hellenism divide, Engberg-Pedersen does not lay open his own hermeneutical presuppositions in his approach, nor his definition of Hellenism and scholarly objectivity as a universalized Enlightenment ideal."[70]

Ehrensperger observes that Engberg-Pedersen and others have revived the image of Paul as a liberal and as the champion of universalism. In contrast, Ehrensperger urges that "Paul uses traditional, scripturally based Jewish tradition, intending to root the identity of his Gentile converts firmly within this tradition. He does not try to identify in any way with Hellenistic culture as such. His universal adaptability in 1 Cor. 9:19ff. can be read as an occasional strategy to suit his own missionary purpose."[71]

---

67. Ibid., 132.
68. Ibid., "Paul's Identity," 3.
69. Ibid. See also ibid., *That We May Be*, 127.
70. Ibid., "Paul's Identity," 3.
71. Ibid., *That We May Be*, 132.

To What Extent was Paul Influenced by Hellenism?

Emphasis on Hellenism[72] often goes along with a perceived antithesis between Judaism and Christianity. "These strands of research operate with the presupposition that Paul is primarily enculturated in Hellenism and therefore to a certain extent alienated from his Jewish roots," Ehrensperger notes. "From this approach, his letters show a universalistic Hellenistic thinker, though at some points (e.g., Rom. 9–11) with unfortunate retrogression into Jewish particularism. Paul could not quite rid himself of the concept of the Jews as God's favorite people!"[73]

Since Hellenism was the prevailing culture of the Mediterranean world, it could not be ignored. There is no question that there was a Hellenistic influence on Judaism in the Diaspora as well as in Palestine.[74] There are significant differences between Jewish and Greco-Roman ways of thinking that persisted during the first century as well as later, although Hellenism did influence Judaism in several ways.[75] In the cultural atmosphere of Roman rule, the Jewish ways of looking at Scriptures were not without significance for Jewish self-understanding.[76]

David Daube has also pointed out how Palestinian Judaism has been influenced by Hellenism. For instance, the early Jewish methods of interpreting Scripture are frequently "derived from Hellenistic rhetoric."[77] Daube also shows that even Hillel's famous seven norms of interpretation are deeply indebted to rhetorical ideas about how to approach and use texts to persuade.[78] First-century Judaism, like Hillel, who lived before Paul, adopted Hellenistic rhetoric in the interpretation of Scripture.

Moreover, "Hillel himself had come from Babylon to Jerusalem as a Diaspora Jew," according to Martin Hengel. As Hengel continues:

> Talmudic tradition says of Gamaliel's grandson, who bore the same name and founded the patriarchy, that in his house five hundred

---

72. I will use "Hellenism" to mean the cultural pattern and way of thinking characteristic of the dominant Greco-Roman power of the first century, as Ehrensperger uses it. See ibid., 50.

73. Ibid., 128–29.

74. Gruen, *Heritage and Hellenism*, xv. See also Boyarin, *A Radical Jew*, 6–7; Davies, *Paul and Rabbinic Judaism*, 320–21.

75. Ehrensperger, *That We May Be*, 52.

76. See Tomson, '*If This Be*,' 28.

77. Daube, "Rabbinic Methods," 239–64.

78. Ibid.

children learned the Torah and five hundred learned Greek wisdom (Sota 49b; BQ 83a), that is, command of the Greek language and Greek rhetoric and training and rabbinic thinking were not absolute opposites. Not only traditional Jewish wisdom schools and schools of the Torah, but also Greek schools, were to be found in Jerusalem from the third century BC onwards.[79]

Does this mean that Pharisees, rabbis, or society as a whole were completely acculturated into Hellenistic thinking? Did they perhaps employ it merely as a technical outward use of a method? Erich S. Gruen notes that the Jews "did not confront daily decision on the degree of assimilation. They had long since become part of a Hellenic environment that they could take as given. But their Judaism remained intact. What they required was a means of defining and expressing their singularity within that milieu, the special characteristics that made them both integral to the community and true to their heritage."[80]

In any case, there is no doubt that the Jewish people's way of thinking in the first century was shaped by the Scripture, despite Hellenistic influence. Likewise, Paul's way of thinking is also shaped by the Scripture. Although Paul was a Diaspora Pharisee, his thought was rooted in Palestinian and Pharisaic rabbinic Judaism. As Peter J. Tomson explains:

> Paul was a hellenizing Jew to the extent that he lived among Greek speaking communities of Jews and Gentiles, wrote letters to them in Greek, and in doing so employed both Hellenistic literary conventions and motifs from popular Stoic and Cynic wisdom. This is only remotely reminiscent of Philo. Scholars agree that apart from such minor and superficial parallels Paul shows no interest in Greek philosophy as such. On the other hand elements from popular Hellenistic and especially Stoic-Cynic tradition are found in Rabbinic literature; but again no interest in philosophy. When the amounts of the authentic and the foreign are weighed up one sees that as far as these Hellenistic motifs are concerned Paul is rather much at one with Palestinian, Pharisaic Rabbinic Judaism.[81]

Although we cannot deny that Paul was also influenced by Hellenism to some degree, the core of his thought is anchored in the Hebrew Bible. After all, if the Scriptures were the main basis of the Jewish way of thinking

---

79. Hengel, *Acts and the History*, 81–82.
80. Gruen, *Heritage and Hellenism*, xv.
81. Tomson, *Paul and the Jewish Law*, 52–53.

in the first century, then it is not too much to assume that they were also basic to Paul's way of thinking.

If Paul is considerably less acculturated than other contemporary Diaspora Jewish authors, as Barclay points out,[82] then to what extent was Paul influenced by Hellenism? It is hard to measure precisely how much Paul had been influenced by Hellenism. This is a matter that scholars will need to research further. Nevertheless, as Davies notes, "any Hellenistic elements which may be found in his [Paul's] thought do not imply that he was therefore outside the main current of first-century Judaism."[83] If, as Hellenized a Jew as a philosopher, Philo's mind was molded by Scripture,[84] then there is no doubt Paul's way of thinking was also shaped by the Scripture.

However, while we acknowledge the degree of Hellenistic influence and its significance, we cannot ignore Paul's own claim of Jewishness in such passages as 2 Cor 11:22 and Rom 11:1, where Paul proudly proclaims his Jewish identity, and in Gal 1:14, where Paul says he "advanced in Judaism beyond many among my people of the same age" being "far more zealous for the traditions of my ancestors." And if we can allow historicity to Acts 22:3, then Paul also claimed an education in Jerusalem.

Since we are concerned mainly with considerations of Paul as Jewish in contemporary scholarship, we will move on from the area of Paul and Hellenism, turning instead to an examination of how various scholars have developed their views of the first-century Jewish context of Paul's hermeneutic and theology.

---

82. Barclay, *Jews in the Mediterranean*, 390. Barclay notes, "It is revealing how little Paul uses allegory in his interpretation of Scripture, and what he finds when he does so (1 Cor 9:9–11; Gal 4:21–31) bears little relation to the theological or ethical mainstream of Hellenistic thought. Paul's ethics are not significantly shaped by the cardinal Greek virtues" (ibid., 391).

83. Davies, *Paul and Rabbinic Judaism*, 320.

84. Cf. Ehrensperger, *That We May Be*, 65. Cf. also Buren, *According to the Scripture*, 26. According to Buren, despite the contradictions and differing traditions we find in the Hebrew Bible, we read the story of Israel "unfolded in the Torah, and celebrated and rehearsed in the Prophets." He continues: "Even for as Hellenized a Jew as the philosopher Philo, this story was the foundation of his thought. Even Israel's Wisdom tradition, which sounds so Hellenistic, was molded by it."

3

More Recent Views of Paul

Since the development of F. C. Baur's Hellenistic assessment of Paul—and the reaction against it by W. D. Davies and E. P. Sanders—many other divergent views have been proposed by scholars.

Davies has pioneered some of the insights that led to the New Perspective on Paul. He takes seriously Paul's Jewish orientation, which Davies demonstrates in Paul's letters.[1] Davies emphasizes that if one wants to understand the complexity of Paul's letters, one must understand them in the light of the Judaism of the first century CE. He also stresses that Hellenistic influence on Jews in Palestine and their close ties with the Diaspora cannot be denied,[2] claiming that "any Hellenistic elements which may be found in his thought do not imply that he was therefore outside the main current of first-century Judaism."[3] Nor can the Pharisaic-rabbinic movement be isolated from the strong apocalyptic vein in Second Temple Judaism or from the mystical undercurrent evident in rabbinic literature.

Although Davies and Daniel Boyarin share, to some degree, a similar view of Hellenistic influence on Palestine Judaism, Davies sees Paul's hermeneutic as Jewish. Boyarin, on the other hand, reads it as Hellenistic. However, Davies shows that Paul thought his gospel was both the

---

1. See Davies, *Paul and Rabbinic Judaism*.

2. A similar view occurs in Boyarin, *A Radical Jew*, 6–7, "I hold, rather, that all of Palestinian Judaism was also Hellenized to a greater or lesser extent, although it is surely plausible that there were major cultural differences between Jews whose daily language was Semitic (Hebrew or Aramaic) and those whose daily language was Greek."

3. Davies, *Paul and Rabbinic Judaism*, 320.

completion of Judaism and its fulfillment. Not only was Paul's thought rooted in rabbinic Judaism, his lifestyle was also closely related to it. Paul was not anti-Torah; he remained a true Jew. Davies shows in his essays in *Jewish and Pauline Studies* that we should interpret Paul as a historical figure rather than simply as a timeless religious genius.[4] The doctrine of justification was not central in his thought. Davies suggests that if we try to read Paul's letters outside of Judaism, we will be inclined to take a position opposed to that context, whereas Paul composed his letters in the context of a dialogue within Judaism.

In Search of the Historical Paul

While Davies's interpretation of Paul emphasizes first-century Judaism, Johannes Munck understands Paul in the context of history and eschatology.[5] Paul was just like one of the Jewish prophets or any other apostle (Peter, John, James, etc.) who was called by God to fulfill God's will in the messianic age. Munck also emphasizes that the epistle to the Romans is best understood in the particular circumstance of Paul's missionary context.[6] He insists, contra F. C. Baur, that Paul did not have any conflict with Jewish Christianity. Indeed, Paul thought Christianity was true Judaism. Moreover, Paul—like Moses—was concerned for his people's salvation. Thus Munck interprets Paul as a missionary for Gentiles and, therefore, assigns his letters to the category of pastoral letters.

C. H. Dodd, on the other hand, attempts to understand Paul's world through both Old Testament and Greek thought, even though he argues that Paul's main background was rooted in Judaism. Dodd stresses that understanding the history of Paul's people along with his religious experience is essential to understanding Paul's theology. In Dodd's mind, Paul was a Hellenistic Jew who was influenced by the "apocalyptic" in Jewish thought.[7] Dodd adds, "The direct influence of non-Jewish Hellenistic thought upon Paul has, I think, been exaggerated. His main background is Judaism, though not altogether the Judaism of the Old Testament or of

---

4. Davies, *Jewish and Pauline Studies*. The use of rabbinic Judaism in Alan F. Segal would differ from Davies in applying the term only to a period from 70 CE; see more detail *in Paul the Convert*, xiv.

5. Munck, *Paul and the Salvation*, esp. 34–35.

6. See also, Munck, *Christ and Israel*.

7. Dodd, *Epistle of Paul*, xxxiii.

More Recent Views of Paul

normal or orthodox Rabbinism, but partly the Hellenized Judaism of the Dispersion."[8] Dodd thought that Paul had not quite got rid of his Jewish patriotism. However, even if Paul was a Hellenistic Jew, this still does not mean Paul's thinking was rooted in Greek philosophy. Perhaps it was more grounded in Jewish thought, as Peter J. Tomson points out.[9]

Krister Stendahl, who has been strongly influenced by Munck's interpretation of Paul, criticizes the traditional church interpretation of the apostle. He believes that the church interpretation blocks out both Paul's original thought and Paul's original intention because it seeks to understand Paul through the lens of the Augustinian and Lutheran view.[10] Stendahl decries the Western individualistic interpretation of Paul.

Instead, Stendahl focuses on the historical description of Paul's mission among Jews and Gentiles. He stresses that Paul's main concern was the Jewish-Gentile problem—that is, the conversion of Gentiles—rather than any universal human problem. Paul was defending the fitness of Gentiles to become full members of the people of God without first becoming Jews. In this understanding of Paul, Stendahl comes close to the emphases of two-covenant theology.

In fact, Stendahl is against the Reformers' interpretation of Paul[11] because he believes they presuppose the Western introspective conscience as a key to interpreting Paul's letters. Stendahl does not explain in detail the Jewish sources of Paul's thought but rather assumes Paul's was a Jewish missionary in the messianic age occupied with fulfilling the mystery of God's plan. Stendahl interprets Paul on the basis of that assumption. In Stendahl's view, Paul was not introspective, had a robust conscience, and was not concerned with his inward feelings or pangs of conscience.

Sanders re-examines first-century Judaism in his book *Paul and Palestinian Judaism*. While Davies believed the law was a gift of God and there was joy in submission to it,[12] Sanders describes first-century Judaism as a "covenantal nomism" rather than as legalism, and although Sanders stresses

---

8. Ibid., xxxii.
9. Tomson, *Paul and the Jewish Law*, 52–53.
10. Stendahl, *Paul Among Jews*.
11. Ibid. Stendahl stresses that the Reformers understood Paul through an antithesis between faith and work, Law and Gospel, Jews and Gentiles, because they read from the framework of late medieval piety. Ibid., 85–86.
12. Davies, *Jewish and Pauline Studies*, 18.

the Jewish background of Paul's thought,[13] he holds that Paul rejected Judaism because he finds the key to Paul in his theory that Paul worked backwards from the Christ event, i.e., from "solution to plight."[14] But Sanders's view contributed enormously to reawakening interest in Paul's theology.

James D. G. Dunn reconceives Sanders's interpretation of Palestinian Judaism. According to Dunn, Paul was a Jew who never ceased to be a Jew. He does not find the same weakness in Judaism that Sanders indicated (that, for Paul, Judaism was not Christianity) but rather criticizes what he terms the nationalistic elements in Judaism. Dunn interprets the law in its sociological function as an "identity marker" and "boundary marker," which Dunn highlights as "the New Perspective" on Paul.[15] Dunn's critique of Judaism is more limited and more precise than Sanders's but seeks to retain some continuity between Paul and Judaism—while remaining critical of it.

A Different Kind of Judaism

Dunn interprets Paul in his Jewish and Pharisaic background, agreeing with Munck and Stendahl that "Paul never speaks of his encounter with Christ as a conversion, only as a calling and commissioning."[16] Therefore, when we interpret Paul, we must recognize that Paul's vocation is more properly understood as a calling rather than a conversion. Paul was first a missionary and only secondarily a theologian. Dunn emphasizes Paul's Jewishness and does not think of him as inaugurating a new religion. Dunn, stimulated by Sanders, has brought forth this New Perspective view on Paul's theology, which centers on a socio-political interpretive approach to Paul's letters.

Alan F. Segal, in his book *Paul the Convert*, underscores Paul's Jewish mysticism, apocalyptic, and incipient rabbinism.[17] Segal shows how Paul's struggles with Judaism and Jewish Christians throw light on Paul's messianic commitment. Segal stresses that we must read Paul's letters in light of the religious experience of knowledge, both in Paul's time and now, in order to fully understand him. Although Paul never left Judaism, "Paul considered himself as part of a new Jewish sect and hoped to convince fel-

---

13. Sanders, *Paul and Palestinian Judaism*, 422–43.
14. See Sanders, *Paul, the Law, and the Jewish People*.
15. Dunn, *Romans* 1:1–8; *Jesus, Paul and the Law*.
16. Dunn, *Romans* 1:1–8, xli.
17. Segal, *Paul the Convert*.

low Christians and Jews of his vision of redemption."[18] Segal suggests that "Paul was both converted and called."[19] Segal shows Paul in his Pharisaic upbringing and lifestyle prior to his conversion, which Segal then discusses in relation to Pharisaic Judaism and the early stages of Paul's rabbinism, Jewish mysticism, and apocalypticism.

Needless to say, Paul's Judaism was a different kind of Judaism. As Segal stresses, "Mysticism in first-century Judea was apocalyptic"[20]—it was not about the revelation of "meditative truths of the universe but the disturbing news that God was about to bring judgment."[21] Paul's mystical encounter with the risen Christ and his experience of a heavenly journey indicate that Paul was a first-century Jewish apocalypticist and a mystic. If this were the case, Paul's ecstatic experience (2 Cor 12) would not have been foreign to a first-century Jew.

We can also find similarities to this experience in ecstatic ascents to the divine throne in other apocalyptic traditions of Judaism. As Segal notes, "Paul's conversion experience and his mystical ascension form the basis of his theology. His language shows the marks of a man who has learned the contemporary vocabulary for expressing a theophany and then has received one."[22]

Segal also asserts that the throne vision of Ezek 1 is one of the central scriptural passages of Jewish mysticism, which later became known as *merkabah* ("throne-chariot") mysticism in rabbinic terms.[23] He has demonstrated how that mystical imagery is revealed throughout the Scriptures, e.g., "a human figure," or "an appearance of the likeness to the glory of the Lord" (Ezek 1:28), and "like a human figure" on the heavenly throne (Dan 7:9–13), etc.

Paul was one of the earliest authors of experiences of such heavenly encounters and a kind of predecessor of Merkabah, as Segal explains. "Techniques of theurgy and heavenly ascent were secret lore in rabbinic literature (see b. Hagiga 13a–15b), which dates from the third century.

---

18. Ibid., xiv. According to Magnus Zetterhoem, "The early Jesus movement was one option of a Jewish way of life among others in Antiquity," in Jewish Christianity Seminar at SBL, 2005.

19. Ibid., 6.

20. Ibid., 34.

21. Ibid.

22. Ibid., 69.

23. Ibid., 39.

Paul alone demonstrates that such traditions existed as early as the first century."[24] Paul's Judaism, therefore, was an apocalyptic and a mystical form of Judaism in the first-century.

William S. Campbell[25] also approaches Paul in his cultural context, specifically emphasizing an election and a covenant background. Campbell interprets Paul's letter to the Romans in a missionary, pastoral, and situational perspective. Since Paul was transformed by the Christ event, his theology is essentially one of transformation. The old is transformed and renewed rather than abandoned or displaced. For Campbell, "The crucial aspect of Paul's understanding of transformation is that it is an ongoing and as yet an incomplete process."[26] Moreover, Campbell argues that Paul's conclusion to Rom 11 is open-ended: "Any other conclusion would not have assisted in discouraging the pride and incipient anti-Judaism of the Roman Gentile Christ-followers."[27]

Campbell strongly emphasizes Paul's understanding that the historical people of God are only the Jewish people. Therefore, Gentile believers can never be termed "New Israel"—and Israel remains Israel. Paul, however, was a product of both Judaism and Hellenism. Campbell sees Paul's main concerns as "obedience to the gospel and the unity of his communities."[28] He also notes that Paul stressed positive aspects of Judaism and Jewish identity in Romans. Campbell writes, "Most telling of all is Paul's conclusion of his letter to Rome which affirms Jewish identity as an abiding reality in the Christ-movement which the strong are obligated to accept and protect."[29]

Campbell also stresses that we must interpret Paul's theology in the framework of Paul's immediate revelation from God and his experience of his call, but always in relation to the context addressed in his letters.

The Political Apostle

Neil Elliott[30] understands Paul's thought in the first-century political context and examines the political dimensions of the theology of the cross. For

24. Ibid., 36.
25. See Campbell, *Paul's Gospel*.
26. Campbell, *Paul and the Creation*, 171.
27. Ibid., 171.
28. Campbell, "Contribution of Traditions," 253.
29. Campbell, *Paul and the Creation*, 119.
30. Elliott, *Liberating Paul*.

Elliott, Paul's perspective on the death of Jesus is apocalyptic. This apocalyptic theology's main purposes are the justification of the covenant people and, through them, the liberation of all creation.

Even though Paul conducted a law-free mission among the Gentiles, he did not abandon his people. Paul had a vision of Isaiah's prophecy of the last day and shared it with the messianic community. As Elliott also emphasizes, Paul's "'conversion' changed not his goal but the strategy he would now adopt to reach that goal."[31] Elliott describes Paul as a political apostle who tried to liberate people from all evil political power rather than from their individual sins. In this respect, Elliott has also contributed to the paradigm shift in the scholarly world's understanding of Paul.

These scholars, unlike Baur and others, attempt to find the real historical Paul in various Jewish contexts. This leads us to ask the inevitable question: Whose Paul is the real Paul? Even though Sanders, Segal, and Dunn believe that Paul is best understood from his Jewish origins, they still maintain, to differing degrees, that Paul left these origins behind once he became a Christian or shortly thereafter—rather than that Paul remained consistent with his Jewish heritage and never turned against it.

We now take some space to consider the views of contemporary scholars who interpret Paul from a Jewish perspective and who regard Paul's embeddedness in Judaism as an abiding and important element throughout Paul's life.

Views of Paul's Embeddedness in Judaism

Some scholars' recent studies show that the Jewish context is a vitally significant element in understanding Paul's thought. Yet such scholars focus on differing aspects of Paul's thought as evidence of his Jewish roots.

For example, J. Christiaan Beker focuses on the apocalyptic,[32] while Peter Tomson turns his attention to halakhah (the legal tradition of Judaism) in Paul,[33] Mark Nanos views Romans through the Jewish perspective of the Shema,[34] and Kathy Ehrensperger emphasizes how Paul thinks within a Jewish symbolic universe.[35] These scholars demonstrate how

---

31. Ibid., 179.
32. Beker, *Paul's Apocalyptic Gospel; Paul the Apostle; The Triumph of God.*
33. Tomson, *Paul and the Jewish Law.*
34. Nanos, *Mystery of Romans.*
35. Ehrensperger, *That We May Be.*

Paul's thought and writing after his encounter with Christ shows a strong connection with his Jewish context rather than a sharp break with Judaism, as some scholars had previously thought.

We will now consider in more specific detail such scholars' various approaches to how and why Paul's thought demonstrates his Jewish roots.

Beker: Apocalyptic

Beker approaches Paul in relation to his Jewish apocalyptic context. Beker also claims that, in Paul's thought, two major themes dominate: "The dialectic of coherence and contingency and the apocalyptic worldview as the basic framework of Paul's gospel."[36] Beker believes Paul, like Jeremiah, had a prophetic call for God's mission.[37] Beker explains Paul's conversion in terms of Paul's life as a Jew rather than simply as a "lightning bolt from heaven."[38] Beker, like Albert Schweitzer,[39] highlights Paul's Jewish apocalyptic context.

However, Beker—rather than speculating on Paul's thought apart from his Jewish roots—tries to determine what influence Paul's life as a Jew may have had on his Damascus experience. For Beker, Paul was an apocalyptist during his Pharisaic career because he was a Pharisee of the Diaspora who fully expected fulfillment of the messianic promises. In other words, "Paul's apocalyptic conviction was not initiated by his conversion to Christ but was formed by his background in the Pharisaic world view."[40]

Beker sees Acts 9:1–2 as evidence that "the apocalyptic structure of his [Paul's] thought remains the constant in his Pharisaic and Christian life."[41] Beker argues that Paul was "an apocalyptic Pharisaic 'missionary' before his conversion,"[42] as evidenced by his letters. Beker also suggests that after his Damascus experience, Paul's thought had changed to some degree regarding the relationship between the Torah and the messianic promises.

---

36. Beker, *The Triumph of God*.
37. Beker, *Paul the Apostle*.
38. Beker, *The Triumph of God*, 107.
39. See Schweitzer, *Mysticism of Paul*. For a more detailed study of Paul's apocalyptic, see Matlock, *Unveiling the Apocalyptic Paul*.
40. Beker, *Paul the Apostle*, 144.
41. Ibid.
42. Ibid.

More Recent Views of Paul

However, the change was not from "'legal casuistic Pharisaism' (Paul the Pharisee) to 'universalistic apocalyptic thinking' (Paul the Christian)."[43] Hence, Paul knew himself as the eschatological apostle who in the last hours of world history was obligated to world mission.[44]

Beker thinks Paul's gospel is formulated within the basic components of apocalyptic thought, which Paul radically modified from Jewish apocalyptic because of his encounter with Christ and because of the Christian tradition he inherited.

Beker gives three lines of evidence to show that Paul modified basic truths drawn from Jewish apocalyptic:

1. Paul does not employ the traditional apocalyptic terminology of "this age" in conjunction with that of "the age to come,"
2. Paul significantly modifies the traditional apocalyptic view of the escalation of the forces of evil in the end time, and
3. Paul rarely uses the terminology "kingdom of God" (or "the day of the Lord"), and when he does, it is mainly in traditional contexts.[45]

These reasons provide the evidence for Beker's conviction that Paul's thought is deeply rooted in a (modified) traditional Jewish apocalyptic. In emphasizing the apocalyptic element of Paul's thought, Beker does see Paul as basing his theology on Jewish apocalyptic, although he does not interpret Paul directly from the Jewish apocalyptic context. There is some transformation of apocalyptic because of Paul's response to the Christ event. However, Beker is not the first scholar to interpret Paul in a Jewish apocalyptic context. Albert Schweitzer also understood Paul within his Jewish background.[46]

Schweitzer had distinguished "between Hellenistic and Semitic concepts of mysticism... But the understanding of so-called mystical elements in first-century Judaism has been largely transformed."[47] He also points out the difference between apocalyptic and Pharisaism and other elements within Judaism. Moreover, he understands Paul in a "purely eschatological

---

43. Ibid., 144.
44. Ibid., 145.
45. Ibid. Beker's view on this may need to be qualified in the light of Rom 14:17, which seems central to Paul's argument in the chapter.
46. Schweitzer, *Mysticism of Paul*.
47. Cf. Davies, *Paul and Rabbinic Judaism*, ix.

context, divorced from Pharisaism and his other first-century currents."[48] Beker, however, explains that Paul's thought was dominated by Jewish apocalyptic motifs rather than Jewish apocalyptic as a literary genre or as a literary source. As Beker states:

> In positioning Jewish apocalyptic as the master symbolism of Paul's thought, I do not suggest that Paul adopts Jewish apocalyptic as a literary genre or uses Jewish apocalypses as literary *"Vorlagen."* Moreover, I am not interested in semantic explorations of the meaning of the concept "apocalyptic" in relation to Paul. Rather, I maintain that apocalyptic *motifs* dominate Paul's thought, that Paul's modifications of the Christian tradition are not due to Hellenistic-Jewish or Philonic influences but are modifications of an *apocalyptic* substratum.[49]

Beker also emphasizes Paul's affinities with Judaism rather than with the Hellenistic world.[50] Moreover, he claims that "four major apocalyptic motifs, however modified by the event of Christ, form the 'coherent center' of Paul's gospel."[51] Beker identifies these components of Paul's thought as the motifs of vindication, universalism, dualism, and imminence. According to Beker, Paul believed in the God of Israel and in the faithfulness and vindication of God in the Old Testament, especially the Psalms (Ps 143:11–12a) and Ezekiel (Ezek 39:25; cf. 39:7, 21; 36:22–23). The Psalmist and Ezekiel were longing for the vindication of God's power over this world. Paul considered "the gospel of Jesus Christ as the inauguration of God's faithfulness,"[52] and "the death and resurrection of Jesus Christ reveal the enduring faithfulness and ultimate vindication of God."[53]

Beker says, "Paul believed in the God of Israel who has confirmed his self-vindication and faithfulness to his promises in the death and resurrection of Jesus Christ and will soon bring them to fulfillment in his whole creation."[54] Beker sees that "Paul characterizes Jesus Christ as the pledge

---

48. Cf. ibid., xi.

49. Beker, "Recasting Pauline Theology," 17–18.

50. Beker, *Paul the Apostle*, 40. Beker points out that Bultmann, in his *Theology of the New Testament*, "follows a topical-dogmatic method that- notwithstanding its often anthropological focus-moves away from the contextual meaning of Paul's themes and language" (ibid.).

51. Beker, *Paul's Apocalyptic Gospel*, 14–15.

52. Beker, *Triumph of God*, 22.

53. Ibid., 21.

54. Ibid.

of God's imminent self-vindication."⁵⁵ Hence, Paul's interpretation of the gospel joins the apocalyptic to the theocentric perspective: the promises of the Old Testament have not been fulfilled in the gospel of Christ but will be fulfilled in the future.⁵⁶ Thus Beker shows how Paul interpreted Jesus within the Jewish apocalyptic motif of the faithfulness and vindication of God.

Beker asserts that universalism is also one of Paul's modifications of Jewish apocalyptic. He writes that "in Jewish apocalyptic the faithfulness and vindication of God is primarily directed to the vindication of those in Israel who are obedient to the Law of God."⁵⁷ However, Paul modified this apocalyptic motif to the universal reign of God rather than to a kingdom confined only to those who are faithful to Torah. Beker observes that Paul saw the death of Jesus Christ as God's universal wrath and judgment. Paul "understood the death of Christ as the apocalyptic judgment on all people, while Christ's resurrection signifies the free gift of new life in Christ for all" (Rom 5:12–19)."⁵⁸ In this way, Beker insists that Paul's apocalyptic motif of universalism is also a modification of Jewish apocalyptic.

He also notes that Paul used the Jewish apocalyptic motif of dualism. This consists of an antithesis between this world and the world to come as well as an enmity between the evil powers of the world and the representatives of the coming age of God's kingdom.⁵⁹ Beker insists that "the dualism between 'this age' and 'the age to come' must be understood in connection with the cosmic anthropology of apocalyptic."⁶⁰ According to Beker, "Paul's Christian apocalyptic modifies the Jewish apocalyptic motif of dualism by both tempering it and intensifying it."⁶¹

Beker explains what this tempering means: "Paul tempers the dualism between this and the coming age, then, by emphasizing continuity in the midst of discontinuity, a continuity that is grounded in God's faithfulness to Israel. Furthermore, the proleptic experience of the new age is manifest in the new life in the Spirit made possible for Christians through the death and resurrection of Jesus Christ."⁶²

---

55. Ibid., 24.
56. Ibid., 22.
57. Ibid., 25.
58. Ibid., 25–26.
59. Ibid., 27.
60. Ibid., 28.
61. Beker, *Paul's Apocalyptic Gospel*, 40.
62. Beker, *The Triumph of God*, 28–29.

For Beker, "Paul denies with Jewish apocalyptic that sin and death are to some extent independent agents,"[63] and affirms that "Christians have been set free from the power of sin and will be set free from the power of death, once death, 'the last enemy' (1 Cor. 15:26), will have been defeated in the final triumph of God."[64] Thus Paul modified the dualistic structure of Jewish apocalyptic thought through the Christ-event.

Finally, Beker demonstrates that Paul's motif of imminence is related to the vindication of God, universalism, and dualism. He says that "Paul strengthens the motif of imminence by linking it to an intense hope in the vindication of God and his universal reign."[65] It is "the universal and cosmic reign of God that will dissolve all dualistic structures of the world and eliminate all suffering."[66] Indeed, Paul intensified this aspect of Jewish apocalyptic "since the death and resurrection of Christ already heralds the incursion of the future into the present."[67]

Beker's study shows how Paul's thought was molded by four central motifs of Jewish apocalyptic, though Paul strongly modified both the imagery and conceptuality of apocalyptic. Ultimately, Beker shows how an understanding of Paul's rootedness in Jewish patterns of thought is essential to comprehending Paul and the gospel, even though Beker does not interpret Paul entirely within the contemporary thinking of first-century Judaism.

Tomson: Halakhah[68] in Paul's Letters

Tomson notes the halakhic element in Paul's letters, which he compares to ancient Jewish sources, including possible Hellenistic influences. Tomson depicts Paul as a Hellenistic Pharisee whose thought was rooted in Palestinian and Pharisaic rabbinic Judaism.[69]

Tomson interprets Paul's unsystematic, yet coherent thought evident in his letters as an example of ancient Jewish midrashic method in which "the nature of midrash is not exegesis proper, and even less so systematic

---

63. Beker, *Paul's Apocalyptic Gospel*, 43.
64. Ibid., 43–44.
65. Beker, *The Triumph of God*, 31.
66. Ibid., 33.
67. Ibid.
68. I will use this spelling of "halakhah" except when I cite others, e.g., Tomson.
69. Tomson, *Paul and the Jewish Law*.

thinking, but the creation of connections between the written verses on the one hand and actual life or thought on the other."[70]

Paul's coherent thought stems from the organic structure of practical life, not from theological adumbrations. Moreover, Paul was primarily concerned about mutual accommodation in Gentile behavior (Galatians), Jewish sensitivities (Romans), and the pursuit of unity in the church. Tomson's study on the halakhic element in Paul's letters shows us the direct relationship between Paul's thought and Jewish sources, specifically halakhic sources.

Tomson demonstrates Paul's Jewishness with reference to the halakhic element in Paul's letters. He believes that the roots of Paul's teaching in the halakhah are extremely important to understanding Paul's thought.[71] Tomson says "that halakha played an essential role in Hellenistic Diaspora Judaism"[72] and that "Hellenistic Jews seem to have had their own halakhic traditions, written or oral, and that they were closely related to the halakhic traditions of Palestinian Jewry."[73] In other words, since Paul was a Diaspora Jew, his usage of halakhic tradition is not much different from that of Palestinian Judaism.

Tomson demonstrates how Paul used halakhic sources in his letters. He describes two main categories, which are "halakhic sources, or those that are intended to formulate halakha, either in 'pure' or in midrash form; and non-halakhic sources such as narratives, apocalypses or adhortations, which contain or reflect halakha in an incidental or fragmentary way."[74] Tomson goes on to say that Paul's letters belong to the second of these categories: non-halakhic sources, which include three different modes.

The first mode is that of "halakha [which was] reflected in behavior or speech of Jews within a narrative."[75] This mode "gives only indirect information on the author's own attitude toward the halakha he describes"[76] and is found in the narrative of Paul's letters. For example, Paul mentioned his circumcision and that of others (Phil 3:5; Gal 2:3) and "his planned

---

70. Ibid., 49.
71. Tomson, *Paul and the Jewish Law*, xiv.
72. Ibid., 263.
73. Ibid., 263–64.
74. Ibid., 259.
75. Ibid., 260.
76. Ibid.

participation in festivals (1 Cor. 16:8)."[77] These examples describe Paul's Jewish surroundings, which give us information on Paul's own attitude toward the halakhah.

In the second mode, Tomson explains, "halakha cited in support of a hortatory argument."[78] This mode "by definition gives direct expression to the author's positive attitude."[79] Tomson further explains, for example, that Paul paraphrased dominical halakha, or halakhic teaching of Jesus on the divorce issue (1 Cor 7:10f.), "on sustenance of Apostles" (1 Cor 9:14), and "on the silence of women during worship" (1 Cor 14:34).[80]

Moreover, in 1 Cor 11: 23-25, Paul cited a "tradition of the Lord," namely "the eucharist tradition which contains halakhic elements on table order."[81] Tomson goes on to say that "while the halakhot on Apostolic sustenance and the silence of women agree with Pharisaic-Rabbinic halakha, the ones on divorce and the table order are closer to Essene halakha."[82]

Apostolic halakhah can be found in Paul's letter in the halakhic formula regarding the remarriage of widows (1 Cor 7:39), which is often compared to Paul's homiletical use of Rom 7:2f. and the instruction concerning head covering of women (1 Cor 11:2-16). Paul used general halakhah in Gal 5:3[83] and in his allusion to the common Jewish liturgical functionary of "deputy of the community" (1 Cor 14:16), as well as "in the prohibition of 'unchastity'" (1 Cor 5:1; cf. 1 Thess 4:3).[84] Finally, Tomson points out that Paul himself formulated halakhah in 1 Cor 10:25-27 regarding "'undesignated food' in pagan surroundings."[85]

In the third mode, "halakha quoted in a work based on the premise that Law observance is obsolete."[86] In this usage, it "expresses a contrast between the author's attitude towards the halakha and the specific tradition

---

77. Ibid.
78. Ibid.
79. Ibid.
80. Ibid., 262.
81. Ibid.
82. Ibid.
83. Tomson notes, "the proselyting halakha which as we just reiterated supports Paul's theological argument against forced judaizing by Gentile Christians" (ibid.).
84. Ibid.
85. Ibid.
86. Ibid., 260.

he happens to utilize."⁸⁷ To be sure, "the author shows no positive interest in the halakha he cites, but neither is he interested in distorting it; adaptation is possible but exact quotation more likely."⁸⁸

Tomson does not find the third mode described above in Paul's writings and demonstrates why he could not find this mode in Galatians. Tomson explains that in the Antioch incident in Gal 2:11–14, the point "is not in the amount of halakha reflected, for information on it is meagre and indirect."⁸⁹ Moreover, "Its sustained and vigorous polemic against forced judaizing and proselyting of Gentile Christians is striking and creates a most unlikely setting for a specific report on a halakhic problem."⁹⁰ Again, Tomson argues that Paul's attitude towards the halakhah remained unaltered even in the midst of law polemic, though the polemic was not central.⁹¹

Tomson also discusses the proselyting halakhah cited in Gal 5:3. "Paul relies on the halakhic distinction between Jews and Gentiles as to the obligatoriness of the commandments," Tomson writes. "His plea against forced observance of the Law is based on the halakha."⁹² Concerning the idol food passage in 1 Cor 8–10, Tomson sees that "Paul does not reject halakha as such but follows a well identifiable halakhic tradition based on a positive relationship to the Jewish law."⁹³

Tomson also suggests that Paul did not reject halakhah in Rom 14–15, but was instead calling for forbearance with those who kept rather than abrogated dietary and purity commandments. In Galatians, Tomson could not find evidence of the third mode, which consists of "halakha cited by an author who himself takes a negative view on halakha."⁹⁴ Thus Tomson finds that Paul used Jewish and Jewish-Christian halakhah in his letters.⁹⁵

Furthermore, Tomson thinks this halakhah, which was formulated by Paul himself, is remarkable regarding the behavior of Gentiles (1 Cor 10:25–27) and that the table fellowship (Rom 14f.) does not fit any category

87. Ibid.
88. Ibid.
89. Ibid.
90. Ibid., 261.
91. Ibid.
92. Ibid.
93. Ibid.
94. Ibid.
95. Ibid.

of mode but rather refers to halakhah because, to some degree, it directly appeals to the reader.[96]

Tomson also believes that in Rom 15, Paul shows a moral appeal for tolerance. Paul used the halakhic principle to imply that the strong should show tolerance toward the weak. In Galatians, Paul had previously said that Gentiles are not obliged to keep Jewish commandments, but according to Romans, the strong are called on to show forbearance toward their delicate Jewish brothers and sisters.[97] This presupposes the halakhic principle that Gentiles are not bound to the Jewish law, but "the message is respect the halakha."[98]

Tomson concludes that Paul never gave up his Jewishness after his Damascus experience but was actually engaged in formulating halakhah for Gentiles. Paul letters contribute to our knowledge of an almost lost literary genre: grecized halakha. Tomson explains, "On the other hand this enhances his Pharisaic background, which as our study showed was not left behind after his 'conversion' on the Damascus road but accompanied him on his further travels, so much indeed that we actually find him formulating halakha for Gentiles in Greek."[99]

In addition, Tomson indicates that Paul's teachings shared greater similarity with the Hillelite tradition than the Shammaite because the Hillelite tradition had an open attitude toward Gentiles regarding social relations, proselytism, and future salvation.[100] Thus Tomson shows us how Paul's thought maintains a direct relationship with Jewish tradition, arguing that "Paul was a hellenizing Jew to the extent that he lived among Greek-speaking communities of Jew and Gentiles, wrote letters to them in Greek, and in doing so employed both Hellenistic literary conventions and motifs from popular Stoic and Cynic wisdom."[101]

Nanos: The Shema in Romans

Understanding of Paul in his Jewish context has also been developed by Mark D. Nanos in his book *The Mystery of Romans*. Nanos emphasizes the

---

96. Ibid., 262–63.
97. Ibid., 263.
98. Ibid.
99. Ibid., 264.
100. Ibid., 266.
101. Ibid., 52.

thorough Jewishness of Paul. For Nanos, Paul's thought functioned entirely within the context of Judaism and, therefore, the historical Paul must be understood in his Jewish context.

Nanos sees monotheism and the Shema as the basis for Paul's argument in Romans.[102] He shows us how Paul's characteristic development of the Shema is the central point of Romans. The Shema is the core of Judaism, in that it emphasizes God's oneness.[103] Nanos also points out that Paul demonstrated "the *universalism* embedded in the monotheistic faith of Israel—for the One God of Israel was also the One God of the nations ('the Lord is One')."[104] For Nanos, Paul's argument that Israel had a special privilege in the Torah is grounded in his monotheistic understanding of the role of Torah.

However, Nanos says, Paul's "argument turns on the *compromise* of God's universal oneness he sees in the denial of equal *access* to those outside Israel and Torah (Rom. 3:29–31)."[105] Moreover, Nanos points out that Paul did not deny the special role of Israel and the Torah but "affirmed both and turned the tables, as it were, on those of Israel who would seek to deny Gentiles equal access to God's promised blessings because they were not part of Israel, for the God who demonstrated his faithfulness to Israel is the one and only God."[106] Nanos believes the Shema[107] of faith (the faith by which Gentiles made confession of the One God without becoming Jews) is not a denial of Israel's election or of the "Torah of faith." On the contrary, it establishes Torah as a witness to the faithfulness of God to "the Jew first and also to the Greek (Rom 1:16)."[108]

Nanos further explains why Paul forbade Gentiles to become Jews. Nanos argues that if Gentiles were not forbidden to become Jewish, it would deny the universalistic oneness of God rather than keeping Torah—which would no longer be a valid act of faith.[109] Nanos goes on to say that Paul saw the Shema of faith (Deut 6:4) in the faith of Abraham (Deut 4:12), who

---

102. Nanos, *Mystery of Romans*, 179–201.
103. Ibid., 80.
104. Ibid., 181.
105. Ibid.
106. Ibid., 182.
107. "Hear [Shema] O Israel, the Lord is our God, the Lord is One" (Deut 6:4). Nanos uses the phrase "the Shema of faith" as Jewish confession of the One God of universe.
108. Ibid., 182.
109. Ibid., 184.

"turned from pagan idolatry to the worship of the One God and walked in righteousness and fulfilled the very intentions of Torah before Torah was even given."[110] According to Nanos, "Paul's linking Torah and the Shema was not unique in Diaspora Judaism," and, surprisingly, "Nor was his linking of the Shema with Israel's election. Even his application of the Shema to a universalistic understanding of the One God for the inclusion of Gentiles was not entirely unique."[111]

Nanos summarizes Romans with this central expression of the Shema of Jewish faith. In Rom 2–4, Paul describes the privilege of the Jew first; "the Torah of faith" itself bears witness both to the election of Israel and to the demonstration of God's faithfulness to all the nations that have faith in the One God. Paul explains the inclusion of Gentiles and their obligation to righteous behavior in Rom 5–8. In Rom 9–11, Paul discusses Israel's responsibility and the current state of affairs. Paul also mentions Gentiles' responsibility to fulfill their eschatological purpose (Rom 12:1–14:4).[112] Nanos indicates that "all these concerns flow from his monotheistic argument for faith in Christ Jesus and the equal inclusion of Gentiles in the people of God through the Shema of faith [Deut. 6:4] that 'establishes' the 'Torah of faith.'"[113]

For Nanos, Paul demonstrated monotheistic faith despite the requirement of purity laws in the context of table fellowship and ethical behavior.[114] Christian Gentiles are theoretically free from purity laws because they are not Jews. In Rom 6, according to Nanos, Paul said Christian Gentiles are obligated to proper behavior even though "they are not under law but under grace." In other words, Christian Gentiles were not free from either the ethical or the purity requirement.[115]

According to Nanos, Christian Gentiles are now "slaves of righteousness," which means "they are not free of the requirements of obedience that follow from their new confession of the Shema. They must obey the

---

110. Ibid., 185.

111. Ibid.

112. Ibid., 187.

113. Ibid.

114. Ibid., 195. By "purity" Nanos means that "Paul and his contemporaries saw the issue of purity in the context of the election of Israel to the worship, as a community, of the One God in the face of idolatry, the very rejection of God and the 'principle source of impurity.'"

115. Ibid., 200.

halakhah for the 'righteous Gentile' laid out in the apostolic decree as developed from the laws given first to Adam."[116]

However, if Paul was monotheistic in his faith—as Nanos has indicated—then his thought was more rooted in Jewish thought than Hellenistic, because the Old Testament God is presented as the God of Jews and also of Gentiles. That is, he is God of the universe. Universalism springs not only from Hellenistic, but also from Jewish thought. Jewish universalism is expressed in the Shema, which is the very heart of Jewish faith: "Hear [Shema] O Israel: The Lord our God, the Lord is one" (Deut 6:4). Jewish universalism does not exclude Jewish particularism but rather embraces Gentile inclusion.

Paul's Thought and Jewish Roots

Recently, Kathy Ehrensperger has argued that Paul's thought grew out of his Jewish roots in spite of the fact that he was educated in Greek culture.[117] Ehrensperger also sees Paul's Jewish heritage as vitally important for understanding his letters in their proper context. She takes seriously Paul statements that he was "a Hebrew born of Hebrews" (Phil 3:5) and "far more zealous for the tradition of [his] ancestors" (Gal 1:14).[118]

Ehrensperger points out that "scholars developed the tendency to see Paul as mostly enculturated in Hellenism in tandem with an image of Paul putting as much distance between him and his Jewish roots as possible."[119] She goes on to say that nineteenth-century scholars—especially in Germany—began to interpret Paul mainly (if not exclusively) in a Hellenistic context. The consequence of this is that Paul the apostle became the hero of a universalistic new religion.[120]

Ehrensperger points to the example of Jews who had a dual identity in Germany during the nineteenth century. In spite of the movement of the Enlightenment ideal of universal humanity, Jews, with their particular identity, never could gain the acceptance of mainstream society. Assimilation was powerless to prevent the rise of anti-Semitism during the

---

116. Ibid.
117. Ehrensperger, *That We May Be*, 125–32.
118. Ibid., 132.
119. Ibid., 126.
120. Ibid.

nineteenth century.[121] Ehrensperger states that "dual identity did not mean that one had to assimilate a part of one's identity to the point of depriving it of its specific contents."[122] Ehrensperger is fully aware that this was a different period of history, but she uses the dual identity of these German Jews to interpret and illuminate aspects of the relationship and interaction between Jewish and Hellenistic identity in Paul's time.

Ehrensperger believes that scholars' understanding of Philo—who wrote at the same time as Paul, who still remained a zealous Jew, and who was almost as distinguished a representative of Hellenistic Diaspora Judaism as Paul himself—is even more true of Paul. While pointing to Hellenistic influences on both Philo and Paul, Tomson shows that the basic substructure of the thinking and reasoning evident in both of their writings is, in distinct ways, Jewish. Ehrensperger agrees and affirms that "it would seem to follow that unless it appears that Paul effectively departed from the ways of Judaism, halakhah must have remained a central factor in his life and thought."[123]

Ehrensperger also concurs with John Barclay,[124] who compares Paul's letters to other writings of Diaspora Jews. In accordance with Barclay's study, Ehrensperger suggests that Paul's Greek is good but not "stylistically grand" and also points out that R. D. Anderson's study shows that "'Paul's Greek styles seems strongly influenced by the Semitic Greek of the Septuagint.'"[125] Anderson states that "the vocabulary of Paul was not that of an average philosopher or rhetorician but it seems rather that it has been formed primarily by the Septuagint."[126]

Ehrensperger argues, based on all these factors, that Paul's thought clearly derives from his Jewish roots, even though he had received a Greek education. She concludes:

> Paul emphasizes that he "advanced in Judaism beyond many among my people of the same age," being "far more zealous for the traditions of my ancestors" (Gal 1:14). After his call Paul committed his life to the "inbringing" of the Gentiles (which possibly implied that he spent more of his time among Gentiles than with

121. Ibid., 129.
122. Ibid.
123. Ehrensperger, *That We May Be*, 131.
124. Ibid. See also Barclay, *Jews in the Mediterranean*, esp. 383.
125. Ehrensperger, *That We May Be*, 131; Anderson, *Ancient Rhetorical Theory*, 281.
126. Ehrensperger, *That We May Be*, 131; Anderson, *Ancient Rhetorical Theory*, 282.

More Recent Views of Paul

Jews); Nevertheless, he shows hardly any attempt to express the gospel in terms of Hellenistic culture . . . Paul uses traditional, scripturally based Jewish tradition; intending to root the identity of his Gentile converts firmly within this tradition. He does not try to identify in any way with Hellenistic culture as such. His universal adaptability in 1 Cor. 9:19ff. can be read as an occasional strategy to suit his own missionary purpose.[127]

These scholars focus on differing aspects of Paul's thought as evidence of his Jewish roots, which is crucial to helping us understand Paul. But specific scholars differ in their views of Paul's concepts of law and covenant. We will now discuss these points to determine what is at the center of Paul's theology.

---

127. Ehrensperger, *That We May Be*, 131–32.

4

Divergent Perceptions of Paul's Theology

THE NEW PERSPECTIVE MAKES it possible to understand Paul's relationship with Judaism more impartially and fairly—yet what it brings to the current debate on Paul's theology is complicated and does not lead to a clear consensus.

The Reformers' understanding of Paul's theology of law has had a powerful influence on biblical scholarship. Luther understood that Paul's usage of "law" in his epistle was referring to the attainment of merit. Luther believed that a misguided view of good works and of merit was the problem of Paul's day. He also thought that the phrase, "works of the law" does not refer to the ceremonial law but to the whole law.[1] Rudolf Bultmann,[2] C. H. Dodd,[3] Charles E. B. Cranfield,[4] and Ernst Käsemann continue to support the Reformers' view that "works of the law" refers to legalism.[5]

---

1. Luther, *Lectures on Galatians*, 124–27, 138–40; ibid., *Commentary on Romans*, 75, 80, 144–46. Luther's definition of a religion of works-righteousness is that one could merit favor with God by doing good works. However, according to Campbell, there is an issue here as to whether legalism or a religion of works-righteousness is the best description of Luther's views. For more detail, see Campbell, "Perceptions of Compatibility," 299–316.

2. Bultmann, *Theology of the New Testament*, 1:259–69.

3. Dodd, *Epistle of Paul*, 49–50, 163–65.

4. Cranfield, *Epistle to the Romans*, 845–62.

5. Käsemann, *Commentary on Romans*, 276–83. Campbell claims this perspective originated with F. Weber in the nineteenth century in Campbell, "Perceptions of Compatibility," 304.

Cranfield indicates that Paul did not think the law had been ended in Christ but that Paul was against legalistic teaching. In other words, Paul never was against law itself, but legalism.[6] Dodd also insists that Paul opposed the legalistic Judaism that Dodd considered to be characteristic of first-century Judaism.[7]

The New Perspective

On the other hand, W. D. Davies—a pioneer of the New Perspective—held that "the gift of the law itself for Jews, because it was not solely commandment, was regarded as an act of grace and a means to grace."[8] Davies goes on to say that "as a Pharisee, Paul would have regarded the law as the perfect expression of God's will. But his 'conversion' compelled him to reassess Judaism and particularly the law."[9] Davies notes that Protestant theologians have often misunderstood the law (Torah) as commandment and mistakenly interpreted Jewish tradition as teaching legalism.[10]

Davies also sees that Paul interpreted the law in the context of the messianic situation. When Paul discussed the law, he related it to Christ. Some rabbis believed the law would be continued in the messianic age; others thought the law would be completely abrogated at that time. Paul was convinced that Jesus, as the Messiah, interpreted the Torah in a new light.[11]

Davies further points out that Paul's response to the law was not monolithic but instead contained various positions. He stresses that "Paul writes polemically and looks at that law with the cold eyes of an antagonist [Gal] . . . With the cross of Christ the writ of the law came to an end (2:21; 3:13, 19; 15:11). Paul is at his coarsest in dismissing those who oppose this view (5:12)."[12]

"Elements of the critique offered in Galatians are repeated," Davies says, "but, in Romans, Paul approaches the law, not from an external view

---

6. Cranfield, *Epistle of Paul*, 845–62.
7. Dodd, *Epistle of Paul*, 49–50, 163–65.
8. Davies, *Jewish and Pauline Studies*, 95.
9. Ibid., 235.
10. Ibid., 93.
11. Ibid., 100–103.
12. Ibid., 103–104.

point as in Galatians, as if it were an object of his dispassionate or clinical theological reflection, but from within, that is, as experience."[13]

For Davies, Paul would have understood that the Torah was an experience of divine grace and, hence, that the antithesis between law and grace is a Christian misinterpretation. Paul was not anti-Torah. Davies consistently argues that "Christ is the end of the law (Rom 10:4) signifies, not that the law has come to an end, but that it has reached its final purpose in him; Christ was the goal to which the law was directed (cf. Rom 3:21)."[14] Davies sees that, for Paul, the gospel was the completion of Judaism rather than the annulment of it.[15]

E. P. Sanders, who was Davies' student, states in his monumental work *Paul and Palestinian Judaism* that the Judaism of Paul's day was a form of "covenantal nomism."[16] First-century Judaism was not legalistic— a religion in which God's acceptance is earned through the merit of righteousness based on work. Sanders' view is similar to that of George Foot Moore,[17] who in 1927 set out a different view than Emil Schürer's[18] work on first-century Judaism. Nevertheless, Davies emphasizes that for the Jew, the law is both a gift and divine will. Naturally, Paul understood that the law was an experience of divine grace.[19] Sanders goes beyond Davies and in a different direction in developing the idea that in Paul's day Judaism was a "covenantal nomism."

Sanders, therefore, insists that when Paul said, "not by works of the law," he did not mean that keeping the law was leading to legalism or self-righteousness, nor that one could not follow it.[20] In other words, in Paul's

---

13. Ibid., 106.

14. Ibid., 237-38.

15. Ibid., 323.

16. Sanders, *Paul and Palestinian Judaism*, 426-27. According to Sanders, "the 'pattern' or 'structure' of covenantal nomism is this: (1) God has chosen Israel and (2) given the law. The law implies both (3) God's promise to maintain the election and (4) the requirement to obey. (5) God rewards obedience and punishes transgression. (6) The law provides for means of atonement, and atonement results in (7) maintenance or reestablishment of the covenantal relationship. (8) All those who are maintained in the covenant by obedience, atonement and God's mercy belong to the group which will be saved" (ibid., 422).

17. Moore, *Judaism*, 100-121.

18. According to Schürer, first-century Palestinian Judaism was falling into legalism (Schürer, *History of the Jewish*, 2:464-87).

19. Davies, *Jewish and Pauline Studies*, 95, 235.

20. Sanders, *Paul, the Law*, 46.

time, Judaism was not legalistic. Hence, Paul did not attack his fellow Jews for seeking righteousness through legalistic works.[21] Rather, Paul attacked the law because of "what he found inadequate in it."[22] Paul actually attacked the notion of Jewish privilege and the idea of election rather than the law.[23] Sanders's point of view is that when Paul attacked righteousness by the law, he was "against making acceptance of the law a condition of membership in the body of those who will be saved"[24] because Paul's conviction is that primary salvation is available to all on the same basis: faith.[25] Sanders cites two reasons Paul gave for why salvation ("the promise," "righteousness") comes by faith and not by the law: "(1) The promise cannot be inherited on the basis of keeping the law because that would exclude Gentiles. But Gentiles cannot be excluded, for God has appointed Christ as Lord of the whole world and as Savior of all who believe, and has specially called and appointed Paul as apostle to the Gentiles. (2) If it is necessary and sufficient to keep the law in order to inherit the promises of God, Christ died in vain and faith is in vain."[26]

For Sanders, Judaism did not provide for salvation by faith, and that lack is what Paul found wrong in Judaism.[27] In other words, Paul rejected the law because salvation comes only through Christ. Sanders calls it working from "solution to plight,"[28] which means Paul first came to believe that salvation is through Christ alone—and *only then* concluded the law is not the way of salvation.

Sanders points out that Paul lacked consistency in his discussion of the purpose of the law. Romans 2 is evidence of his self-contradictions. Yet, Sanders believes, Paul showed "coherency," even though he is not a "systematic" thinker.[29] Davies, on the other hand, as already noted, thinks that

21. Ibid., foreword to *Paul and Rabbinic Judaism*, xiv.
22. Ibid., *Paul, the Law*, 47.
23. Ibid.
24. Ibid., 48.
25. Ibid.
26. Ibid., foreword to *Paul and Rabbinic Judaism*, xvi.
27. Ibid., xvi.
28. Sanders, *Paul and Palestinian Judaism*, 442–47.
29. Sanders, *Paul, the Law*, 144–47, 314. Räisänen's view on this is stronger than Sanders. He argues that Paul's view of the law is plagued throughout by inconsistencies and contradictions (Räisänen, *Paul and the Law*). Also, he emphasizes, "Paul the theologian is a less coherent and less convincing thinker than is commonly assumed" (ibid., "Paul's Theological Difficulties," 314).

Paul thought the gospel was the completion of Judaism[30] and that the law has reached its final purpose in which Christ was the goal towards which the law was directed.[31]

In Sanders's view, Paul faulted Judaism for not being Christianity.[32] His contrary claim is that Paul denies "the election of Israel and faithfulness to the Mosaic law."[33] Even though Paul left Judaism, "his ethical views were basically Jewish."[34] Sanders separates Pauline Christianity from Judaism: "I am inclined toward the view τέλος in 10:4 means primarily end."[35]

However, for Sanders, Paul did not reject the law because no one could obey it perfectly[36] or because devotion to the law led to legalism. Rather, Paul rejected the law because he thought that salvation was available only through Christ. Paul had no quarrel with the law in itself, according to Rom 7.[37]

A Problem with Judaism

James D. G. Dunn—who coined the phrase "the New Perspective" as a description of his and Sanders's work—agrees with Sanders's that first-century Judaism was not legalistic. However, Dunn disagrees with Sanders's view that Paul did not have a problem with Judaism at all.

Dunn criticizes Sanders for wrongly portraying Paul as arbitrary and contradictory in his theology of law and justification.[38] In his commentary on Romans, Dunn carefully shows that Paul never thought Judaism was legalistic. But this does not mean Paul did not see fault in Judaism at all. Dunn's point is that "works of the law" is not referring to legalism but to "national righteousness."[39]

---

30. Davies, *Paul and Rabbinic Judaism*, 323.
31. Ibid., *Jewish and Pauline Studies*, 237–38.
32. Sanders, foreword to *Paul and Rabbinic Judaism*, xiv–xvii.
33. Ibid., *Paul, the Law*, 208.
34. Ibid., 144.
35. Ibid., 39.
36. Räisänen, "Legalism and Salvation," 68. Räisänen's view is that Paul thought righteousness is not by the law because it is impossible to do the entire law (the "quantitative" answer).
37. Sanders, *Paul, the Law*, 143–62.
38. Dunn, *Romans*; ibid., *Jesus, Paul and the Law*, 183–205; ibid., *Theology of Paul*, 334–85.
39. Ibid., *Jesus, Paul, and the Law*, p. 183–213, esp. 198.

The Jews believed that they were the only people of God, as symbolized in their identity markers: circumcision, food laws, and Sabbath. Gentiles could become people of God only if they were willing to be circumcised and to keep the food law, purity laws, and the Sabbath. These identity markers were what distinguished Jews from Gentiles in the Greco-Roman world. Yet circumcision was primary.[40] Therefore, first-century Jewish people understood "works of law," as their national badge rather than as an attempt to earn God's favor. They kept these observances to demonstrate the covenant status they already possessed.[41]

Dunn goes on to say, however, that Paul criticized this definition of the people of God on the basis that God had now fulfilled the covenant he promised to Abraham: that he would be a blessing to the nations (Gal 3:8; Gen 12:3; 18:8). Hence, participation in the covenant should no longer be only a Jewish privilege. Moreover, the covenant should no longer to be identified by such distinctively Jewish observances as circumcision, food laws, and the Sabbath.[42]

Dunn says that Paul tried to become "freed from the ethnic constraints which he saw to be narrowing the grace of God and diverting the saving purpose of God out of its main channel—Christ."[43] Paul wanted all who put their faith in Jesus as Messiah to be included in the people of God and did not wish to make the observance of Jewish rituals a central issue. Dunn argues that "Paul's negative thrust is against the law taken over too completely by Israel, the law misunderstood by a misplaced emphasis on boundary-marking ritual, the law become a tool of sin in its too close identification with matters of the flesh, the law sidetracked into a focus for nationalistic zeal."[44]

Dunn interprets works of the law as the marks of Jewish privilege. Thus Paul was against Jewish national privilege but not against the law.[45]

40. Ibid., 191–92.
41. Ibid., 194.
42. Ibid., 195.
43. Ibid., *Romans*, 1:lxxi–lxxii.
44. Ibid., lxxii.
45. Ibid., *Jesus, Paul and the Law*, 215–41. In this last part of his book, Dunn indicates that Räisänen, Hübner, Stuhlmacher, Sanders, Bruce, Schreiner, and Westerholm disagree with his understanding of "works of the law" (Dunn, 206–14, 237–41). See also Cranfield, "Works of the Law," 89–101. John Barclay agrees with Dunn that the issue in Galatians is not Jewish legalism but national righteousness, or the law in terms of badges of Jewish Identity (Barclay, *Obeying the Truth*, 235–42). Francis Watson also examines

For Dunn, Paul was polemically against first-century Jews who demanded that Gentiles adhere to Jewish nationalistic practices in order to become part of the people of God, rather than against legalism as such. His view is different from Sanders's, who finds no flaw in the Judaism of Paul's time. Yet Dunn does see that Paul had a problem with certain aspects of Judaism.

Does this mean that Paul and the Jewish Christians abandoned their Jewishness (the law)? Dunn asserts that Paul did not want to give up his Jewishness and the badges of his national religion. But because the Jews believed in Jesus as Messiah, "faith in Jesus as Christ becomes the primary identity marker which renders the others superfluous,"[46] and these observances were certainly not obligatory. Finally, Dunn understands τέλος in Rom 10:4 as "Christ is the end of the old epoch and of Israel's exclusive privileges with it."[47]

Throughout Romans and Galatians, Dunn uniformly interprets the law or works of the law as Jewish national righteousness, privilege, or identity marker. In the end, therefore, despite his agreement with aspects of Sanders, Dunn is more negative toward the law than Sanders.

In his book *Paul and the Law*, Heikki Räisänen agrees with Sanders and Dunn that Judaism was not legalistic. But Paul portrayed Judaism as legalistic.[48] Räisänen goes back to the traditional understanding, supporting Sanders's notion that Paul's view of the law is plagued by inconsistencies and contradictions.[49] Indeed, Räisänen emphasizes Paul's inconsistencies and arbitrariness even more heavily than Sanders.

However, Räisänen believes that Paul distorted first-century Judaism by describing it as legalistic, while he portrayed his own theology as gracious because his only concern was to defend and promote the Gentile mission.[50] Räisänen argues that Paul had a theological problem with law.[51]

Romans from this perspective and comes to a conclusion similar to Dunn's (Watson, *Paul, Judaism*, 88–176).

46. Ibid., *Jesus, Paul and the Law*, 196.

47. Ibid., *Romans*, 2:596.

48. Räisänen, 163–98.

49. Ibid., 142, 199–202. Räisänen tries to prove Paul's inconsistencies and contradictions throughout the book.

50. Ibid., 176–77.

51. Ibid., 14–15, 140.

Räisänen, therefore, criticizes Paul for being responsible for a distortion of first-century Judaism.[52]

He also asserts that Paul was critical of the law because Paul's Pharisaic experience was in his past. Räisänen states that Paul's life under the law was a form of slavery because he was unable to fulfill the high standard of law—even though, after his conversion, he was free from that burden of the law.[53] However, Räisänen holds that because of Paul's own conversion and the inclusion of Gentiles into the people of God, Paul did misrepresent the law even as he lived apart from the law.

J. Christiaan Beker, in his book *Paul the Apostle*, carefully investigates Paul's theological method rather than sharing Sanders and Räisänen's concern with the relationship between Judaism and Paul or with Paul's view of the law. However, Beker's study still contains a significant discussion of the coherence of the law and the relationship between Paul and Judaism.

Beker suggests that we must understand Paul's theology of the law within the context of the specific historical situation. For Beker, Paul's theology emerged as the interaction between a central conviction, the approaching cosmic triumph of God, and the specific historical concerns of the communities to which he wrote.

Beker emphasizes that Paul's inconsistency and illogical theology were the result of his central conviction about certain urgent historical situations (e.g., Gal 3:10–29).[54] Beker argues that "Galatians does not render a consistent picture of the relation between law and gospel."[55] When Paul opposed Judaizers in Galatians, he could not avoid the antithetical arguments: faith versus works of the law.[56] On the other hand, in Romans, Paul discussed "the function of the law within the compass of God's faithfulness and salvation-historical plan."[57] The two different views Paul showed from Galatians to Romans were the result of the interplay between the contingent situation and the coherence of the gospel.

Unlike Sanders or Dunn, Beker interprets "works of the law," as "doing the works of the law" (the *mizwoth*). In Gal 3:11-12, Paul did not reject

---

52. Ibid., 154.
53. Ibid., 229–36.
54. Beker, *Paul the Apostle*, 52–56.
55. Ibid., 57.
56. Ibid.
57. Ibid., 107.

"doing" but rather doing in the context of the law. Beker strongly emphasizes this point:

> Paul does not oppose motivation or intent to doing; he does not blame Judaism for adhering to an alleged externality of "doing work" rather than researching the inner impulses of the heart, and he does not psychoanalyze the mistaken intent of the Jew. Rather, Paul opposed "the works of the law" primarily because the system of Judaism has come to an end in the new lordship of Christ. Paul's new allegiance to Christ is the primary reason for this stance toward the law, and it is the new posture that makes him say that works of the law condemn before God. Works of the law are not inherently wrong because they are works; they are primarily wrong because in the new dispensation of Christ they are clearly shown not to have been fulfilled by the Jews.[58]

Beker denies that the interpretation of "works of the law" is legalistic, but he insists that Paul rejected the Jewish idea of salvation. Beker argues that the coherent center of Paul's contingent theology about the law lies in his radical view of the nature of sin. Thus Paul rejected the Jewish notion that repentance and sacrifice were completely effective against sin. Jesus's death on the cross is the only way to deal with the power of sin.

For Beker, "the function of God's holy law was taken up and absorbed by Christ in whom 'the just requirement of the law was fulfilled' (Rom 8:4) and its deadly function under sin was abrogated. Christ was both the fulfillment and end of the law (Rom 10:4)."[59]

Nevertheless, Beker emphasizes that the Jews in Paul's day were not legalistic. Romans 7 cannot be interpreted as a picture of the struggle of the Jew to rely on self rather than on God for salvation.[60] Beker could not accept Sanders's view that in Rom 1–5 Paul argued backwards from salvation in Christ to a necessary plight under the law. Rather, Paul's argument was that the Jews had transgressed the law and were therefore subject to the power of sin. Thus, they needed the death of Christ for their redemption. Paul was simply trying to convince Jews to have faith in Christ for their own salvation.[61]

---

58. Ibid., 246.
59. Ibid., 243.
60. Ibid., 239.
61. Ibid., 242–43.

According to Beker, Paul's argument about the Jewish plight under the law would have been understandable to the Jews of his day, since Paul's point was that all Jews have transgressed the law rather than simply that their works were legalistic. Nevertheless, Beker has a more positive view on Paul's inconsistency concerning the law in his letters than either Räisänen or Sanders.

"Covenant Nomism"

John G. Gager also responds to Räisänen's statement concerning Paul's inconsistency, stating that it is nothing new because, in the late fourth century, John Chrysostom was also defending Paul against the criticism of heresy and inconsistency in his *Homilies on Romans*.[62]

Nevertheless, Gager and Lloyd Gaston build their theology solidly on Sanders's concept of "covenant nomism."[63] In other words, since Judaism is a religion of grace, Paul did not find anything wrong in the law. According to Gager, Paul never said that Jews needed to obey the law perfectly to be saved, or that they were under a curse because of the law, or that they were legalistic. Gager believes that "Paul had no argument against the Jewish law in relation to Israel and the Jews."[64]

Gager argues that Paul's message concerned Gentiles rather than Jews.[65] Paul's statement that salvation does not come through the law relates to the Gentiles—not to the Jews. Since Gentiles were not in covenant with the God of Israel, the law given to Israel could never save them. For this reason, if Gentiles tried to be saved by the law, the law would curse them.

Gager goes on to say that Paul never criticized Jews for not accepting Jesus as their Messiah. Instead, Paul criticized them for wrongly demanding that Gentiles keep the law, because Jesus came to save Gentiles from the law.[66]

---

62. Gager, *Reinventing Paul*, 8.

63. See Gager's *Reinventing Paul* and *The Origins of Anti-Semitism* as well as Gaston's *Paul and the Torah*. Gager and Gaston are much in agreement with one another.

64. Gager, *Reinventing Paul*, 57.

65. Ibid., 77–143.

66. Ibid.

Gager thus subscribes to the two-covenant theory:[67] the covenantal nomism of the Old Testament is God's way of salvation for Israel, while Gentiles are saved through the faithfulness of Jesus Christ. In other words, Jews were saved by the gracious covenant God had already made with Israel, while Gentiles were saved according to a different covenant.

Gaston also points out that Paul demonstrates in Romans a two-covenant theology. Gaston puts it like this:

> Romans 3:21–31 is clearly about the inclusion of the Gentile . . . The "human being" who is justified in verse 28 must mean primarily the Gentile if the connection with the following verse is to be understood: "Or is it of Jews only that God is God? Not also of the Gentiles?" Then comes one of those extraordinary statements to be found only in Romans which indicate that Paul is moving close to the two-covenant theology of F. Rosenzweig. "If indeed God, who will justify the circumcised out of [his] faithfulness, is one, [he will justify] also the uncircumcised through the same [*tes*] faithfulness." Inclusion of Gentiles does not mean exclusion of Jews . . . The inclusion of Gentiles was always the goal of the Torah, which has now been realized through the righteousness of God manifested in the faithfulness of Jesus Christ.[68]

For Gaston, Paul's main point in Rom 9–11 was to make readers know that God had chosen Israel by grace also, and would save Israel by grace alone because God is faithful to his promises to Israel. Therefore, all Israel will be saved. Gentiles should know this condition because they have been called into the people of God on exactly the same basis.

Moreover, Paul was against Israel for its failure to acknowledge that the righteousness of God for Gentiles, which is the goal of the Torah, had now been manifested. Therefore, Gaston insists, God's righteousness is for both, without changing one into the other—namely, through the two-covenant theology.[69]

Sanders and Dunn disagree with this two-covenant theory. Gaston and Gager both lament the anti-Semitism that has so influenced Christian theology. Perhaps, however, Gager's radical view contributes usefully to Jewish-Christian dialogue today.

---

67. Ibid., 59–61, 152. Stendahl also shares some similarities to the two-covenant perspective; Paul's gospel was only for the Gentiles, but this is as far as he goes. See Stendahl, *Paul Among Jews*, 2.

68. Gaston, *Paul and the Torah*, 122–23, 134.

69. Ibid., 142–50.

Reaction and Differentiation

Hans Hübner[70] continues to interpret the law according to the view of the Reformation in general. Hübner criticizes Sanders for failing to see that Paul attacked "legalistic works-righteousness."[71] He says that Paul, in Galatians, was against Jewish legalistic religion.[72] Hübner also insists that Christians do not have to keep the law because the law has been abolished.[73] On the other hand, in Romans, Hübner sees that the law has some positive role for believers.[74]

For Hübner, Christ is the end of the law—although only the misuse of the law has been set aside with the coming of Christ, not the Torah itself.[75] Paul's differing statements in Romans and Galatians, according to Hübner, stem from Paul trying to maintain a good relationship with James. Since Paul thought his work would be in vain without James's approval, he rethought his theology of law in Romans.[76]

Stephen Westerholm attempts to read Romans as Luther did.[77] He maintains that, for Paul, salvation was only through Christ, not through observance of the law, because no one obeys it perfectly. Westerholm also emphasizes that the Spirit plays a central role in Pauline ethics, and that Gentiles were not bound to keep the ceremonial law. "Its ceremonial aspects were never intended for any but Jews," he says. "But even its moral demands now have a different character."[78]

On the other hand, Westerholm points out that Luther's mistake was to read the legalism of Roman Catholicism into the theology of Paul's Jewish opponents. Westerholm did not find evidence that first-century Judaism is fundamentally a legalistic religion in the Pauline text.[79]

---

70. Hübner, *Law in Paul's Thought*.

71. Ibid., "Pauli Theologiae Proprium," 445–73.

72. Ibid., *Law in Paul's Thought*, 53.

73. Ibid., 18–42. Hübner interprets Gal 3 as no one can fulfill the whole law, and if one is obligated to circumcision, then there is an obligation to obey the whole law. That is why Paul rejected circumcision in Galatians.

74. Ibid., 65.

75. Ibid., 65, 138.

76. Ibid., 61–65.

77. See Westerholm's *Israel's Law* and *Preface to the Study of Paul*.

78. Westerholm, *Preface to the Study of Paul*, 92–93.

79. Ibid., *Israel's Law*, 105–222.

Westerholm nevertheless asserts that Paul had a different view of the Judaism of his day. Jews were pursuing the law with misplaced zeal. Paul rejected the law as a way of salvation, but he did not reject it because he considered it legalistic. Christ's coming has set aside the way of law. Thus, Westerholm is not totally against the traditional view on the law, and yet he gives some consideration to the New Perspective on Paul.

Frank Thielman's study shows that Paul did not regard all Jews as legalists or Judaism generally as a legalistic religion.[80] Thielman, unlike Sanders, finds that the Second Temple period literature of Judaism and the Pauline letters shows a clear pattern of plight to solution rather than vice versa. Jewish literature indicates that human beings could not obey the law. Thus, Paul did not argue that Christ provides the solution to humanity's inability to obey the law. Thielman maintains that "Most Jews in Paul's time understand that works of the law do not justify."[81] He concludes that while Christ is the end of the curse of the law, Christ is not the end of all aspects of the law.

Timo Laato shows in his work *Paul and Judaism* that Paul saw Judaism as legalistic because of its synergism. In his perspective, Paul had a different view than Judaism in his understanding of anthropology. Laato explains how, unlike the more optimistic Jewish view, Paul thought human nature was dominated by sin and by the flesh. Paul believed that people have no ability to keep the law and that salvation depends on God's grace alone. Thus, Paul rejected the synergistic theology of Judaism. Paul was, according to Laato, a "monergist," which means one who totally depends on the grace of God in Christ.

Daniel P. Fuller, in his explanation of the relationship between the law and gospel, emphasizes the unity of the Testaments.[82] Paul understood that one divine covenant shows throughout Scripture. This covenant of salvation is always by grace, although good works are also necessary for justification. He maintains that, in Galatians, "works of the law" referred to a legalistic distortion of the law, while in Rom 10:4, Christ is the goal of the law rather than Christ being the end of the law.

Mark D. Nanos also suggests that Paul was not against the law in Galatians. Paul's message is not about being against Israel, or "against Torah observance by Jews who do not share faith in Christ. It is the message of

---

80. See Thielman, "From Plight to Solution."
81. Thielman, *Paul and the Law*, 239.
82. Fuller, *Gospel and Law*; see also ibid., "Paul and the Works of the Law," 28–42.

Torah, the source of Wisdom; it expresses the plight of Israel in the midst of the nations, of the psalmist or the prophet in the den of his accusers."[83] For Nanos, in Gal 2:11–21, the Antioch incident means not "freedom from the Law, but freedom for Torah observant Jews to reconsider the halakhic implications for themselves of the inclusion of Gentiles in the people of God as full equals."[84] Therefore, Nanos sees Paul as a Torah observant Jew even after his encounter with Christ.

As we can see, Paul's theology of the law is still interpreted by many scholars in the traditional way, which assumes that "works of the law" refers to legalism and that the law is now ended. However, some scholars do not think the law has been ended and argue only that Paul was against legalistic teaching. Other scholars read Paul's letter following the Tübingen school's perspective of a very negative view of Judaism. Still others believe that Paul considered Christ to be the goal of the law (Rom 10:4) rather than that the law has come to an end. Thus, the new scholarly perspectives on Paul show no real consensus, though it is possible to identify certain scholars within a particular perspective.

No Real Consensus

Sanders's contribution to the scholarly world was to show that the Judaism of Paul's day was a form of "covenantal nomism" rather than being legalistic. Paul did not regard Judaism as legalistic. Therefore, Paul did not attack his fellow Jews for "legalistic works" righteousness. Rather Paul attacked the law because of "what he found inadequate in it."[85] Indeed, Paul did not find any fault in the law itself, but noted that in Judaism there is lack of provision for salvation by faith. For Sanders, Paul denied the election of Israel and the Mosaic law. Moreover, although Paul left Judaism, he did not become a Gentile but was instead instrumental in the creation of a third entity.[86]

Even if we accept that this view is correct—that Paul did not find fault in the law—how could Paul possibly abandon his past to create the third entity of (former) Jews and Gentiles in Christ? For Sanders, Pauline

83. Nanos, "Inter- and Intra-Jewish," 404.
84. Ibid., 403.
85. Sanders, *Paul, the Law*, 47.
86. As Sanders writes, "the rules governing behavior were partly Jewish, but not entirely, and thus in this way too Paul's Gentile churches were a third entity" (ibid., 178).

Christians are neither Jews nor Gentiles. But did not Paul say in 1 Cor 7:18–20 that Jew remains as Jew and Gentile remains as Gentile? This indicates that Paul honored different ethnic groups but did not encourage them to give up their ethnic identity entirely.[87] For Paul to disconnect with the law he believed to be holy seems unlikely. Nevertheless, Sanders does help us to discover the Jewishness of Paul to some degree, although not entirely. The question still remains: Who was the real historical Paul?

As we have seen, scholars' views on Paul's theology concerning the law and two-covenant theology have developed divergently. Some still see Paul through the lens of Western Christian culture, in which universalism is to be preferred to ethnic particularity. Others go to extremes in order to restore the Jewishness of Paul. Thus, while Sanders does, to some degree, help us to discover the Jewishness of Paul as distinguished from the "Gentilizing" Paul, he still portrays Paul as being against the law and Judaism. The fact is, there is no real consensus on the historical Paul in contemporary scholarship.

The Center of Paul's Theology

The New Perspective and its pioneers brought divergent new interpretations not only of Paul's view of law and covenant but also of the center of Paul's theology. If Judaism was not legalistic in Paul's time, Paul did not have to preach the message of justification by faith to Jews. Naturally, the Reformers' understanding of Paul is faced with new questions: What was the Reformers' view on the center of Paul's theology, and how has this view developed until today?

Martin Luther interpreted Rom 1:16–17 as the center of the entire biblical message of salvation because he saw that Paul taught the justification of the sinner by faith alone.[88] However, in 1904, William Wrede

---

87. See chapter 6.

88. Luther, *Luther's Works*, 34:337. Luther expressed his experience thus: "At last, by the mercy of God, meditating day and night, I gave heed to the context of the words, namely, 'In it the righteous of God is revealed, as it is written, "He who through faith is righteousness shall live."' There I began to understand that the righteousness of God is that by which the righteous lives by a gift of God, namely by faith. And this is the meaning: the righteousness of God is revealed by the gospel, namely, the passive righteousness with which merciful God justifies us by faith, as it is written, 'He who through faith is righteous will live.' Here I felt that I was altogether born again and had entered paradise itself through open gates. There a totally other face of the entire Scriptures showed itself

asserted that justification by faith was not the central teaching in Paul's theology but rather a polemical response to the Judaism of his day.[89] Albert Schweitzer supported Wrede's view when he observed that "the doctrine of righteousness by faith is a subsidiary crater, which has formed within the rim of the main crater—the mystical doctrine of redemption through the being-in-Christ."[90] For Schweitzer, justification by faith was simply a "subsidiary crater" in Paul's theology; eschatological redemption was the vital element in Paul's thought. For Schweitzer, in Paul the main crater is a central Christ mysticism.

In 1961, Krister Stendahl stressed the difference between the converted Pharisee Paul and Martin Luther, who was driven by pangs of conscience.[91] By emphasizing that Paul's theology has been misunderstood because it has been read through the lenses of Luther and Augustine, Stendahl claims that the doctrine of justification was not the center of Paul's message of salvation. The reason Paul said that justification is available only through faith in Jesus Christ and not through works of the law is because Paul wanted to make sure that Gentiles understood they could share the same privileges of salvation as Israel through faith in Christ.[92] Stendahl claims that "the center of gravity in Paul's theological work is related to the fact that he knew himself to be called to be the Apostle to the Gentiles, an Apostle of the one God who is Creator of both Jews and Gentiles."[93]

W. D. Davies, who holds that the law was a gift from God and the joy of first-century Judaism, thought that the influence of the Reformation—which emphasized justification by faith as the heart of the gospel—accounts for the difficulty that we have in understanding Paul's thought.[94] "The center of Paulinism lies not in the relation of gospel and law," he says,

---

to me. Thereupon I ran though the Scriptures from memory. I also found in other terms an analogy, as, the word of God, that is, what God does in us, the power of God, with which he makes us strong, the wisdom of God, with which he makes us wise, the strength of God, the salvation of God, the glory of God. And I extolled my sweetest word with a love as great as the hatred with which I had before hated the word 'righteousness of God.' Thus that place in Paul was for me truly the gate to paradise" (ibid.).

89. Wrede, *Paulus*, 72.
90. Schweitzer, *Mysticism of Paul*, 225.
91. Stendahl, *Paul Among Jews*, 185–86.
92. Ibid., 15–40, 78–96.
93. Ibid., 15.
94. Davies, *Jewish and Pauline Studies*, 238.

"but in Paul's awareness that with the coming of Christ the age to come was becoming present fact, the proof of which was the advent of the spirit."[95]

Starting from his view that first-century Judaism was "covenantal nomism," Sanders opposes the Reformation's view of justification as the center of Paul's theology. He discusses Albert Schweitzer's distinction between a peripheral justification and a central Christ mysticism in Paul, but Sanders does not think that justification by faith is so important. For him, the center of Paul's thought is "participation in Christ."[96] Sanders, moreover, asserts that Paul considered participation in Christ to be much more important than justification.[97] Sanders's evaluation of Paul's theology on justification is very similar to Stendahl's.

Since Stendhal, Davies, Sanders, and Dunn all agree that, in Paul's time, Judaism was not a works-righteousness religion, the traditional view of the center of Paul's thought starts to collapse rapidly among scholars.

J. Christiaan Beker, like Schweitzer, says that Paul's central thought is "the Christ-event in its apocalyptic meaning," but Beker emphasizes that the real center for Paul is "the triumph of God."[98] "Paul's apocalyptic theocentrism, then, is not to be contrasted with his Christocentric thinking," he asserts, "for the final hour of the glory of Christ and his Parousia will coincide with the glory of God, that is, with the actualization of the redemption of God's created order in his kingdom."[99]

Alan Segal focuses on 2 Cor 4:4 as the center of Paul's thought. He writes, "the center of Paul's gospel is the identification of Christ as the Glory of God" and adds that "Paul's vocation is to make known the identification of Jesus Christ as the Glory of God."[100]

Neil Elliott offers a different perspective: that the heart of Paul's theology is not about individual salvation or Gentiles' inclusion, but instead "the apocalyptic theology centers on the vindication of God's ancient purposes for the covenant people, and through them for the liberation of all creation."[101]

---

95. Ibid., 239.
96. Sanders, *Paul and Palestinian Judaism, Paul, the Law*, 5.
97. Ibid., *Paul*, 65–76, esp.74.
98. Beker, *Paul the Apostle*, 362–63.
99. Ibid., 363.
100. Segal, *Paul the Convert*, 156–57.
101. Elliott, *Liberating Paul*, 138.

Divergent Perceptions of Paul's Theology

Hans Hübner, however, still retains, in general, the original Reformer's view on the center of Paul's theology. Hübner strongly insists that the center of Paul's theology is "legalistic works-righteousness" and wonders why Sanders cannot see this in Paul's epistles.[102]

In spite of all these divergent views on the center of Paul's thought, Peter Stuhlmacher, Ernst Käsemann, and Rudolf Bultmann still assure us that "justification by faith" is Paul's central theme.[103] Bultmann, like Luther, emphasizes that justification by faith is the center of Paul's theology. He tends to approach Paul in an eschatological dimension through his own existentialist approach, with its emphasis on the individual.[104]

Yet Käsemann and Stuhlmacher view justification by faith not only as individual salvation (on the model of Luther), but also assert that it has a corporate and cosmic aspect.[105] Käsemann, in fact, makes a substantial correction to Bultmann's theology in opposing his existentialist individualism.

The New Perspective on Paul has brought forth divergent views regarding the center of Paul's theology. The question still remains, however: What is central to Paul's theology? An interesting way of approaching this complicated issue is proposed by Brad Young, who indicates that "Paul's conceptual theology is circular thought but not linear... In circular thought the conceptual theological ideas are connected together in continuous motion."[106] If Paul's thought is seen as primarily circular and evolving, then we might see that his view of Jesus as the goal of the Torah is intertwined with several thoughts he wove together in order to present the concept of Messiah. Perhaps the question of what is the center of Paul's theology is itself problematic in light of this Jewish way of thinking.

---

102. Hübner, "Pauli Theologiae Proprium," 445-73.

103. See Stuhlmacher, *Revisiting Paul's Doctrine*; ibid., *Paul's Letter*; Käsemann, *Commentary on Romans*; ibid., *Perspectives on Paul*; Bultmann, *Theology of the New Testament*; and Schlatter, *Romans*. Schlatter interprets the Romans' theme as the righteousness of God in the context of eschatology, as does Schweitzer.

104. Bultmann, *Theology of the New Testament*, 1:318-19.

105. Käsemann, *Perspectives on Paul*, 32-59; Stuhlmacher, *Reconciliation, Law*, 68-93.

106. Young, *Paul the Jewish Theologian*, 40.

The Next Step

Whereas the Reformers' exegesis was to generalize Paul's understanding of law,[107] the New Perspective brought fresh attention to Paul's understanding of law, covenant, and to the quest for the center of his theology. Because of this New Perspective, we are able to understand Paul's relationship with Judaism more impartially and, hopefully, with less bias.

However, the New Perspective on Paul, in spite of its contribution, also has to answer some questions. The current debate on Paul's theology is complicated and leads in divergent directions. Yet questions still remain: What did Paul really intend to say about the law? Was there a center to his thought? What did he consider to be the relationship between faith and the law? How do we find answers to these questions? The only way to progress in the current debate is to return to the biblical text, read it in its context. It is in this—Paul's Jewish roots—that we find a vital element in understanding Paul's thought. Following this line of thought, let us continue the attempt to understand Paul's letters from a Jewish perspective in light of contemporary scholarship.

Up until now, the focus of the present investigation has been mainly descriptive. Its aim has been to observe how current scholars' tendency to view Paul mainly from his Hellenistic thought or from his Jewish roots has emerged in general and how, in various scholars' views, hermeneutics and theology on Paul has been developed.

While the New Perspective discloses Paul's Jewishness to some degree, I wish to demonstrate why Paul remains a Jew in the light of contemporary scholarship. After his encounter with Christ, Paul neither broke with Judaism, nor was he opposed to the Jewish people—as we shall see.

---

107. Luther understood that Paul's usage of "law" in his epistle referred to the attainment of merit (Luther, *Lectures on Galatians*, 33, 124–27, 140, 266; ibid., *Commentary on Romans*, 75, 80, 144, 146). In other words, the Reformers thought Judaism was a religion of merit.

5

How Paul Uses Scripture

PAUL'S ATTITUDE TOWARD SCRIPTURE is a vitally significant element in understanding his Jewishness—and his interpretation of Scripture was from a Jewish perspective rather than from some private theological perspective of his own.

The older view among scholars has been that Paul had his own theological ideas and simply added Scripture texts to support or illustrate them.[1] For example, Heikki Räisänen believes that Paul distorts first-century Judaism (the Torah) by describing it as legalistic while portraying his own theology as gracious in order to defend and promote the Gentile mission.[2]

In contrast to Räisänen, W. S. Campbell emphasizes that after Paul's encounter with Christ, Paul still acknowledged that the Jews were entrusted with the oracles of God and that "he argues as a Jew of his own time from the scriptures he shares with his own people."[3] Paul never abandoned his previously learned methodology, and he continued to describe social grouping on the basis of Scripture, even if "he bends his Pharisaic exegesis to new ends."[4]

Campbell stresses that Paul never believed the Torah is wrong or completely irrelevant despite the fact that faith—not Torah observance—defines

---

1. Dodd, *According to the Scriptures*, 16–25.
2. Räisänen, *Paul and the Law*, 62, 82, 154, 176–202.
3. Campbell, *Paul's Gospel*, 143.
4. Ibid., "Contribution of Traditions," 239–40.

the Christian community.[5] He goes on to say that "it signifies rather a fresh understanding of the place of Torah in the divine purpose. He now realizes that there are specific limits to the Torah's scope and perhaps too that there are temporal limits now that the Messiah has come."[6]

Moreover, Campbell points out that the earliest Christians understood the Scriptures both as Torah and as prophecy of the fullness of time in the eschatological context. Paul "stands in this *pesher* tradition."[7] According to Luke, Jesus's own exegesis strongly reflected the *pesher* type of interpretation, which focused intensely on the fulfillment of prophecy (Luke 4:16–21).

Paul, however, was challenged to interpret Scriptures to guide his communities to live the life of the end time, the coming age. Campbell agrees that "Paul's perspective on the meaning of scripture has changed, reflecting the change from one community to another."[8] Campbell goes on to underline that Paul's "emphasis as apostle to the Gentiles is on the entry requirements for the new covenantal community, in which the performance of the special laws of Judaism are not binding. His emphasis is necessarily different from that of Judaism."[9]

Campbell shares Terence Donaldson view's on Gal 3:13–14, in which Paul argues for the inclusion of the Gentiles.[10] Paul saw the "cross as the eschatological redemption of Israel that sets the stage for the inclusion of Gentiles."[11] Campbell believes that Paul radically reinterpreted the Scripture here with "a Jewish pattern of thought in which the inclusion of the Gentiles is seen as a consequence of the eschatological redemption of Israel."[12]

He argues that—though Paul's radical reinterpretation is the result of his interpretation of the Jewish Scripture in the eschatological context—Paul did not misuse the Scripture but rather argued in a way that

---

5. Ibid., 240.

6. Ibid.

7. Ibid., 240–41. "*Pesher* interpretation" means focusing strongly on the fulfillment of prophecy; Luke showed that Jesus' own exegesis reflects the *pesher* type (Luke 4:16–21).

8. Ibid., 241.

9. Ibid.

10. Donaldson, "Curse of the Law," 106.

11. Campbell, "Contribution of Traditions," 242.

12. Ibid.

his non-believing-in-Christ Jewish brothers would understand and even accept. Campbell suggests that Paul, as a faithful Jew, interpreted Torah in the light of the cross. In other words, rather than misusing Scripture for his own ends, Paul showed himself to be a faithful Jew through his inclusive *pesher* form of interpretation.

Then the question is: Did Paul truly twist Scripture (the Torah) to support his own tendentious arguments? I concur with Campbell's view that Paul used Scripture according to a Jewish *pesher* pattern rather than simply using it to support his own ideas. Paul was a Pharisee who was an interpreter of Scripture. After his encounter with Christ, Paul still remained a Pharisee. Even though some Pharisees would have rejected and misrepresented Paul, Paul does not seem to reject Pharisaism as such. Many years after his encounter with Christ, Paul still insisted that he was a Jew (2 Cor 11:22; Rom 11:1) and, in a broad sense, as Pinchas Lapide trenchantly observes, Paul never underwent conversion out of Judaism: "instead he pursued a vision of vocation which he intentionally described in words originating from the callings of Jeremiah, Isaiah, and Ezekiel."[13]

Paul, Pharisees, and the Use of Midrash

The Pharisees were not only the grand interpreters, but also generated new practices in the first century.[14] As William Dean has indicated, interpreters are speaking "not from beyond history, but only from historical events and interpretations in their own previous lives, events and interpretations which they continually reinterpreted to meet new needs."[15] Likewise, Paul's interpretation of the Old Testament was not from beyond his background, but was rooted in his previous life and in the historical events of the Jesus movement. Paul continues to reinterpret the Scripture in apocalyptic context.

The Pharisaic traditions are always open to redevelopment through responsive interaction with new social situations and through new religious experience. As we have already discussed, Peter J. Tomson has demonstrated how Paul, in the epistle to the Corinthians, constantly formulates halakhah for Gentiles in the Pauline communities.

13. Lapide and Stuhlmacher, *Paul: Rabbi and Apostle*, 47.

14. See Schürer, *History of the Jewish*, 2:336–403. See also Safrai, "Talmudic Literature," 121–35.

15. Dean, "Hebrew Law," 7. Cf. Lee, *Galilean Jewishness*, 116.

Pinchas Lapide, an orthodox Jewish theologian, also sees Paul as a formulizer of halakhah for Gentiles. He says that "Paul prescribes a new *halakha* for his young congregations, containing dozens of statutes, regulations, prohibitions, and requirements, some of which seem to be even stricter than the unascetic ordinances of orthodox rabbis."[16]

Mark D. Nanos, as also already noted, has pointed out that Paul writes Romans in the context of the Shema, which, as the core of Jewish faith, emphasizes God's oneness.[17] In this context, Paul interprets, or reinterprets the Scripture in eschatological context for "the Jew first and also to the Greek." Paul confirms Jewish Scriptures as a witness to the gospel. Nevertheless, for Paul, the Scripture is his primary source of faith and practice, not simply a source just used for proof texts to inculcate in converts. Moreover, there is usually a real coherence between the original context and content of the passage he cites and its use in his arguments.

Paul's Jewish heritage enabled him to attain deeper meaning for himself in the coming of Jesus than would have been the case if he had known only the Gentile perspective. Paul learned from the Old Testament how, more than four hundred years before the law was given in Sinai, God revealed to Abraham his character and purpose—that is, God's righteousness, grace, and the election of Israel. For Paul, God's character and purpose was being fulfilled in Jesus Christ.

Paul probably never had any doubt that either God's character or his salvation plan would be changed by the coming of the Messiah, because all these things God intended were perceived to be recorded in the Scriptures of Israel. Thus, Paul views his teachings as founded in the Hebrew Scripture. In 1 Cor Paul writes, "For I delivered to you as of first importance what I also received, that Christ died for our sins according to the Scripture, and that He was buried, and that He was raised on the third day according to the Scriptures" (1 Cor 15:3–4).

According to Richard Longenecker, Paul quotes directly from the Scripture eighty-three times in his letters.[18] The richness of quotations and Paul's frequent echoes of Scripture show that Paul's mind was fully saturated

---

16. Lapide and Stuhlmacher, *Paul: Rabbi and Apostle*, 37.

17. Nanos, *Mystery of Romans*, 179–87.

18. Longenecker, *Biblical Exegesis*, 107. Longenecker included Romans (forty-five times), 1 Corinthians (fifteen times), 2 Corinthians (seven times), Galatians (ten times), Ephesians (four times), and Pastoral Epistles (two times).

with the Scripture.[19] Paul's reliance upon the Scripture in halakhic dialogue was particularly the characteristic of Pharisaism. However, in distinction to the Pharisees, Paul affirmed the validity of Scripture for illuminating the significance of the coming of Jesus Christ.

His interpretation is typical of Pharisaic interpretation in the first century. The Pharisees' interpretation was "more inductive in nature,"[20] and "it made new judgments based upon new circumstances, and recognizes these judgments as normative interpretations of God's immediate presence."[21] Paul considered the gospel to be both the completion of Judaism and its fulfillment.[22] In this context, Paul interpreted the Scripture in the new circumstances and for the new aeon. "It was rather that the texts themselves were interpreted by living communities," Campbell says, "and what was happening to these people in their daily life was a powerful influence in their interaction with the text ... The interpretation is not fixed by its past, but its real meaning is discovered in the living dynamic of the spirit at work in an ever-new and ever-changing present."[23]

In other words, Paul formed his interpretation of Scripture in interaction with events of daily life in the community. For Paul, this method of interpretation was nothing new because he had already been trained as a Pharisee to interpret the Scriptures in the context of new circumstances and new events.

Dan Cohn-Sherbok, in his book *Rabbinic Perspectives on the New Testament*, has also carefully shown Paul's use of the exegetical methods and modes of exegesis found in rabbinic literature. As Cohn-Sherbok has

---

19. See Hays, *Echoes of Scripture*.

20. See more detail in Lee, *Galilean Jewishness*, 116.

21. Ibid., 116. For example, Qumran viewed Scripture thus. According to Gerald Bray, "An examination of these scrolls reveals that the exegetes of Qumran knew and used many scribal techniques, though they had their own approach to interpretation which at times was quite different. In particular, they believed that Scripture could be interpreted without regard to its context, that it had secondary meanings which were independent of its plain meaning, and that variant texts were nevertheless valid forms of Scripture ... In particular, Qumran had a concept of ongoing divine revelation which supplemented the Torah with additional prophecies. True to the general tendency of the time, the Torah itself gave way to this prophetic form of interpretation, which is the true hallmark of Qumran ... Today this form of interpretation is known as *pesher* ('solution')" (Bray, *Biblical Interpretation*, 60).

22. Davies, *Paul and Rabbinic Judaism*, 323.

23. Campbell, "Contribution of Traditions," 243.

demonstrated, Paul's exegesis is not alienated from its Jewish roots, as seen in his conclusion:

> The preceding analysis of Paul's exegesis of Scripture compared with that found in rabbinic literature bears out his claim. Of course certain aspects of rabbinic exegesis, such as the expansion of scriptural law, are absent from the epistles. Yet like the rabbis, Paul attempted to show that Scripture is sacred, that it is susceptible of interpretation, and that properly understood, it guides the life of the worthy. In proclaiming his Christian message, he employed standard techniques of scriptural exegesis, occasionally even using some of the rules of rabbinic hermeneutics. In this sense, Paul's teaching and preaching are rooted in Pharisaic Judaism.[24]

Paul, a Pharisee, was a grand interpreter, and he reinterpreted (as did others in his time) from his own perspective, if not always from that of other Jews. He never abandoned or misused the Torah but was intent on revealing a new meaning through Christ. As Longenecker has also pointed out, "Paul's basic thought patterns and interpretive procedures were those of first-century Pharisaism."[25]

Paul's Form of Argumentation

Much of Paul's form of argumentation in his letters is Jewish.[26] When Paul wrote letters, he addressed them to his new community as a Jewish missionary and apostle who was appointed by God, like Jeremiah, even before he was born (Gal 1:15). In Romans, Paul demonstrates that his interpretation was rooted firmly in Jewish Torah rather than just in his own personal understanding of the gospel. In Romans, Paul explicitly quotes from Scripture forty-five times (more than half of his total quotations are found in Romans).[27]

Moreover, Paul shows at the beginning and at the end of his epistle to the Romans references to the "holy" and "prophetical writings" which foretold the coming of Christ. At the beginning, Paul declares the gospel was "promised beforehand through His prophets in the holy scriptures,

---

24. Cohn-Sherbok, *Rabbinic Perspectives*, 83.

25. Longenecker, *Biblical Exegesis*, 126.

26. See Sanders, *Paul, the Law*, 160–62; Davies, *Jewish and Pauline Studies*, 91–122; Beker, *Paul the Apostle*, xviii, 135–52.

27. Longenecker, *Biblical Exegesis*, 108–09.

concerning His son, who was born a descendant of David according to the flesh" (Rom 1: 2–3). At the end, Paul concludes his letter with Scripture, saying that the mystery that was kept secret since the world began "but now is manifested by the scriptures of the prophets, according to the commandment of the eternal God, has been made known to all the nations, leading to obedience of faith" (Rom 16:26).[28]

Paul also stresses the significance of the Scripture in Rom 15:4, saying, "For whatever was written in earlier times was written for our instruction, that through perseverance and the encouragement of the scriptures we might have hope." For Paul, the Old Testament was "not only the Word of God but also his mode of thought and speech."[29] He lived in the world of the Scripture. As Kathy Ehrensperger points out:

> Rather, as Campbell, Nanos, *et al.*, have emphasized, the Scriptures are seen as the symbolic universe within which Paul lives, within which he is rooted in his thought and life before as well as after his call. Thus he is perceived as living, thinking and acting from within this symbolic universe whilst working out the implications of life in Christ for his Gentile communities.[30]

When Paul quoted from the Old Testament, he used the various LXX versions, often from memory. Perhaps he might also have been influenced by a Targum, or translation of a Hebrew text. Paul's method of quotation of Scripture was very common in the Jewish practice of his time.[31]

When Paul interpreted the Scripture, he used the exegetical methods of his time—but in the light of the Christ-event—and therefore it is sometimes difficult to discover the precise Old Testament basis of Paul's thought. For example, recently Philip F. Esler has argued that behind Rom 1:18–32 lies the scriptural story of Sodom and its use in Ezek 16,[32] an interpretation that has not been noted until now.

---

28. Rom 16:26 is disputed—vv. 25–27 may be an addition. According to Dunn, "The textual history has been repeatedly reviewed and a fair consensus achieved for the conclusion that vv 25–27 were first added to an abbreviated (Marcionite) version of the letter (= 1:1–14:23), then incorporated into the longer original (see particularly Lietzmann; Barrett, 10–15; Kümmel, Introduction 314–17; Gamble; Cranfield, 6–9; Wilckens 1:22–24; Lampe). S. H. Schmidt, Bruce, and Hurtado still wish to defend the authenticity of vv 24–27 as Paul's original conclusion to the letter" (Dunn, *Romans*, 1:912–13).

29. Ellis, *Paul's Use*, 10.
30. Ehrensperger, "scriptural Reasoning," 33.
31. Thackeray, *Relation of St. Paul*, 180–203.
32. Esler, *Conflict and Identity*, 145–52.

The fact that Paul mainly quoted literally from Scripture does not require much comment. Thus Cohn-Sherbok refers to historical analysis, noting that:

> In this type of exegesis a conclusion is reached on the basis of an historical analysis of a text or situation ... Paul affirms in Romans 9:6–9 on the basis of the historical events recorded in Gen. 21 concerning Hagar and Ishmael and Sarah and Isaac, that Abraham's true descendants include only Isaac and his progeny: "Neither because they are the seed of Abraham, are they all children; but, in Isaac shall thy seed be called" (Rom 9:7).[33]

Paul also used the Old Testament literally for his exhortation and ethical teachings. According to Brian Rosner's study of 1 Cor 5–7, "the Jewish scriptures are a crucial and formative source for Paul's ethics. The major lines of Paul's ethics in 1 Corinthians 5–7 have been reliably traced back into the scriptures, in most cases by way of Jewish sources."[34]

For Paul, the Scriptures are "not only witness to the gospel (Rom 3:21), but are also a guide for ethical conduct, written for our instruction (1 Cor 10:11)."[35] In other words, Paul relied on traditional use of Scripture both for doctrine and ethics. But by "use" we do not mean misuse; rather, as Rosner goes on to say, "the word 'use' is thus used in this book in its wider sense to include not only explicit use of Scripture but also what might be called implicit and instinctive use of Scripture."[36]

The form known as "pearl-stringing" is also one of the midrashic exegetical methods. This type of midrashic exegesis collects passages from different portions of Scripture in support of a particular argument. Paul employed this method of arguement in Romans. For example, he argued

---

33. Cohn-Sherbok, *Rabbinic Perspectives*, 72–73. According to Bray, an example of Paul's literalistic exegesis can be found in both Rom 4:17–18 and Gal 3:8, 16, which Paul regards as the prototype of salvation history (Bray, *Biblical Interpretation*, 66). It also can found in Rom 7:7 (Exod 20:12–17), 1 Cor 6:16 (Gen 2:24) and 2 Cor 13:1 (Deut 19:15).

34. Rosner, *Paul, Scripture, and Ethics*, 177. According to Rosner's study, even though Paul used few quotations from the Old Testament, "the Scriptures not only directly influenced Paul's ethics through his use of Scripture, but also indirectly through his familiarity with Jewish moral teaching, which itself distilled and developed Scripture. In part, Paul heard the moral demands of Scripture through this Jewish 'filter' when he formulated the ethical instruction recorded in his epistle. He did not receive his Bible in a vacuum" (ibid., 57).

35. Ibid., 194.

36. Ibid., 17.

this way in Rom 3:10–18, Rom 9:12–19, and Rom 10:18–21. Moreover, it can also be found in Gal 3:10–13.

Paul used allegorical interpretation first in 1 Cor 9:9–12, where it is additional to the literal sense, and second in Gal 4:21–31, where Hagar and Sarah are used to reveal a hidden symbolism that is in the literal sense of the original text.[37] The use of allegory was far more restricted in Paul's time: "Most of Jewish midrashic literature brings out ethical and devotional aspects of the Bible, sometimes drawing out and applying what is manifestly there, and sometimes imposing meanings on the texts, although the norm in Judaism is not to make a *midrash* that violates the *p'shat* (simple sense) of the texts."[38] Paul's use of allegory is subordinate to his main argument and also illustrative of it. However, allegorical exegesis did play a part in all the known branches of first-century Judaism.

When Paul argues in his letters, he sometimes uses an *a fortiori* argument (Rom 5:15–12; 11:12, 24; 2 Cor 3:7–8). The seven rules of Hillel's rabbinic exegesis[39] were later increased to thirteen by R. Ismael ben Elisha (110–130 CE). However, among the seven rules of Hillel, the first rule is *Qal wa-homer*, which is known as "light and heavy." In other words, what applies in less important cases will apply in more important ones as well.

Paul often used this device when he made an argument. For example, it can be found in Rom 11:12, 24 and Rom 5: 9–10: "but if . . . how much more." Perhaps Paul's use of this form of argument is not necessarily arguing from the Scripture, but rather using the primary rabbinic rule of scriptural interpretation in Paul's time.

---

37. Eastman, "Cast Out," 309–36.

38. Stern, *Jewish New Testament Commentary*, 559.

39. 1. *Qal wa-homer*: This is deduction. What applies in less important cases will apply in more important ones as well. 2. *Gezerah shawah*: A deduction from "an equal decree." The use of the same word in different contexts means that the same considerations apply to each context. 3. *Binyan ab mikathub 'ehad*: The application of a specific regulation found in one biblical passage to another passage where no specific is given; that is, the inference of a general rule from some single biblical verse. 4. *Binyan ab mishene kethubim*: A principle can be established by relating two texts to each other; that principle can then be applied to other texts. 5. *Kelal upherat*: The inference of a single specific regulation where Scripture provides a general principle, as well as the obverse inference of a general principle where Scripture provides only specific rule. 6. *Kayoze bo bemaqom 'aher*: A difficulty in one text may be resolved by comparing it with another similar passage, though verbal correspondences are not required. 7. *Dabar halamed me 'inyano*: A meaning may be established by the context. See more detail in Sandmel, *Judaism and Christian Beginnings*, 114.

In Romans, an application of Hillel's sixth rule is found in a similar passage. As Dan Cohn-Sherbok cogently demonstrates,

> This rule (the sixth in Hillel's system) is intended to solve a problem by means of a comparison with another passage in Scripture. For example, in Rosh Hashanah the question why Moses had to hold up his hands during the battle with Amalek (Ex. 17:11) is answered by referring to Num. 21:8 . . . Like the rabbis Paul occasionally appeals to this exegetical rule. In Rom. 9:14, for example, Paul cites the narrative in Gen. 22:5 concerning the birth of Esau and Jacob where we read that God distinguished between unborn twin infants . . . This scriptural passage proves the freedom of God in achieving His ends . . . "So then," Paul concludes, "He has mercy on whom he wants to have mercy, and he hardens whom he wants to harden" (Rom. 9:18). Again in Rom. 11:2 Paul asks whether, since Israel is disobedient and contradictory, God has cut off His people. In answer Paul quotes an analogous case in 1 K. 19 concerning Elijah . . . God decreed: "I have left myself seven thousand men who have not bowed the knee to Baal" (Rom. 11:4). Thus Elijah was not alone; these Israelites as well were as faithful as he. "So also at the present time," Paul states, "there has come into being a remnant" (Rom. 11:5). The body of Jewish Christians, exceptions to the general unbelief of their race, form a group analogous to the seven thousand who refused to worship Baal, and it is in this sense that God has not cast off His people.[40]

As we can see, he clearly observes that Paul's interpretation of Scripture resembles that of rabbinic Judaism.[41] Furthermore, in Romans, Hillel's second, fifth, and seventh rules are applied to the following verses: second rule to Rom 4:1–12; fifth rule to Rom 13:8–10; seventh rule to Rom 4:10. This usage adds credence to the supposition that Paul was trained at the feet of Gamaliel (Acts 22:3) if we allow some value of historical reliability to Acts.

As Ellis points out, despite the fact that Paul "never introduces his *haraz* (הרז) [combined quotations] in the explicit rabbinical manner, i.e. The Law says . . . the Prophets say . . . the Writings say . . ."[42] we can find

---

40. Cohn-Sherbok, *Rabbinic Perspectives*, 79–80.

41. Ibid., 79–80. Schoeps thought that Paul was a Hellenistic Jew who lacked knowledge of Scripture and rabbinical opinions. As Schoeps writes, "the whole thing is, of course, pure speculation, and shows not the slightest dependence on Scripture or reminiscence of Rabbinical opinions" (Schoeps, *Paul*, 183).

42. Ellis, *Paul's Use*, 49–50. *Haraz* means two forms of combined quotations: merged,

examples of Paul's use of *haraz* in Rom 9–11, 15. Also, "examples of the *haraz*, so frequent in Rom. 9–11, 15, are numerous in the Talmud. The conjunction is usually 'and' or 'and then', though sometimes a longer connective occurs."[43]

Furthermore, "A *haraz* reminiscent of Rom. 9–11 is found in the same section of the tractate in which Moses, Jeremiah, Moses, Ezekiel, Moses and Isaiah are cited successively with the writer's name being adduced in the Pauline manner."[44] All of these instances indicate that Paul's mind was operating in a way that would later become very typical of rabbinic exegesis.

Paul's typological exegesis is also crucial because it is firmly grounded in the historical significance of "types." His usage implies the "continuity" of God's purpose throughout the history of God's covenant and plan—continuity through transformation. Paul used such figures as Adam, Abraham, Moses, and Jonah in Romans for "types" of Jesus Christ.[45]

The most common form of Jewish exegesis in Jesus's time is the nomological method, which, as Gerald Bray observes, is an approach that leads to an "'ultra-literal' interpretation, in which words are taken completely out of context and to mean something which goes against the plain meaning of the text."[46]

It can be argued that there are instances in Paul's letters where the original meaning is abandoned. For example, in Rom 9:33, there are two

---

or amalgamated quotations, and chain quotations, or *haraz*.

43. Ibid., 49–50.

44. Ibid., 50.

45. Hays has indicated that "Paul reads Scripture under the conviction that its story prefigures the climactic realities of his own time" (Hays, *Echoes of Scripture*, 161). But Hays opposed the view that Jesus is the antitypical fulfillment of the scriptural figures, he says, "Paul's typological linkages center on the people of God as the culmination of God's redemptive activity rather than on Jesus as the antitypical fulfillment of scriptural figures" (ibid., 162).

46. Bray, *Biblical Interpretation*, 57. The reason for this is that, as Bray says, "Rabbinical Midrash, in its concern to draw out the 'deeper meaning' of the text, to explain its obscurities and difficulties, and to apply it to the contemporary situation, was quite prepared to adopt methods of interpretation which went far beyond what the text actually said, but which they still believed were doing no more than bringing out its 'plain meaning.' They achieved this result partly by reading Scripture as a legal document, in which examples of behaviour could be taken out of context and made to apply in ways which went well beyond anything the text actually said" (ibid.).

quotations of passages from Isa 28:16 and 8:14 that speak of "Jehovah as the Rock." Paul applies them to the image of Christ.[47]

This type of messianic interpretation was made not just by Paul, but also by Jewish writers before him. Paul used messianic interpretation in many passages; for example, Rom 10:15 (Isa 52:7); 11:26 (Isa 59:20f.; 27:9) and Rom 15:3 (Ps 69:9). When Paul interpreted the Red Sea crossing as a baptism (1 Cor 10:1–4), he reflected the Pharisaic tradition that the Exodus was a baptism.[48]

Thus, Paul interpreted the Scripture in the light of messianic fulfillment. Paul "viewed the whole scope of Old Testament prophecy and history from the standpoint of the Messianic Age in which the Old Testament stood open, fulfilled in Jesus Christ."[49] It is much more fitting to claim that Paul interpreted the Scripture in the context of the Christ-event.

Paul was recalling certain Pharisaic treatments of the biblical narrative and "reinterpreting them from the dual perspective of corporate solidarity and messianic fulfillment in the person of Jesus of Nazareth."[50] Paul used the Pharisaic tradition's interpretation to convince his audiences that Jesus was the Messiah. In this sense, Paul's form of argumentation was rooted firmly in the Pharisaic tradition's interpretation.

Two Examples of scriptural Interpretation in Romans

Romans 10:5–8

In Rom 9–11, Paul explicitly quotes from Scripture twenty-five times,[51] largely dealing with the issue of Israel. Paul's use of the Scripture in Rom 9–11 is very intricate. However, Joseph A. Fitzmyer claims that in Rom 10:5f. Paul "merely borrows phrases from Deuteronomy and applies them to Christ."[52] Fitzmyer also says that Paul contradicts himself in quoting from Lev 18:5 to refer to the "'uprightness that comes from the law' and the Deuteronomy passage as that which 'comes from faith.'"[53]

47. Thackeray, *Relation of St. Paul*, 189.
48. Bray, *Biblical Interpretation*, 66.
49. Ellis, *Paul's Use*, 116.
50. Longenecker, *Biblical Exegesis*, 120.
51. Ibid., 108–109.
52. Fitzmyer, *Romans*, 588.
53. Ibid.

How Paul Uses Scripture

It does appear that Paul contradicts himself here. But Paul's logic is hard to understand precisely because there is little or no conceptualized logic in Pharisaic theology, but rather organic thinking and complexity. In other words, Paul was not a systematic thinker, but that does not mean he was not coherent.[54] As we noted previously, Kathy Ehrensperger emphasizes that Paul's thought is firmly rooted in Judaism, and Paul can be better understood in his Jewish context rather than in the context of the Western philosophical tradition:

> The move towards Scriptures does not imply a naive return to some "original" pure text or original truth, but neither is it an uncritical application of so-called "rational" forms of thinking and reasoning in the Western philosophical tradition. The Jewish movement finds significant affinities between Jewish forms of reading and reasoning and postmodern thought. It challenges the notion of there being just one single discourse of reasoning and rationality, that is, that of Western science and logic, as the valid model for the "right" way of thinking . . . scriptural reasoning as described above is inspired and nurtured by classic rabbinic forms of conversation—as conversations around texts in relation to community life before God—and relates such conversations to contemporary academic conversations around texts and questions of philosophy, theology and methods.[55]

However, did Paul really twist the Scripture in Rom 10:5 by quoting selectively in order to apply the passage to Christ? How one interprets the Greek word, δέ ("but") at the beginning of verse 6 will determine whether these two verses are viewed as *connected* to each other or as *contrasted* with each other. The Greek word δέ covers meanings which, in English, are divided into the three areas: 1) "and," "moreover," "furthermore," 2) "but," "rather," "in contrast," "on the contrary," 3) "but only if." The traditional interpretation of δέ in verse 6 as the contrast conjunction[56] "but" is not a balanced interpretation. The meaning is not necessarily adversative. Since Paul did not use the Greek word ἀλλά ("but"), we need to consider all the options in his use of the word δέ.

After understanding the meanings of δέ, we must then ask three questions as follows:

---

54. Tomson, *Paul and the Jewish Law*, 58.
55. Ehrensperger, "scriptural Reasoning," 33–34.
56. Dunn, *Romans*, 2:602.

1. Does Paul quote the Scripture to support righteousness by faith only in contrast to the law?[57]

2. Does Paul quote the Scripture in support of both righteousness by the law and righteousness by faith?

3. Does Paul interpret Christ as the goal or fulfillment of the law (v. 4)?[58]

57. According to the following scholars, Christ is the "termination" of the law in Rom 10:4. Bultmann notes, "For to them Christ is the 'end of the law' (Rom10:4); 'in him' or 'through him' we have freedom from the Law (Gal 2:4). For freedom he set us free (Gal 5:1); to it we were 'called' (Gal 5:13). The Christian Church is the congregation of the free, while Judaism is under bondage to the Law, as the Sarah-Hagar allegory (Gal 4:21–31) sets forth" (Bultmann, *Theology of the New Testament*, 1:340). Dodd claims, "The way they have chosen is a false one, because Christ is an end to law, so as to let every believer have righteousness. He must have put an end to law, for otherwise 'righteousness' would not be available for every believer... Therefore the Jewish way of righteousness through works of the Law must be wrong" (Dodd, *Epistle of Paul*, 165). Sanday and Headlam assert, "Their own method was based on a rigid performance of legal enactments. But that has been ended in Christ. Now there is a new and a better way, one which has two characteristics; it is based on the principle of faith, and it is universal and for all men alike" (Sanday and Headlam, *Romans*, 277). Käsemann says, "'The Mosaic Torah comes to an end with Christ because man now renounces his own right in order to grant God his right (3:4). In the eschatological change the creature who wants to possess his own right is replaced by the Creator who has the right and who is acknowledged in the ὑποταγη, of faith. Even for Israel no other possibility of salvation exists. Failing to understand the law, it falls into illusion and is overthrown" (Käsemann, *Commentary on Romans*, 283).

58. In Rom10:4, these following scholars try to take τέλος in both senses of "end" and "goal" of the Law. Barth writes, "For the end of the law-its sense and meaning-is the righteousness of God... All human religion is directed towards an end beyond itself (iii.21); and that *end* is Christ. For Christ is the goal of all the needs and longings and endeavours of men" (Barth, *Romans*, 375). Campbell emphasizes that "it is not a static abrogation of the law that Paul intends by the word τέλος because τέλος itself a dynamic concept embodying the idea of one phase ending, coinciding with the inception of another. Christ as the τέλος of the law is not so much abrogation of the law, but 'an act of transition, of transformation of its (the law's) servitude from death to life'" (Campbell, *Paul's Gospel*, 63). Cranfield believes, "For Christ is the goal of the law, and it follows that a status of righteousness is available to everyone who believes" (Cranfield, *Romans*, 519–20). Barrett notes, τέλος means that "Christ is the end of the law, with a view not to anarchy but righteousness. He puts an end to the law, not by destroying all that the law stood for but by realizing it" (Barrett, *Romans*, 184). Bruce states, "The word 'end' has a double sense... Christ is the goal at which the law aimed, in that he embodies the perfect righteousness which it prescribes... since Christ is the goal of the law, since in him the law has found its perfect fulfillment, a righteous status before God is available to everyone who believes in him, and that implies the termination of the law's function (real or imagined) as a means of acquiring such a righteous status" (Bruce, *Romans*, 190). And Dunn claims, "Christ is the end of the old epoch and of Israel's exclusive privileges with it. The word 'end' therefore is probably intended in the primary sense of 'termination,

First, Käsemann and others assert that Paul contrasts the law and gospel. Käsemann claims that "this is the contrast between the old and new aeons under the banner of the law on the one side and of the promise and the gospel on the other."[59] If this had been the case, Paul probably would have realized he would not reach his non-believing Jewish brothers. In verses 6–8 Paul was not trying to convince his hearers that the righteousness based on faith in Christ is different from the righteousness based on the Torah, but rather that they are the same: the same righteousness based on the same trust and leading to the same eternal life. It is not unlikely that Paul knew what Jesus himself said about the law according to Matt 5:17: "Do not think that I came to abolish the Law or the prophets: I did not come to abolish, but to fulfill." Anthony T. Hanson has reviewed this passage and notes, "The contrast is not between what Moses says and what Christ says, but between two ways of life, the way of Torah-obedience and the way of faith, both equally recorded by God."[60] Joseph Shulam has a more convincing interpretation.

"To prove his point that faithfulness to God in Yeshua [Jesus] is the goal of the Torah," Shulam says, "Paul uses a familiar rabbinic exegetical technique. He cites two biblical verses (Lev. 18:5 and Dt. 30:11–14) which attribute different grounds to the finding of 'life' to establish a new principle—that eternal life is found through faithfulness to Yeshua's [Jesus's] death and resurrection and is therefore open to all who call on the name of the Lord (cf. Isa. 28:16, Joel 2:32)."[61] Although Shulam's interpretation cannot be ruled out, the next interpretation is more likely, given the context.

Paul interprets Christ as the goal of the law in verse 4. Rather than standing in contrast to this idea, this verse then leads to a discussion of righteousness based on faith. These verses (vv. 5–6) show *how* Christ is the goal of the law. Paul is not trying to point out that the Scripture contradicts itself. As Campbell argues, "Instead of setting out a contrast between law-righteousness (v. 5) and faith-righteousness (v. 6) . . . Paul intends both quotations to support his claim that the righteousness now realized in Christ

---

cessation' . . . It is possible that Paul intended 'end' here to have also the fuller or further sense of 'fulfillment, goal' . . . Christ is the realization of God's final purpose in choosing Israel initially" (Dunn, *Romans*, 1:596–97).

59. Käsemann, *Commentary on Romans*, 286.

60. Hanson, *Technique and Theology*, 149.

61. Shulam, *Jewish Roots*, 347.

is that to which Moses also pointed. The righteousness ἐκ τοῦ νόμου (v. 5) is thus seen to be the righteousness of faith (and not law-righteousness)."[62]

R. Nahman b. Issaac has stated that "it is Habakkuk who came and based them all on one [principle], as it is said, 'But the righteous shall live by his faith'" (Hab 2:4).[63] Likewise, Paul stated it in Rom 1:17, wherein the Scripture is summed up as the "righteousness of faithfulness." Paul tried to make plain that righteousness was now revealed in Christ. Paul did not have a new arrangement of the Torah to make a new theological system, but only an interpretation in strict connection with Christ Jesus, whom Paul had encountered.

In Rom 10:6–8, Paul quoted Deut 30:11–14 to show that righteousness requires trust, which the Old Testament itself also teaches. When Paul uses part of the quotation, he assumes the passage will recall to the reader's mind the entire passage it belongs to.[64] In this passage, Paul uses the method of Rémez (רמז)[65] to teach his audiences that Jesus is the Messiah, rather than simply quoting from the Scripture. Here Paul has assumed that his audience remembers that God's requirement in Deuteronomy is that Israel trusts in the Messiah when he comes—"the prophet like me" whom Moses wrote about (Deut 18:15–19). Modern interpretation tends to think of Paul as looking up a scroll to find his citations. But if he did not carry all of the Bible with him, he could only do so when near a synagogue. We should think instead in terms of careful memorization in a predominantly oral culture.

A majority of scholars have understood other passages in Romans in the same manner. In Rom 9:25, Paul apparently quoted passages from Hosea out of the original context and applied them to the calling of the

---

62. Campbell, *Paul's Gospel*, 65. See also Badenas, *Christ*, 79–80, 144–51. For a contrary view, see Esler, *Conflict and Identity*, 286–88.

63. Talmud, Makkot 24a.

64. According to Safrai, in the first century CE the majority of Jewish boys receive a formal education. Most male children in Palestine in Jesus's time attend school, even those from poor families. A child begins in the bet sefer at about the age of five or six, and learns to read the Scripture, the Written Law. At about at eleven students move to the *bet talmud* where they study the Mishnah, the Oral Law. In other words, the majority of Jewish men memorized the Scripture in Paul's time, so when Paul uses a part of a quotation, the readers perhaps can recall the rest of passage from Scripture. See more in Safrai, *The Jewish People in the First Century*, 2:945–57.

65. Rémez: the wording of Scripture is regarded as providing clear hints or clues in the direction of the overtone and inference. See more in Sandmel, *Judaism and Christian Beginnings*, 115–16.

Gentiles. Hosea originally addressed these passages to the Northern Kingdom, scattered tribes of Israel.[66] Fitzmyer observes that "Paul freely adapts the prophetic utterance to the coming of the Gentiles to faith." Fitzmyer goes on to say that in verse 26,

> The prophet's words refer to the call to Israel to return, and the "place" probably is to be understood as Jerusalem. But the words are now transferred by Paul to the call of the Gentiles, and there really is no need to try to specify the "place," which just happens to be part of the quotation. More important, the OT passage cited echoes Paul's own designation of Christians as "children of God" (8:21), now applied to Gentile Christians. Whereas Paul quoted Hosea's promise apropos of the Gentiles, he will next quote Isaiah's admonition apropos of Israel.[67]

Then, the question is: If Paul was randomly picking and choosing from Scripture to prove his own ideas, how could he persuade his non-believing brothers who knew the text? Or did Paul use the Scripture in a rabbinic method that neglected the original context? C. H. Dodd read Rom 9:25 as follows: "First, that Gentiles should be included is established by Hosea's prophecy . . . It is rather strange that Paul has not observed that this prophecy referred to Israel, rejected for its sins, but destined to be restored: strange because it would have fitted so admirably the doctrine of the restoration of Israel which he is to expound in chap. xi."[68] Dodd thought Paul should have used Hosea's prophecy to refer to Israel but that Paul misused this prophecy for Gentiles.

C. E. B. Cranfield,[69] C. K. Barrett,[70] and F. F. Bruce,[71] along with Francis Watson[72] all agree that Rom 9:25 refers to Gentiles. Watson especially wonders why Paul, in Rom 11:1–10, wrote that the Jewish Christian remnant is seen as a sign that God has not rejected his people. In Rom 11:1f., "'his people' (τὸν λαὸν αὐτοῦ). refers to the present generation of Jews, and Paul as a representative of them describes himself as 'of the seed of

---

66. Cranfield, *Epistle to the Romans*, 2:499. See also Watson, *Paul, Judaism*, 168.
67. Fitzmyer, *Romans*, 573.
68. Dodd, *Epistle of Paul*, 160.
69. Cranfield, *Epistle to the Romans*, 2:499–500.
70. Barrett, *Romans*, 178.
71. Bruce, *Romans*, 184.
72. Watson, *Paul, Judaism*, 162–63.

Abraham'. This is diametrically opposed to 9:6ff. In 9:25, λαόν μου refers to Gentile Christians."⁷³

In the context of Rom 9, Paul's main issue is about Israel, not the inclusion of Gentiles. Therefore, in Rom 9:25, Paul used the Hosea quotation primarily to apply to Israel, and immediately following this, two other Scripture quotations are applied to Israel in support of Paul's assertion in verse 25. Campbell points out that verse 25 *is not referring to Gentiles*, saying:

> It would be most unlikely for Paul to use the Hosea citation with reference to Gentiles when this was not its original purpose and especially since it is immediately followed by two other scriptural citations that clearly apply to Israel. I would maintain that the Hosea citation is taken by Paul to apply primarily to Israel and thus the three citations all have the same point of reference, Israel. Rejected Israel, like the northern tribes, will be restored. This is Paul's primary thesis, but in and with the restoration, another "non-people," the Gentiles, will also be blessed. Paul does apply the Hosea citation in a secondary sense, typologically, to Gentiles also, but only after he has first used it to refer to Israel. Like Hosea, he envisages the reuniting of the twelve tribes into one people, that is, the hardened and the remnant parts of Israel will one day be reunited.⁷⁴

Campbell goes on to emphasize that:

> The most surprising factor in Romans 9 is the somewhat unexpected twist with which Paul makes use of his powerful argument about the divine freedom. Instead of arguing that God is free and therefore can cast off Israel, Paul turns this around and asks, What if, as is the case, God patiently endures his people Israel (Barrett 1961, 189). When we follow closely the manner and sequence of Paul's argument in ch.9, and recognize that the primary interest is in God's activity with Israel, then ch.11 and its ending are not

---

73. Ibid., 168. But see also Thackeray, *Relation of St. Paul*, 186–88. Thackeray notes, "This is in accordance with the practice of the Rabbis, who held that there was an infinite fullness of meaning in the Scriptures. 'Every word of the Torah can be expounded in 70 different ways' is one of the many similar Jewish sayings. This neglect of the context is quite justifiable in passages which are merely used by way of illustration and not to introduce a logical argument, or where the Apostle without expressly quoting a passage couches his argument in the familiar language of the O.T." (ibid., 186–87).

74. Campbell, "Divergent Images," 199, now included in Campbell, *Unity and Diversity in Christ*, 67–90.

such a surprise after all, because the "surprise" has already been tentatively introduced in 9:22ff.[75]

Hanson points out in his book *Studies in Paul's Technique and Theology* that in Rom 9:25–26, Paul is referring to the remnant and nothing else. Hanson elaborated it as follows: "Paul probably means to indicate that these words apply to the remnant in the last days and to nothing else," Hanson says. "It is, however, tempting to follow the lead of many scholars and see a reference here to Northern Israel. If so, then we do have a double meaning here: the words apply primarily to the situation in Hosea's day, and secondarily to the remnant in Paul's day."[76]

Hanson's view confirms that Paul's main concern is the Jewish people. Paul uses these texts from Hosea midrashically. Hosea was not referring primarily to Gentiles but to Israel itself. Therefore, Paul's meaning, "which does not conflict with what Hosea wrote but is not a necessary inference from it, is that 'God's people' now includes some Gentiles."[77]

Romans 2:24

Some scholars[78] also think that Paul did not do justice to the Old Testament text of Isa 52:5[79] in Rom 2:24, "God's name is blasphemed among the Gentiles because of you." Paul quoted Isa 52:5, καὶ νῦν τί ὧδέ ἐστε τάδε λέγει κύριος ὅτι ἐλήμφθη ὁ λαός μου δωρεάν θαυμάζετε καὶ ὀλολύζετε τάδε λέγει κύριος δι' ὑμᾶς διὰ παντὸς τὸ ὄνομά μου βλασφημεῖται ἐν τοῖς ἔθνεσιν. But Paul's quotation here is slightly different from LXX. Paul quoted in Rom 2:24, "τὸ γὰρ ὄνομα τοῦ θεοῦ δι' ὑμᾶς βλασφημεῖται ἐν τοῖς ἔθνεσιν."

However, Runar M. Thorsteinsson demonstrates in his book *Paul's Interlocutor in Romans 2* why Paul did not disregard the original meaning. Thorsteinsson sees the issue of proselytes (and potential proselytes) as the

---

75. Ibid., 200.
76. Hanson, *Technique and Theology*, 154.
77. Stern, *Jewish New Testament Commentary*, 392.
78. Byrne, *Romans*, 101; Harvey, *True Israel*, 78. Cf. Thorsteinsson, *Paul's Interlocutor*, 219; Käsemann, *Commentary on Romans*, 71; Fitzmyer, *Romans*, 318–19; Hays, *Echoes of Scripture*, 45.
79. Isa 52:5. שְׁמִי מִנֹּאָץ:עַתָּה (מִי־לִי) [מַה־לִּי]־פֹה נְאֻם־יְהוָה כִּי־לֻקַּח עַמִּי חִנָּם (מֹשְׁלוֹ)וְתָמִיד כָּל־הַיּוֹם [מֹשְׁלָיו] יְהֵילִילוּ נְאֻם־יְהוָה

key to Paul's words in Rom 2:17, "But if you call yourself a Jew" (implying this person was not in fact a Jew). Therefore, Thorsteinsson states,

> Paul was not at all concerned with an indictment of Jews, but of a Gentile interlocutor . . . He was probably well aware of the fact that Isaiah 52:5 referred not to the misdeeds of Israel but of other nations, and thus that it could suit his purpose in an indictment of a Gentile interlocutor. Hence, Paul's citation of Isaiah is neither a "stunning misreading of the text" nor a "low blow," but a natural application of its basic meaning.[80]

In other words, according to Thorsteinsson, Paul does not say that the person addressed in Rom 2:17 is a Jew, but only that he claims to be a Jew, wants to be called a Jew, or simply calls himself a Jew.[81]

Other scholars claim that, in the original context of Isaiah, God's name is blasphemed because Israel is being oppressed by other nations. In other words, because Israel, God's people, were in exile, Gentiles had blasphemed God's name, but in Rom 2:24, Paul used the Isaiah quotation to refer to Israel's misdeeds. For example, "According to both the Hebrew original and the LXX it was Israel's misfortune that led to the reviling of God's name by the nations," states Brendan Byrne. "Paul, however, interprets the LXX phrase 'on account of you' as 'because of your fault,' thereby converting what was originally an oracle of compassion towards Israel into one of judgment."[82]

Again, Richard Hays criticizes Paul for misreading Isa 52:5—even though Paul understood the context of the Isaiah passage to be a portent of God's grace toward Israel. Hays argues that Paul's use of Isa 52:5 is "a stunning misreading of the text" in which "Paul transforms Isaiah's oracle of promise into a word of reproach."[83]

Thomas Schreiner does not find that Paul's interpretation of Rom 2:24 is not consistent with the original sense of the passage.[84] According to Schreiner, some Jews in Paul's time thought that Rome's conquest of Palestine was a sign that they were still being punished for their sins and hence were still in "exile," just like the Israelites in the original passage.[85]

80. Thorsteinsson, *Paul's Interlocutor*, 221.
81. Ibid., 197–98.
82. Byrne, *Romans*, 101.
83. Hays, *Echoes of Scripture*, 45–46.
84. Schreiner, *Romans*, 134–35.
85. Cf. Stanley, *Arguing with Scripture*, 148.

But Christopher D. Stanley opposes this view, saying, "But Paul gives no indication that he was thinking in these terms, and even if he was, this does not explain how the quotation relates to Paul's accusations in vv. 21–23, which bear no evident relation to the situation of Israel in Isa 52."[86]

As we can see, divergent views on Rom 2:24 exist among scholars. However, if Paul misquoted the text, then the question arises: Why was Paul intentionally misreading the text? How is it possible that Paul, a scholar of Torah, could make such a misquotation? Why did Paul not use other scriptural texts to prove God's judgment of Israel's disobedience? Did Paul use this text as evidence of indictment of the Jews?

If Paul wanted to argue for Israel's misdeed, he could have perhaps used Ezek 36:20f. to support his argument, just as any of the other rabbis of his time would have done.[87] Then why did Paul use Isa 52:5? Romans 2:24 perhaps gives some explanation for Paul's choice.

Thackeray gives some explanation of the use of the quotation from Isa 52:5 in Rom 2:24. He again indicates that Paul used the Scripture as freely as his contemporaries.[88] In other words, in Rom 2:24, Paul's neglect of the original context is justifiable.

Although both Thackeray's view and Thorsteinsson's interpretation of Rom 2:24 cannot be ruled out, I propose my understanding of this verse from the perspective of a prophetic context. We can throw light on this passage if we understand that Paul was speaking in prophetic language in the manner of a prophet. The prophet's job was not only to point out the sin of the Jewish people, but also to see his sinful people restored.

In Isaiah, we can see that the prophet repeatedly warned the people that Jerusalem and Judah would be judged because of their wickedness (Isa 1–6). Isaiah went on to predict that the exile would be the result of their sin(s) (Isa 39). Yet he also held to the hope that the kingdom would be restored. In the last twenty-seven chapters of the book, Isaiah comforted the people with the promise from God (Isa 40–66). Given the whole context of Isaiah, Paul would have understood that the exile was occasioned because of their sin. If Israel repented from their wickedness, then no exile (i.e., punishment) would occur, nor would the Gentiles have uttered any blasphemy of God's name. Thus, Paul emphasized that the reason God's

---

86. Ibid.

87. Ezekiel was used by many of the rabbis to support the charge that the reviling of God's name was because of Israel's misdeed. Cf. Cranfield, *Epistle to the Romans*, 171.

88. Thackeray, *Relation of St. Paul*, 188–89.

name was blasphemed by Gentiles was their (Jewish people's) sin(s), just as Isaiah indicated (Rom 2:17–23).

If we connect Isa 52 to other chapters in Isaiah, we can see why Paul used this quotation to prove that Jews of his day were also unrighteous and deserving of the divine judgment accorded Gentiles.[89] Paul understood from the first chapters of Isaiah's book that the exile had occurred because of Israel's wickedness before God. In other words, since Paul considered Israel's sin to be the cause of the exile, he naturally also blamed Israel for causing dishonor to God's name among the Gentiles in his day.

Likewise, Paul was saying that Jews who claim to be God's people but do not follow God's Torah are, by their sins, dishonoring God's name among the Gentiles. For Paul, any disobedience to God was sin, whether Israel's wickedness in Isaiah's time or the Jews' disobedience to the Torah in Paul's time.

However, Paul did not mean to say they were forever condemned but simply points out their moral condition before God, especially since they had the Torah, which the Gentiles did not have. We should understand Rom 2–3 in the context of Rom 9–11.[90] In Rom 9–11, Paul was as optimistic about Israel's future as the prophet Isaiah was in Isa 52 (Rom 11). In this reading, Paul was not misreading the Old Testament text of Isa 52:5 in Rom 2:24.

The Consistency of Paul's Interpretation

Paul was interpreting and reinterpreting the Scripture from the Jewish perspectives of corporate solidarity and messianic fulfillment in the Christ event.[91] Paul's method of midrash on Scripture is explained by E. E. Ellis: "With this in mind the first century exegete had a twofold task, to 'search the Scriptures', and to discern 'the signs of the times'; he learned from the scriptures the nature of God's purpose, and from current events he sought indication of the fulfillment: When the scripture rightly interpreted coin-

---

89. Stanley states, "Apparently, Paul did not anticipate that the Romans would be able to consult the original context of Isa 52" (Stanley, *Arguing with Scripture*, 148). But any audience familiar with Isa 52 (in which Isaiah spoke of Yahweh's covenant loyalty to his people and his merciful attitude toward them) would also be familiar with the whole context of Isaiah; therefore, this audience would understand what Paul was saying.

90. I will discuss Rom 9–11 in chapter 6.

91. Longenecker, *Biblical Exegesis*, 121.

cided with the event rightly understood, then you had the argument from prophecy."[92] However, Paul's custom of teaching that Jesus was the Messiah indicates that Paul saw Jesus as the eschatological fulfillment of prophecy.

Paul acknowledges in the crucified and risen Jesus the promised Messiah. His interpretation of the Torah is in the context of the Christ, Jesus. For Paul, it would have been unacceptable to distort the Torah, but he did not hold that his interpretation concerning Christ was a distortion. In other words, Paul did not arrange the Scripture in order to make a new theological system but rather to testify the strict connection with the Christ, Jesus, whom Paul encountered.

Moreover, as E. P. Sanders points out, Paul did not formulate but rather interpreted the conviction that Jesus is the Christ. "Though I wince at the possible anachronism of the phrase," Sanders says, "I think that Paul had found a canon within the canon. He did not formulate it . . . Behind this reading of the Scripture we see the great convictions which determined Paul's career: God has appointed Christ for the salvation of the world, for the salvation of all without distinction."[93]

Even though Sanders believes that Paul left Judaism because salvation comes only through Christ,[94] he also confirms that Paul's form of argumentation is Jewish. Paul's letters are the result of his interpretation of the Scripture—not the other way around. Nevertheless, Paul consistently interpreted the Scripture with his Pharisaic training in interpretation of Torah even after he encountered Jesus Christ, which indicates that he remained consistent with his Jewish heritage and never turned against it. In this line of thought, Paul was a faithful Jew who interpreted the Torah in the light of Jesus the Messiah.

Now let us re-examine those texts in the Pauline letters that are controversial among scholars in order to review Paul's attitude toward Judaism and toward Jews who did not believe in Christ.

---

92. Ellis, *Paul's Use*, 135.
93. Sanders, *Paul, the Law*, 162.
94. Ibid., *Paul and Palestinian Judaism*, 442–47.

6

Paul, Judaism, and Unbelieving Jews

PAUL CONTINUED AS A faithful Jew even after his encounter with Christ. After his experience on the road to Damascus, he did not—as some scholars believe—break with Judaism,[1] found an independent religion,[2] and become more or less biased against his Jewish people.[3]

Let us review some texts that are used to support this view, and re-examine their interpretation.

How Does Luke Portray Paul?

Scholars frequently cannot completely escape their own presuppositions or move beyond particular ways of thinking when they interpret Paul's letters, yet it is important to read Paul's letter from a Jewish perspective because Paul was a Jew. I understand Paul from the primary source of his own letters while stressing his Jewish roots—but I also hold that, in a limited form, we can use Acts as an additional historical source.

Even though some years ago a majority of New Testament scholars voiced extreme skepticism concerning the interpretation of Paul in Acts, Martin Hengel urges that there must be a realistic recognition that Acts

---

1. Ibid., *Paul, the Law*, 178, 207–208.
2. Burton, *Critical and Exegetical Commentary*, 44.
3. Jervell, *Unknown Paul*, 36. Jervell does not suggest Paul was against either Judaism or Jewish people in Acts and Romans, but he argues that Paul showed a different attitude toward Jews earlier in 1 Thess 1:14–16 and Galatians.

contains much valuable and accurate information about Paul's mission—even though the writer's theological tendencies are quite apparent.[4] F. F. Bruce also indicates:

> This [Acts] is our principal secondary source for the life and work of Paul, and the present work is based on the conviction that it is a source of high historical value. The differences between the portrait of Paul drawn in his undisputed letters and that drawn in Acts are such differences as might be expected between a man's self-portrait and the portrait painted of him by someone else for whom he set either consciously or (as in this instance) unconsciously. The Paul of Acts is the historical Paul as he was seen and depicted by a sympathetic and accurate but independent observer, whose narrative provides a convincing framework for the major epistles at least and may be used with confidence to supplement Paul's own evidence.[5]

We, therefore, should not ignore the fact that the book of Acts is an historical source that can assist as a supplementary source for building an understanding of Paul.

Jack Finnegan has also pointed out in his book *The Archeology of the New Testament* that there is historical accuracy in much of the material in Acts.[6] For example, Acts 17:8 employs the phrase τοὺς πολιτάρχας ("city authorities"). This unique term, used in Acts only with regard to Thessalonica, has been verified as fitting precisely within this historical context. Such data in the book of Acts are pointers that Acts should not be ignored as a secondary source for Pauline theology and mission.[7]

In any case, Luke portrays Paul as a genuine Jew who labored for the ministry of the gospel, first for Jews and then for the Gentiles. Paul was educated in the school of Gamaliel (Acts 22:3), one of the foremost sages of

---

4. See Hengel, *Acts and the History*. Hengel notes, "Luke is no less trustworthy than other historians of antiquity" (ibid. 60).

5. Bruce, *Paul*, 16–17.

6. Finegan, *Archeology of the New Testament*, 108.

7. Wette (1780–1849) raised the issue that the Lucan portrait of Paul (Acts 9:1–30; 15:1–35) differs from that of Paul's epistle (Gal 1:13–2:21). According to Gasque, Wette was the one to start criticism of the reliability of Acts (Gasque, *History of the Interpretation*, 24–26; cf. Marguerat, *First Christian Historian*, 2). Baur also pointed out that Paul's speeches in Acts (13:39; 21–26) and the council of Jerusalem (Acts 15) do not sound like Paul's epistle (Gal 2:11–14), though Baur accepted Paul's report as factual (Baur, *Paul the Apostle*, 109–74). On the other hand, Baur did question the historicity of Acts. For more detail on the historicity of Acts, see Marguerat, *First Christian Historian*.

the late Second Temple period. Luke depicts Paul claiming to continuously live a Pharisaic lifestyle of the "strictest sort" (Acts 23:6; 26:5).[8]

After his Damascus road experience, according to Luke, Paul was still accepted as a teacher in numerous synagogues (Acts 13:15; 17:2-3; 18:4; 19:8, etc.). Paul returns to the Temple to pray (Acts 22:17), participates in vows and offerings (Acts 18:18; 21:20-28), and observes the festivals (Acts 2:5-6, 16). In Num 6:1-21, the Nazirite vow is described as a minimum length of thirty days, during which the devotee abstains from alcohol and from cutting his hair. When the Nazirite vow is finished, his hair is completely shaved off and he offers a sacrifice in the temple at Jerusalem. The vow should be in thanksgiving to God for past blessings or a petition for future ones.

If Luke's report is correct, even though Paul shaved off his hair completely in Cenchreae and not in Jerusalem, his vow was valid because the shaving of the hair was permissible elsewhere (*m. Naz.* 3:6; 5:4).[9] Thus Paul cut his hair in Cenchreae and offered the sacrifice in Jerusalem (Acts 23:21-26). The significant point, though, is that according to Luke, Paul's action indicates that he abandoned neither the Torah nor his Jewishness.

Luke also indicates that even after many years of ministry, Paul could adamantly maintain that he had "done nothing wrong against the Jewish law" (Acts 25:8) and had not "violated the customs of our ancestors" (Acts 28:17). Furthermore, according to Luke, Paul tried to persuade people to understand that Jesus is the Messiah using both the law of Moses and the prophets (Acts 28:23).

---

8. Marguerat, *First Christian Historian*, 133. Marguerat indicates that the Lukan portrait of Paul "does not cease to demonstrate his scrupulous obedience to the law of Moses (Acts 16:3; 21:20-26; 24:14) and to claim his Jewish identity: 'I am a Jew, born in Tarsus in Cilicia' (Acts 22:3)" (ibid.). Tannehill also notes that Luke shows Paul continuously lived as a Pharisee despite his role as witness of Jesus the Messiah (Tannehill, "Rejection by Jews," 95). On the other hand, Witherington opposes the idea that Paul lived as a Pharisee (Witherington, *Acts of the Apostles*, 740). Witherington points out that in Acts 22:3, "The tense of the verb 'live' here is aorist making it clear that Paul is speaking about his past at this point, though in 23:6 he speaks in the present tense on this subject. In Acts 23 Paul is talking about his belief in the resurrection. In this regard he could still say he was affirming something distinctively and essentially Pharisaic" (ibid.). However, if we look at Acts overall, it seems that Paul continued to be a Jew even after his Damascus experience, as Jervell notes (Jervell, *Luke and the People*, 153-54). Also, in Acts 22:3, Paul uses the aorist to explain that he was trained in the law. In Acts 23:6, he still remains a Pharisee, though he has a different view than the unbelieving Pharisees regarding Jesus as Messiah.

9. See the Talmud mishnah *Nazir* 3:6 and 5:4.

Paul, Judaism, and Unbelieving Jews

Therefore, according to Luke, Paul was not only a zealous Jew before his Damascus road experience but also still remained a Jew after his Damascus road experience. According to this perspective, Paul would have thought his gospel was both the completion of Judaism and its fulfillment and also that his pattern of life was closely related to it. Not only was Paul not anti-Torah, he also remained an observant Jew.[10]

Even though Paul was an ambassador to Gentiles, his priority was, as Nanos notes, "first to the Jew then to Gentiles."[11] Luke's account also indicates that when Paul went on a missionary journey, he always visited synagogues first to proclaim and testify from Torah that Jesus is the Messiah (Acts 13:4, 14; 14:1; 16:13; 17:1-2, 10, 17; 18:4; 19:8; 28:17). These incidents are further indication that Paul was a Jew who was committed to the Jewish people and to the Torah.

Moreover, according to Luke's depiction, Paul did not "gentilize" Jews because they had become followers of the Messiah. For example, in Acts 15, Paul disagreed with some Jews who required Gentile Christians to be circumcised according to the custom of Moses in order to belong to God's people. Paul did not require Gentile believers to become Jews, but rather allowed them to remain as Gentiles (Acts 15:2-3; 1 Cor 7:8).

Likewise, Paul did not require Jews to live like Gentile believers. Luke's view suggests that the issue at the Jerusalem Council was whether Gentile believers should or should not be circumcised and become Jews; the issue was not about Jewish believers ceasing to be Jews. Luke's account of Paul brings us to the conclusion that Paul still practiced his Jewishness after becoming a follower of Christ. He never ceased to be an observant Jew.

New Testament scholarship is particularly divided on the question of the historical reliability of Luke's portrait of Paul. Some scholars point out that certain aspects of Luke's view of Paul contradict Paul's own claims. One example concerns Paul and the church of Jerusalem. In Acts, Paul appears to visit Jerusalem three times (Acts 9:20f.; 11:30; 15:2), but according to Paul, he visited Jerusalem on two occasions (Gal 1:16f.; 2). This discrepancy has led to the assumption that Luke is incorrect. Somehow, some scholars

---

10. Davies, *Paul and Rabbinic Judaism*, 321-34; ibid., *Jewish and Pauline Studies*, 91-121.

11. Nanos, *Mystery of Romans*, 21-40. Nanos writes that in "Paul's apostolic ministry God is demonstrating the irrevocable priority of Israel in the faithful fulfillment of his promise to the fathers... For Paul, the pattern of salvation history has been and always will be, even in the midst of confronting misguided exclusivity on the part of some of the children of Jacob, 'to the Jews *first* and *also* to the Greek'" (ibid., 21).

have proposed to treat the visits of Acts 11:30 and 15 as duplicated accounts of the same event, which would indicate the inaccuracy of Luke's information.[12]

Concerning Paul and the Jewish law, Luke describes Paul as supporting Jewish ritual observances in two passages: once when recommending the circumcision of Timothy (Acts16:1–3), and again when he submitted to James's suggestion regarding the vow and its accompanying shaving of the head (Acts 21:17–26).[13] For some scholars, Luke's information is contradictory to Paul's epistles. However, certain scholars have supposed on the basis of Gal 2:3 that at the Jerusalem Council Paul had opposed the demand that Titus should be circumcised.[14]

Yet another example regarding the issue of Paul and the Council decrees is that according to Luke, Paul agreed to the apostles' injunctions involving the enforcement of certain ritual prohibitions on the Gentile

---

12. Cf. Cadbury and Lake, *Beginnings of Christianity*, 5:195–96. Longenecker does not think that Luke's report of Paul's three Jerusalem visits is inaccurate (Longenecker, *Luke-Acts*, 405). Longenecker writes, "Here it is sufficient to say that the simplest solution that provides the most satisfactory and convincing reconstruction and leaves the fewest loose ends is that Galatians 2:1–10 corresponds to the famine visit of Acts 11:27–30. On such an understanding, and taking the temporal conjunctions 'then' (*epeita*) of Galatians 1:18 and 2:1 as referring back to Saul's conversion (AD 33, allowing some flexibility in rounding off the years), his first visit to Jerusalem can be dated about 36, and his famine visit some fourteen years after his conversion, about 46. On such a basis, the reference in Galatians 2:2 to Saul's having gone to Jerusalem 'in response to a revelation' (*kata apokalypsin*) should probably be related to Agabus' prophecy of 11:28" (ibid.).

13. Cf. Wilson, *Luke and the Law*. In contrast to this view, according to Witherington, "Once the full weight of 2 Cor. 11:24 is appreciated, having a half-Jew circumcised on one occasion or observing a Jewish rite of purification on another (cf. Acts 21:23–26) seems perfectly possible for Paul" (Witherington, *Acts of the Apostles*, 477). Longenecker also points out in *Luke-Acts*, "Having urged Paul to follow their proposed course of action, the leaders of the Jerusalem church go on to assure him that this in no way rescinds their earlier decision to impose nothing further on Gentile converts than these four injunctions given for the sake of harmony within the church and in order not to impede the progress of the Jewish Christian mission" (Longenecker, *Luke-Acts*, 520).

14. Cf. Windisch, qtd. in Cadbury and Lake, *Beginnings of Christianity*, 2:320. According to Witherington, Paul did not contradict Acts 16:1–3 in Gal 2:3. Witherington notes, "For utilitarian reasons, Paul could very well have circumcised a colleague who came from a mixed marriage, all the more since his mother was Jewish and thus Timothy was a Jew by rabbinic law . . . Paul's intrinsic attitude to the act of circumcising a Jewish Christian is expressed in I Cor. 7. 19: 'Circumcision is nothing and the foreskin is nothing'" (Witherington, *Acts of the Apostles*, 476).

converts, but the decrees in Acts would have been repugnant to Paul's own claim in Gal 2.[15]

However, regarding Timothy's circumcision (Acts 16:1–3), the traditional interpretation is that Paul circumcised *Timothy* for missiological reasons.[16] But David J. Rudolph points out some problems in light of the literary context.[17] He notes, "The traditional interpretation of Acts 16:3 wrongly assumes that Jews at this time did not ask questions."[18] Therefore, Rudolph adds:

> Paul considered Timothy a Jew on the basis of matrilineal descent. Timothy identified as a Jew and lived as a Jew (Acts 16:1; cf. 2 Tim 1:5; 3:15). The young man was uncircumcised probably because his Gentile father had not permitted it. Now the circumstances were different and Timothy desired to fulfil his covenant responsibilities. Paul thus circumcised Timothy to confirm a pre-existing covenantal identity ... There is no evidence in the literary context that Paul regarded circumcision as a Jewish cultural expression detached from its first-century meaning as a sign of the covenant.[19]

In Jewish law, if a child had a Gentile father and a Jewish mother, then this child was a Jew. In that case, why had Timothy never been circumcised? "Timothy should have been circumcised and raised as a Jew," Longenecker says, "but in Greek law the father dominates in the home. Apparently the Jewish community at Lystra was too weak or lax to interfere

---

15. Catchpole, "Paul, James," 428–44. Bruce does not view Luke's report in Acts 15 as contradicting Paul in Gal 2:11–14. It seems that the dating of Gal 2 and Acts 15 is a significant point to Luke's report accuracy. As Bruce writes, "part of Paul's autobiographical narrative in Galatians probably provides the background to Acts 15. In Gal. 2:11–14 Paul tells how (presumably sometime after the conference of Gal. 2:1–10) Peter visited Antioch and (in accordance with his convictions and general practice) shared meals freely with Gentile Christians there" (Bruce, *Books of the Acts*, 284). See also Longenecker, *Luke-Acts*, 440–41. Some have dated the controversy of Gal 2:11–14 before the conference of Gal 2:10. See, for example, Munck, *Paul and the Salvation*, 100–103. Knox supposes that "the Antioch controversy preceded the first missionary expedition of Paul and Barnabas: that it was, in fact, the controversy that made the Antiochene church decide 'to launch a vigorous Gentile mission'" (Knox, *Acts of the Apostles*, 49; cf. Bruce, *Book of the Acts*, 284). I will discuss the Antioch Incident in Gal 2:11–14 in chapter 6.

16. See Witherington, *Acts of the Apostles*, 476–77.

17. See Rudolph, "A Jew to the Jews," 29–33.

18. Ibid., 30.

19. Ibid., 31.

with the prevalent Greek customs . . . Therefore, it was both proper and expedient for Paul to circumcise him."[20]

Rudolph goes on to note, "Luke's explanatory statement ('because of the Jews who were in those places') does not mean that the *act of circumcision* was an expedient, but that *the timing of the circumcision* was an expedient."[21] Therefore, the passage should be interpreted: "and he took him and had him circumcised [at that time] because of the Jews who were in those places."[22] Rudolph concludes, "Paul thought that the optimum time for Timothy to be circumcised (in order to confirm his covenant identity as a Jew) was prior to visiting his home region. The covenant-keeping motive for circumcision would have been *well received* by the Lystra Jewish community and would have opened hearts to Paul's message."[23]

If this were the case, then Luke's portrayal of Paul's Jewishness in Acts 16:1–3 is a reliable source. Rudolph notes that among commentators who argue for the historical reliability of Acts 21:17–26, there are some issues the commentators do not address. "Typically 1 Cor. 9:20 is cited as a prooftext to explain Paul's actions," he remarks.[24] Rudolph adds:

> If becoming "all things to all people" refers to Paul's open table-fellowship with Jewish and Gentile families during the course of his missionary journeys, and to the adaptation he exhibited by accommodating to his hosts within the limits of God's law, then it is not judicious for exegetes to use 1 Cor. 9:19–23 as a hermeneutical key to explain Paul's ritual purification in the temple described in Acts 21:17–26 (cf. 24:18) . . . As Barrett points out, "if Paul was not consistently law observant, then his testimony would have been a lie and a deceit, something not covered by 1 Corinthians 9" (Barrett 1998:1013). The thesis thus encourages a revisiting of the meaning of Acts 21:17–26 and its mirror text (Acts 15).[25]

Rudolph does not see Luke's portrayal of Paul in Acts 21:17–26 as contradicting 1 Cor 9. Stuart Chepey's study in Acts 21:23–27 similarly shows that Luke's information is historically plausible. He concludes:

---

20. Longenecker, *Luke-Acts*, 958.
21. Rudolph, "A Jew to the Jews," 32.
22. Ibid.
23. Ibid.
24. Ibid., 59.
25. Ibid., 205.

> Luke's information regarding Nazirite behavior in 21.23–7a is historically plausible as it stands, and there is no basis for the rationale that Luke misconstrued his facts. The reference to the purification process of all five individuals, all due to corpse contamination and all taking place simultaneously, is easily conceivable given what is known about Nazirites in the period Luke composed his account . . . In addition, Luke's narrative use of the Nazirite custom is sound. There is no reason to suppose Luke's use of Nazirites in Acts 21:23–4, namely as a means of portraying Paul as a pious, Law-minded Jew, stands out as odd either when comparing Luke's account with early rabbinic or other sources of the period. Not only would Nazirites have been thought of as pious individuals (in some cases), but by purifying himself along with four impure Nazirites and covering their costs to restart their avowed periods, Paul would have had a high chance of being seen participating and promoting Mosaic cult ritual associating himself with Law-minded Jews.[26]

Furthermore, according to Lüdemann, Acts 21 is a historically reliable source. "If we inquire concerning the historical reliability of the source," Lüdemann says, "the answer must be unconditionally positive. The individual elements are confirmed as probable or at least possible by other reports independent of Acts 21 . . . Our analysis of the traditions underlying Acts 21 can then be summarized as follows: Luke uses a connected source, which in fact does deal with Paul's last trip to Jerusalem and which is of great historical value."[27]

Another point where scholars differ concerns Luke's portrayal of Paul's education (Acts 22:3).[28] Hengel says that Luke's portrayal of Paul's education in Jerusalem is historically reliable. He points out that Paul was educated not in the Diaspora but in Jerusalem, as Luke reports. Hengel remarks:

> There is no reason to doubt that he was in the school ("sat at the feet") of Gamaliel 1, the son (or grandson) of the great Hillel (Acts 22.3). Even later, the Hillel family always had a particular interest in the Diaspora, the Jewish mission, and Greek language and culture. Hillel himself had come from Babylon to Jerusalem as a Diaspora Jew . . . Unfortunately far too little attention has been paid to the significance of Paul's own remark that he was a Pharisee and

26. Chepey, "Nazirites," 173–74.
27. Lüdemann, *Opposition to Paul*, 58–59.
28. See chapter 2.

as such was "blameless in the law" (Phil. 3.6), or that he exceeded by far the majority of his contemporaries in *iudaismos*, i.e. in study of the law (Gal. 1. 14). We know nothing of any form of organized Diaspora Judaism or of Pharisaic schools outside Jerusalem before AD 70. Evidently it was only possible for a Pharisaic pupil seeking to be a scribe to make a real study of the law in the holy city itself.[29]

Moreover, Paul's mission started "first for the Jew, then for the Gentiles" (Rom 1:16) in keeping with Luke's report. Hengel notes:

> There is one further indication that Paul tried to carry on his mission in Jerusalem. According to Rom. 1.16; 11.14; and I Cor. 9.20 he felt obliged to present his message not only to the Gentiles but always also to the Jews, and in Rom. 15.19 we find a remark to which too little attention has been paid, namely that he has preached the gospel of Christ 'from Jerusalem and the surrounding area' (or less probably: 'and in a wide circle') to Illyricum. This information must have some support in historical reality; we can hardly assume that the apostle is not telling the truth here... Perhaps Luke here is following a tradition which is connected with Paul's own testimony in Rom. 15.19, according to which the Pauline mission started in Jerusalem itself.[30]

As we have seen, New Testament scholarship is divided on the question of the historical reliability of Acts in general and on Luke's portrait of Paul in particular. Despite the controversy among scholars regarding Luke's portrayal of Paul and concerning Paul's own testimony, some important studies show significant elements of historical reliability in Acts, especially in regard to Paul's Jewishness in Acts (16:1-3; 21:17-26; 22:3). Therefore, we should attribute some value to Luke's portrayal of Paul even if some of Luke's view of Paul is disputed.

Did Paul Turn His Back on Judaism?

Though Luke is one of the earliest interpreters of Paul, some scholars do not accept Luke's picture of Paul. In commenting on Gal 1:13-17, certain scholars also argue that Paul rejected Judaism because of the contrast he drew between his former life in Judaism and his present life in Christianity.

29. Hengel, *Acts and the History*, 81-82.
30. Ibid., 87.

However, as we have already noted, Paul's own claim was that he truly was a Hebrew of Hebrews (2 Cor 11:22). Thus, Paul still believed himself a Jew who was called by God to witness the gospel first to Jew and then Gentile (Rom 1:16).

Divergent Views on Galatians 1:13–17

Nevertheless, there are many divergent views on Galatians 1:13–17 among scholars. "For you have heard of my previous way of life in Judaism," Paul wrote in Gal 1:13–17:

> how intensely I persecuted the church of God and tried to destroy it. I was advancing in Judaism beyond many Jews of my own age and was extremely zealous for the traditions of my fathers. But when God, who set me apart from birth and called me by his grace, was pleased to reveal his Son in me so that I might preach him among the Gentiles, I did not consult any man, nor did I go up to Jerusalem to see those who were apostles before I was, but I went immediately into Arabia and later returned to Damascus.

Scholars' views on this passage have diverged over the years. We will explore and evaluate each of these views before we proceed to my understanding of this text.

In 1921, Ernest De Witt Burton claimed in *A Critical and Exegetical Commentary on the Epistle to the Galatians* that in Gal 1:13–14, Paul refers to:

> The prevalent Judaism with its rejection of Jesus in contrast with the faith of the followers of Jesus as the Messiah. The very use of the term in this way is significant of the apostle's conception of the relation between his former and his present faith, indicating that he held the latter, and had presented it to the Galatians, not as a type of Judaism, but as an independent religion distinct from that of the Jews. Though the word Christianity was probably not yet in use, that fact was in existence.[31]

Burton also indicates that by the use of the term Ἰουδαισμός in verse 14, Paul is describing his life from the general national point of view—but it cannot be understood to have specific reference to the sect of the

---

31. Burton, *Critical and Exegetical Commentary*, 44.

Jew Among Jews

Pharisees.³² In Burton's view, Paul rejected Judaism and founded an independent religion.

Donald Guthrie, in his 1973 commentary on Gal 1:13, interprets this text to mean that Paul already regarded Christianity as having separated from Judaism.³³ Guthrie's position is that even though the effect of faith on morals in Judaism held much that was good, Judaism had rejected Christ. Thus Judaism, as a religious system, was in direct antithesis to Christianity. Guthrie also says that "Paul could never tolerate any presentation of Christianity which regarded it as a form of Judaism."³⁴ Guthrie argued that in verse 15, Paul gave literal dates for his calling to the gospel: "The idea behind the expression is of a distinct delimiting of boundaries. No longer was he confined within the limits of Judaism, but he was still confined, nevertheless, to the purposes of God."³⁵ Guthrie concludes that Paul's disdain for Judaism is reflected here.

George Lyons, in his 1985 dissertation *Pauline Autobiography*, agrees with Guthrie that Gal 1:13–17 reflects that Paul converted from Judaism to Christianity.³⁶ Lyons holds that the emphasis in this section works to contrast Paul's former position against Paul's present position.

"The formulation of Paul's autobiographical remarks in terms of 'formerly-now' and 'man-God' serves a paradigmatic function," Lyons says, "to contrast Paul's conversion from Judaism to Christianity with the Galatians' inverted conversion . . . Even the verb μετατίθημι which describes their desertion of Paul and his gospel in 1:6 has the connotation of a reverse conversion, apostasy, treachery, desertion."³⁷ As a result, Lyons comes to the same conclusion as Guthrie, though with a different explanation.

In contradistinction to Guthrie and Lyons, Beverly Roberts Gaventa does not find that Paul draws a contrast in Gal 1:13–17.³⁸ Rather, Gaventa thinks that Paul explains his faithfulness to God rather than his separation from God. As Gaventa states, "Verses 13–14 set the state for this inbreaking by characterizing Paul's life 'in Judaism,' . . . He had been acceptable, even successful, by the standards of his own people. Especially his action as a

---

32. Ibid., 46.
33. Guthrie, *Galatians*, 67.
34. Ibid.
35. Ibid., 68.
36. Lyons, *Pauline Autobiography*, 150.
37. Ibid.
38. Gaventa, *From Darkness to Light*, 24–29.

persecutor confirmed his zeal. Paul does not describe this period as a time when he was separated from God, but as a time of apparent faithfulness."[39]

Gaventa goes on to ask, "How is the prophetic imagery of vv. 15–17 connected with Paul's self-understanding?" As Gaventa explains:

> That particular faithfulness is interrupted and, indeed, overthrown by the revelation of Jesus Christ; Paul draws on prophetic imagery in vv. 15–17 in order to convey the radical impact of the revelation. While this may imply that he views himself as standing within the prophetic tradition, it does not mean that what has occurred to Paul may be subsumed under the category of "call." What Paul describes in Gal. 1:11–17 includes a commission but it is not limited to that commission.[40]

In other words, Gaventa does not think Paul thought of himself as having been called from Judaism to Christianity; rather, Paul describes how Jesus the Messiah intervened with him. Paul was standing within the prophetic tradition. Gaventa also observes that "Paul gives no indication of remorse or guilt concerning his past"[41] because, in Gal 1:13–14, "Paul has portrayed himself as one who maintained faithfully all that pertained to Judaism."[42]

Richard N. Longenecker (1990),[43] unlike Burton, thinks that in verses 13–17 Paul:

> Speaks of his life in Judaism, his conversion to Christ, and his commission to a Gentile mission, obviously rebutting rumors to the contrary. As for his life in Judaism (vv. 13–14), he denies that he was in any way prepared for preaching a law-free gospel to Gentiles. Far from it! Rather, he was a faithful and zealous observer of the Jewish religion and way of life, even to the point of persecuting Christians and trying to destroy "the church of God."[44]

Longenecker regards verses 13 and 14 more positively than other scholars in their perspective on Judaism. In verse 13, he observes that "Paul's evangelistic practice, it seems, included certain of his own experiences in

---

39. Ibid., 28.
40. Ibid.
41. Ibid.
42. Ibid., 26.
43. See Longenecker, *Galatians*.
44. Ibid., 26.

proclaiming the gospel, though these were twisted by his opponents for their own purposes."[45]

Longenecker also notes that "'Ioudaismos,' meaning 'the Jewish religion and way of life,' appears in the New Testament only here and at v 14 ... Whatever its origin, it became for Jews an honored title."[46] Longenecker goes on to say that:

> more important, however, in days when the keeping of the Mosaic law was considered by Pharisaic Jews to be the vitally important prerequisite for the coming of the Messianic Age (cf. *b. Sanh.* 97b-98a; *b. B. Bat.* 10a; *b. Yoma* 86b), Paul could well have validated his actions against Christians by reference to such godly precedents as Moses (cf. Num. 25:1–5), ... Phinehas (cf. Num 25:6–15), ... and the action of Mattathias and the Hasidim in rooting out apostasy among the people (cf. 1 Macc 2:23–28, 42–48).[47]

For Longenecker, Paul was transformed from being "a zealous proponent of the traditions of Judaism (vv. 13–14) to a proclaimer of the Christian gospel that has as its content God's Son and as its legitimate sphere of outreach to the Gentiles (vv. 15–16a)."[48] However, he sees some connection between God's sovereignty in Paul's life in Judaism and his life as a Christian, for he was "set apart from birth." As Longenecker explains, "But it was the call of God, and the encounter by Christ which together formed the basis for Paul's proclamation of God's Son to the Gentiles."[49]

R. Alan Cole (1991) believes, like Donald Guthrie,[50] that "it is quite clear that already Paul regards Judaism as a different religion."[51] Cole also argues that "Betz is incorrect in saying that, at that time, Paul was only 'changing parties' within Judaism, from Pharisaism to Christianity; the break was too total and violent for that, and both sides were clearly conscious of it."[52] Cole again explains that Paul implicitly says that he left Judaism because, "It is not that Judaism was a false faith; but, to Paul, it was only a past step along the road that finally led to Christ (3:24). To go back

---

45. Ibid.
46. Ibid., 27.
47. Ibid., 28.
48. Ibid., 35.
49. Ibid.
50. Guthrie, *Galatians*, 67.
51. Cole, *Galatians*, 86.
52. Ibid.

to Judaism now would be unthinkable (3:3), while to remain in Judaism after Christ's coming would be to refuse to accept Israel's Messiah (Acts 18:5–6)."[53] In other words, what Cole is saying is that Paul left Judaism because Judaism's function—to lead to Christ—was finished.

According to James D. G. Dunn (1993),[54] Paul's use of the words "the former life in Judaism" implies that "Christianity and Judaism were already separated,"[55] but "only in the sense that 'Judaism' constituted a particular claim to and interpretation of Israel's covenant and heritage which Paul had once embraced but now questioned, 'Judaism' as characterized by the attitudes and life-styles documented in verse 13 and 14."[56] Dunn sees, as does Alan F. Segal,[57] that Paul's conversion was "from one Jewish movement, the Pharisees, to another, the Christians."[58] Dunn does not think Paul left Judaism in Gal in 13–17.

J. Louis Martyn (1997) notes the sharp contrast between verses 13 and 15 because of the locution ὅτε δε:

> In v 15, employing the expression *hote de*, he begins to speak about the period that followed that call. For the locution *hote de* there are two possible translations; "but when," indicating a sharp contrast between the two periods in Paul's life; and "and when," pointing to a continuity in which the second period is a supplement to the first . . . There are two strong reasons for electing the first of these translations, seeing here a sharp contrast. (1) In v 12 Paul emphasizes a contrast between tradition and apocalypse. He then continues that contrast in the next two sentences . . . (2) As we have noted earlier, it is only by looking back that Paul can say he was earlier persecuting the church of God (v 13). At the time, sure that God was active in the nomistic traditions he had received in the religion of Judaism, he was altogether certain that God could not possibly be active in the messianic sect whose members confessed as God's Messiah a criminal put to death by crucifixion (cf. 3:13). With God's apocalyptic call, however, he saw that in his earlier life he had been tragically mistaken as to the locus of God's activity. It did not lie in the traditional, nomistic zeal that led him to persecute the church . . . Paul means to refer to a contrast, "but

---

53. Ibid., 55.
54. See Dunn, *Epistle to the Galatians*.
55. Ibid., 57.
56. Ibid.
57. Segal, *Paul the Convert*, xiv.
58. Dunn, *Epistle to the Galatians*, 57.

when" thus the translation with which v 15 begins; but all of that came to an end.⁵⁹

Martyn goes on to say:

> It follows that Paul does not speak in 1:15–16 of being converted from one religion, Judaism, to another, Christianity. Nor, in speaking to the Gentile Galatians, does Paul denigrate Judaism. As the whole of the letter shows, he is consistently concerned to say that the advent of Christ is the end of religion. With his call, then, he neither remained in the religion of Judaism nor transferred to a new religion, from which vantage point he could comparatively denigrate his earlier religion. Referring to God as *ho kalesas* ("the One who calls"; 1:15), Paul speaks of God's calling him into existence as an apostle of Jesus Christ. That call is not for Paul a religious event; it is the form taken in his own case by God's calling into existence the new creation.⁶⁰

According to Martyn, Paul brings Judaism (or religion) to an end because he is a new creation by virtue of the calling of his God in the eschatological context. Martyn only solves the problem of Paul by asserting that to be in Christ is not to be in the past of any religion—a very odd solution, as Mark D. Nanos indicates.⁶¹

Ben Witherington III (1998) also notes a contrast between "Judaism" and "the assembly of God" in verse 13. Witherington suggests that the assembly of God should be distinguished from Judaism because "the heritage of Israel is seen by Paul as being claimed by and fulfilled in the Christian assembly and not elsewhere," and he goes on to say that "Paul's days of being bound to observe Torah as someone under the Mosaic covenant were over, it was what he 'formerly' (ποτε) did."⁶² However, "Paul continues to regard himself as ethnically a Jew, so that he can speak of his kinsmen and kinswomen according to the flesh, or of 'my people' (cf.1:14; 2:15), but his point is that he is no longer a part of the social and religious and political system known as Judaism. The issue then and now is of course how one defines what a true Jew is (cf. Rom. 9)."⁶³ Witherington sees that, for Paul,

---

59. Martyn, *Galatians*, 163–64.
60. Ibid., 164.
61. Nanos, "How Inter-Christian Approaches," 250–54.
62. Witherington, *Grace in Galatia*, 99.
63. Nanos, *Irony of Galatians*, 98.

the Mosaic covenant was over rather than fulfilled in Jesus Christ. Thus, Witherington naturally comes to the conclusion that Paul left Judaism.

In 2002, Nanos brought a new view of the Galatians' problems in his book *The Irony of Galatians*. According to Nanos, the Galatians' situation differed from what former scholars have proposed. He says:

> The addressees are righteous Gentiles within Jewish subgroups, that is, synagogue communities. Paul writes to the Galatian communities ἐκκλησίαις—which language implies several groups meeting at several cities, towns, or villages—who are suffering marginalization for considering themselves already full members of the larger Jewish communities as though they had completed proselyte conversion . . . Paul is himself an example of status and observance, and his message in this letter does not abrogate the identity or observance of Torah for Jewish people (i.e., Israelites) in the least but is instead predicated upon their continued validity for himself and other Jewish members of this movement.[64]

Nanos also notes:

> This approach to the Galatian situation recognizes that within intra-Jewish contexts it was entirely plausible that Jewish communal groups without affiliation with Jesus Christ could assert that it was possible for Gentiles to be included among the righteous people of God now—these Gentiles needed but to complete the ritual process of conversion that provided proselyte Jewish status . . . Galatians exemplifies the characteristic of a letter of ironic rebuke: the ironic nature of the letter is present on the very surface of Paul's language.[65]

He sees that Paul in Galatians was arguing in an intra-Jewish debate rather than abandoning Judaism. Nanos reads that, in Gal 1:11–2:21, "Paul defines his own independent revelation of the good news of Christ in tandem with the independent revelation enjoyed by the Jerusalem apostles (1:11–13, 15, 18; 2:1–2, 5, 7–9). He is not concerned to oppose his apostleship, mission, or message to that of the Jerusalem apostles."[66] Nanos argues that "Paul's appeal is not a message proclaimed against Israel, or against Torah observance by Jews who do not share faith in Christ. It is the message of Torah, the source of Wisdom; it expresses the plight of Israel in

---

64. Ibid,. 6–7, 9.
65. Ibid., 318–19.
66. Nanos, *Galatians Debate*, 402.

the midst of the nations, of the psalmist or the prophet in the den of his accusers."⁶⁷ Nanos goes on to say, "Only in the context of Paul's polemic against influencers who seek to conform (sub)groups of Gentile believers in Christ to the halakhic group norms of the larger Jewish communities do Paul's negative comments carry weight. Otherwise, Jewish identity and Torah observance are considered an advantage: Paul maintains the privilege of being 'a Jew by nature, and not a Gentile sinner' (2:14)."⁶⁸ He emphasizes that Paul never left Judaism, but what Paul says must be contextualized within intra-Jewish debates in Galatia.

Evaluation

Whereas Gaventa and Nanos understand this text within its Jewish context, Longenecker draws some contrast between Paul's former life and his present situation, yet Longenecker still reads this text in its Jewish background. James D. G. Dunn also comments on this text within a Jewish context to argue that Paul had not completely separated Christianity from Judaism this point in time. On the other hand, Dunn believes that somehow, sooner or later, Christianity had to break with Judaism to exist on its own.⁶⁹ However, I do not see any indication of Paul's intention to separate himself from Judaism in favor of Christianity either here or anywhere else.

In contrast, Guthrie, Burton, Lyons, Cole, Martyn, and Witherington all interpret this text to mean that Paul left Judaism—though each for different reasons. First, because Guthrie and the other scholars mentioned above understand "Judaism" in a twentieth-century form of contrasting religions, they claim that Paul left Judaism because Judaism had rejected Christ. In their opinion, Paul set Judaism in direct antithesis to Christianity.

But in the first century, according to Shaye J. D. Cohen, the definition of *Ioudaismos* is not "Judaism" but "Jewishness."⁷⁰ He says:

> As is well known, 2 Maccabees is the first work to use the word *Ioudaismos*. We are tempted, of course, to translate this as "Judaism," but this translation is too narrow, because in this first occurrence of the term, *Ioudaismos* has not yet been reduced to a designation of a religion. It means rather "the aggregate of all

---

67. Ibid., 404.
68. Ibid., 404–405.
69. Following the critique by Campbell, *Paul's Gospel*, 147.
70. Cohen, *Beginnings of Jewishness*, 106.

those characteristics that make Judaeans Judean (or Jews Jewish)." Among these characteristics, to be sure, are practices and beliefs that we would today call "religious," but these practices and beliefs are not the sole content of the term. Thus *Ioudaismos* should be translated not as "Judaism" but as Judaeanness.[71]

According to Cohen, Paul did not talk about Judaism in Gal 1:13, but of his devotion to Jewishness. Paul did not use Ἰουδαϊσμός as the concept of the religion that is Judaism. Martin Hengel has also indicated that, in the first century, the definition of Ἰουδαϊσμός is "the nation and exclusive belief in the one God of Israel, together with observance of the Torah given by him,"[72] rather than Ἰουδαϊσμός as a religious system.

According to these two studies, Guthrie's understanding of Ἰουδαϊσμός only as a religious system is revealed to be questionable. Paul's Judaism was not in direct antithesis to Christianity. Rather, after his encounter with Christ, he still believed the Shema and observed the Torah. In this context, Paul did not observe Torah as a means of salvation, but rather tried to convince his opponents that he was a true Jew and a true apostle for Gentiles. Guthrie is not the only scholar who believes Paul left Judaism. Lyons does as well, but for a different reason. He puts the stark paradigmatic contrast between Paul's life "formerly" and his life "now." "The whole of Paul's autobiographical narrative in Gal 1:10–2:21 appears to be framed by this temporal contrast, 'formerly-now,'" he says.[73] Consequently, Lyons concludes that Paul converted from Judaism to Christianity.

However, the contrast itself may not imply that Paul left Judaism, because Paul could still compare his life "formerly" and "now" while still within Judaism. Leaving his former way of life does not mean Paul left Judaism. The reason is that Paul probably considered Jesus to be the fulfillment or goal of Judaism (Rom 10:4).[74] As Nanos points out, the Galatian debate is an intra-Jewish debate.

Burton also indicates that in Gal 1:13–14 Paul contrasted the faith of the followers of Jesus as the Messiah over against the prevalent Judaism, which rejected Jesus. Paul used the word "Judaism" here to make a distinction between Paul's independent religion and that of Jews. Thus, for Burton, Paul rejected Judaism and founded an independent religion. But Paul

---

71. Ibid., 105–106.
72. Hengel, *Judaism and Hellenism*, 1–2.
73. Lyons, *Pauline Autobiography*, 147.
74. See more detail in Campbell, *Paul's Gospel*, 60–63.

probably did not say in Gal 1:13–17 that he left Judaism because he made a distinction between his life before and after his encounter with Christ. Rather, Paul simply tried to distinguish for his hearers his situation before and after his calling. Paul did not necessarily put Judaism in antithesis to Christianity or found an independent religion.

Cole insists that Paul regards Judaism as a different religion and left it because its function was finished and had now led to Christ. If this is the reason why Paul left Judaism, he did not have to—because he regarded Judaism as a tutor or schoolmaster to Christ (Gal 3:24). In other words, after a child learns the alphabet, he or she does not abandon it but rather builds on that foundation or grows out of it. And after a child graduates from elementary education, he or she does not have to go back to learn the alphabet again, nor oppose it. Likewise, Paul does explain his way of life before and after his encounter with Christ. He develops from what he previously learned, but he used it positively to grow within the faith of which Jesus is Messiah.

For Martyn, Paul brings Judaism (or religion) to an end because Paul is the new creation by the calling of God. He draws a sharp contrast between verses 13 and 15 because of the locution ὅτε δέ. Martyn says that Paul's former life in Judaism was nomistic. After God's apocalyptic call, Paul realized that he had made a mistake as to the locus of God's activity. If this was the case, the question is: What kind of mistake does Martyn talk about? If the mistake was that Paul neither recognized Jesus as Israel's Messiah nor recognized the inclusion of Gentiles without their circumcision, then "but when" in verse 15 could read in that way, which would mean that all of Paul's misunderstanding[75] is ended rather than that Judaism is ended.

According to Nanos's observation of Martyn's definition of religion, "'the various communal, cultic means . . . by which human beings seek to know and to be happily related to the gods or God,' in particular, it 'is a human enterprise.'"[76] The problem with Martyn's interpretation of Gal 1:13–14 is that he regards Judaism as a religion even though he says that Gal 1:13–14 is not referring to Judaism. And "he forgets that Paul's Scriptures claim for Abraham the same basis for circumcision as well as for Moses the same basis for the giving of the commandments, to name just

---

75. See ibid., 142–43.
76. Nanos, "Inter-Christian Approaches," 250–54.

two examples—cannot help but reflect the view that not only is Christian Judaism bankrupt, but [also] . . . non-Christian Judaism."[77]

The same God of Abraham, Isaac, and Jacob was revealed to Paul in the apocalyptic age to confirm, through Jesus the Messiah, the promises for the salvation of both Israel and Gentiles. Paul, as Cohen pointed out, was not talking about Judaism in Gal 1:13 but rather about his devotion to Jewishness.[78] The fact that Paul accepted Jesus as the Messiah of Judaism cannot mean that he abandoned his Jewishness. In this context, Paul's main argument did not set aside Judaism. Rather, Paul explained his thoughts regarding inclusion of Gentiles before and after God's revelation. Paul did not wipe out God's redemption history, which is Israel's history, because for Paul, God promised the Messiah through Israel's prophets who testify in the Scriptures (Rom 1:1–2). After all, Paul in all likelihood believed that Jesus the Messiah had completed Judaism in the eschatological context. In Rom 10:4, Christ *confirmed* the promises, not annulled them—he is their τέλος or goal.

Witherington has a different reason to explain why Paul left Judaism: because the Mosaic covenant was over. Was it? In 2 Cor 3:4–18, Paul discusses the Mosaic covenant and the new covenant. As W. S. Campbell indicates,[79] if the new covenant is not used in the sense of "new" but rather of the renewed covenant, then the Mosaic covenant is not terminated but instead has some continuity in Christianity.[80] Campbell cites W. D. Davies, who says each new moon is not an entirely "new moon" but the old moon in a new light.

However, Witherington notes that Paul's Christianity was discontinuous with Judaism. Yet Paul continued to regard himself as ethnically a Jew. For Paul, birth or ethnic identity alone was not sufficient to be a true member of the people of God, which comes by faith. This question of who is a true Jew is nothing new in Jewish circles. Paul defined the true identity of the "Jew" in like manner (Rom 2:23–29). Therefore, these verses do not imply that Paul had abandoned Judaism. Although Paul's interpretation of

---

77. Ibid., 250–54. Martyn changes the contrast to be between religion versus true faith rather than Judaism, but Nanos shows that despite the change in terminology, it comes to the same view in the end.

78. Cohen, *Beginnings of Jewishness*, 105–106.

79. Campbell, *Paul's Gospel*, 68–79.

80. I will discuss this Mosaic covenant in further detail later.

"true Judaism" and of "Jew" differed from some of his contemporaries, he still regarded himself as a true Jew.

In other words, as Dunn has pointed out:

> If Paul's use of "Judaism" here indicates a certain distancing of himself from the characteristic self-understanding of most of this fellow Jews, he still regarded himself as a Jew (ii.15; i.14—"my people"); and his description of the sect of Jesus Messiah as "the church of God" indicates a firm claim that the new movement with which he now identified was wholly part of and continuous with the Israel of old.[81]

Paul also indicated that the Christian's God is "God of Israel" (Gal 6:16).[82] Hence, Paul did define the true identity of the Jew within an intra-Jewish debate, but not as some new invention or new creation without antecedents.

As we can see, these scholars intend to read this text (Gal 1:13–17) as a negative evaluation of Judaism. The result is that they come, through various reasons, to different conclusions concerning the Jewishness of Paul. Davies has indicated that, for Paul, the gospel was both the completion of Judaism and its fulfillment. Not only was Paul's thought rooted in Second Temple Judaism, his lifestyle also was closely related to it. Paul remained a true Jew.[83] Moreover, as Davies has noted, "Paul's letters were composed in the context of a dialogue within Judaism. They were later read outside and over against that context. Context determines content."[84] What then, is Paul's focal point within this text?

Paul's Focal Point

The question is: What point was Paul really trying to make in Gal 1:13–17? Whoever Paul's opponents were in Galatia, the Galatians influenced by Paul's opponents were deserting Jesus Christ (1:7). These opponents were probably Judaizers[85] who wanted the Galatian Christians to be circumcised

---

81. Dunn, *Epistle to the Galatians*, 57.

82. This text has been controversial among scholars. I will discuss it in the next chapter.

83. Davies, *Paul and Rabbinic Judaism*, 321–22.

84. Ibid., *Jewish and Pauline Studies*, 99.

85. For more detail, see *Dictionary of Paul*, s.v. "Judaizers," 512–17. Campbell, unlike those who take the traditional view, has pointed out that Paul's opponents may not

and keep the law (5:3) in order to become God's people. Paul addressed the Galatians and his opponents sarcastically. In the beginning (Gal 1:1), Paul adamantly emphasized the authority of his apostleship. The verse implies that Paul's opponents questioned (or undermined) Paul's apostleship, perhaps because Paul was not one of Jesus' disciples, and thus Paul's opponents thought Paul's apostleship was inferior to the Jerusalem apostles (Gal 1:1).

In Gal 1:6f., Paul begins to argue that he has authority to preach the gospel, and he insists that his gospel is the true gospel. Paul is beginning here to defend his gospel. First, in verses 13-14, when Paul mentions "his former manner of life in Judaism (Jewishness),"[86] Paul indicates that he thought if Gentiles wanted to become God's people, they first had to become circumcised and keep the law. Thus, he was an extremely zealous Jew who persecuted Christian Jews who brought Gentiles to God's family without circumcision. In other words, Paul was probably talking about his own experience *before* he encountered Jesus Christ. Paul himself, like the Judaizers, was formerly against those Gentiles who did not become Jews in the proper way through circumcision.

Paul was simply trying to distinguish between before and after his calling when he used the phrase "my former manner of life in Judaism."[87]

---

have been Jewish Christians but were perhaps non-Christian Jews who resented Paul's interference with their adherents (ibid.). Davies has identified Paul's opponents in Galatia as nationalistic Jews who urged those Gentile Christians to give up Paul's advice and observe the law and circumcision (Davies, *Jewish and Pauline Studies*, 127). Cousar lists five potential groups of Paul's opponents: 1) Jewish Christians from Jerusalem, 2) Jewish Christians with no support from Jerusalem, 3) Jewish Christian with gnostic views, 4) Gentile Christians who felt that Paul's teaching had departed from its Jewish base, and 5) Judaizers who wanted submission to the law and partly radicals who "felt themselves exempt from moral issues" (Cousar, *Galatians*, 5). See also Sumney, *Identifying Paul's Opponents*.

86. Cohen indicates that "the most distinctive of the distinctive characteristics of the Jews was the manner in which they worshipped their God, what we today would call their religion. But Ἰουδαϊσμός, the ancestor of our English word 'Judaism,' means more than just religion. For ancient Greeks and contemporary social scientists, 'religion' is only one of many items that make a culture or a group distinctive. Perhaps, then, we should translate Ἰουδαϊσμός not 'Judaism' but 'Jewishness'" (Cohen, *Beginnings of Jewishness*, 7-8). According to Esler's study, Ἰουδαῖοι means "Judeans" but not "Jews" (Esler, *Conflict and Identity*, 63-74).

87. Hengel has indicated that "the Greek counterpart to 'Judaism,' Ἰουδαϊσμός, derives from the middle of the period with which we are to deal. It appears for the first time in the account of the persecution under Antiochus IV in II Maccabees or its source in Jason of Cyrene, and conveys what even the ancient world found to be an astonishing state of affairs: the word means both political and genetic association with the Jewish nation and

But some scholars, on the basis of Phil 3:4–11, have argued similarly in support of the proposition that Paul left Judaism. But these verses do not support that, despite the use of derogatory terms such as "rubbish." As Arnold Fruchtenbaum says, "Paul compares what he has in the Messiah to what he had in Judaism. The comparison is that what he had in Judaism he declared 'rubbish' . . . But what he says is 'rubbish' is only in comparison to what is so much greater—not that the thing itself is by nature."[88] This comparison certainly does not mean that Paul changed his religion.

Some scholars put the contrast as we see above between Gal 1:13–14 and Gal 1:15–17 for several different reasons. Burton has pointed out that Paul drew the contrast between the prevalent Judaism, with its rejection of Jesus, and with the faith of the followers of Jesus as the Messiah.[89] Burton is perhaps right here, but this contrast[90] still does not imply that Paul founded an independent religion or a different religion. Rather, "Paul defines his own independent revelation of the good news of Christ."[91]

In verses 15–16, God initiates his call to Paul to realize his misunderstanding that a Gentile could not become one of God's people without becoming a Jew first. Now Paul knows that Jesus is the Messiah and that God has given him authority to preach the gospel to Gentiles. In other words, Paul's authority for having an apostleship to the Gentiles rested in the fact that he was appointed by God, not by man. For Paul, his apostleship was independent of and also identified with or authenticated by other apostles in the Jerusalem community (Gal 2:7). Paul points out that his apostleship is equal to that of the other apostles, perhaps because he was concerned that his opponents may have claimed superior authority for James and, by implication, for themselves.

As Leon Morris has indicated, "Paul makes it clear that becoming a Christian was not a bright idea that occurred to him. It [his becoming a Christian] was not that he became dissatisfied with Judaism and, looking

---

exclusive belief in the one God of Israel, together with observance of the Torah given by him" (Hengel, *Judaism and Hellenism*, 1–2).

88. Fruchtenbaum, "Danger of Throwing," 67.

89. Burton, *Critical and Exegetical Commentary*, 44.

90. Koptak draws a contrast between a commitment to the human traditions of Judaism and faith in the divinely revealed gospel in Koptak, "Rhetorical Identification," 163.

91. Nanos, *Galatians Debate*, 402.

around for a way that appealed to him more, settled on Christianity."[92] Rather, Paul was a follower of the Messiah, Jesus, by God's calling.

In verses 15–16, Paul had an experience both of conversion and of calling. Paul's calling was more like prophetic calls (cf. Jer 1:5). Such language emphasizes Paul's role as one called to proclaim the word of God and points to the divine origin of the word that is proclaimed. The Greek word μετάνοια means "change of mind," or "repentance," which in English can signify "conversion." It means "a change in which one adopts a new religion" or "transformation"; that is, as water is converted to ice.[93] Paul did not change Judaism to another religion but insisted on transformation. If "Paul considered himself as part of the new Jewish sect,"[94] then Paul truly believed that his messianic Judaism was true Judaism. As Davies has argued, "Paul was not thinking in terms of what we normally call conversion from one religion to another but of the recognition by Jews of the final or true form of their own religion."[95] Also, Betz, along with Segal, has pointed out that "at the time of his conversion the two religions were still one and the same, so that the most one could say is that he was converted from one Jewish movement, the Pharisees, to another, the Christians."[96]

For Paul, it was a significant change. As Campbell articulates in similar vein:

> Yet even the assertion that Jesus is Messiah was not for Paul tantamount to a rejection of Judaism, or the founding of an entirely new religion but, rather, expressing the profound conviction that the final expression and intent of Judaism had been born. For this reason we believe that it is inadequate to speak only in terms of Paul's conversion—as if he were moving from one religion to another; and likewise only in terms of his call—as if he were continuing in an unaltered faith. The conversion-call combination emphasizes both continuity and change.[97]

Likewise, in Gal 1:13–17, the context is more within an intra-Jewish debate than outside. Moreover, Paul himself also testified in 2 Cor 11:24 and Rom 11:1 that he continued to be committed to Judaism. Finally, Paul's

---

92. Morris, *Galatians*, 54.
93. *American Heritage Dictionary*, 2nd college ed., s.v.v. "conversion," "convert," 320.
94. Segal, *Paul the Convert*, xiv.
95. Davies, "Paul and the People," 27.
96. Betz, *Galatians*, 69.
97. Campbell, *Paul's Gospel*, 74.

motto is to preach "the gospel to the Jew first and also to Gentiles" (Rom 1:16).[98] In light of all these factors, one could conclude that Gal 1:13–17 does not imply that Paul left Judaism.

Therefore, the focal point of Paul's message in Gal 1:13–14 is Paul's own practice, wherein he fought against the Gentiles having to become Jews in order to be recognized as having full standing or equality before God (vv. 13–14). Before his calling, Paul might have argued against Gentile inclusion, but when God revealed the Messiah, Jesus, to him and appointed him as an apostle for Gentiles (vv. 15–16), Paul understood that the Gentiles were not required to become Jews in order to be in God's family.

In other words, for Paul, his gospel to Gentiles was rooted in divine revelation and divine calling. In this sense, it is unlikely that Gal 1:13–17 implies that Paul had left Judaism some time prior to his writing to the Galatians.

Did Paul Advocate Exclusion of the Jews from Salvation?

Galatians 4:21–31 is also a disputed text among scholars who hold that Paul excluded Jews from salvation. First, I will discuss Paul's allegorical use of Scripture in Gal 4:21–31 and different kinds of views on Gal 4:21–31—the traditional view, the "new consensus" view,[99] and Susan G. Eastman's study on "cast out" (Gal 4:30)—in order to bring out the most likely view of Gal 21–31.

Paul's Use of Scripture in Gal 4:21–31

I have noted previously that Paul uses allegory—a Jewish method of argument—in his own discourse. In Gal 4:21–31, he uses this device to communicate with both his opponents and followers. However, some scholars' view that Paul's argument here is not early rabbinic seems to ignore the plain evidence of the text. As Witherington has noted, "[t]here is strong evidence that Pharisees like Paul and before him Jewish teachers like Hillel had received rhetorical training, even in Jerusalem."[100] David Daube,

---

98. Nanos, *Mystery of Romans*, 21–40; Jervell, *Unknown Paul*, 52–76.

99. Eastman calls some contemporary scholars' new interpretation in Gal 4:21–31 a "new consensus" (Eastman, "Cast Out," 309–36).

100. Witherington, *Grace in Galatia*, 322.

however, has noted that the early Jewish methods of interpreting Scripture are frequently "derived from Hellenistic rhetoric,"¹⁰¹ thus indicating some interaction. Furthermore, as R. Alan Cole notes, "Paul's exegesis is certainly not allegorical in the extreme sense of the exegesis of Philo, who is no rabbi; for Philo, Sarah stands for 'philosophy' and Hagar for 'lower education.'"¹⁰² According to R. P. C. Hanson, "the practice of allegorizing was much more widespread among Rabbis trained in a Palestinian tradition in Paul's day than has hitherto been realized or than later rabbinic literature was willing to admit."¹⁰³ But Paul did not use allegory as his primary hermeneutical strategy, as many scholars have noted.¹⁰⁴

Many scholars have preferred to call Paul's use of Scripture here "typological" or "figurative" rather than "allegorical" because it differs from the allegorical treatments of first-century Alexandrian Jew Philo and the late third- and early fourth-century Alexandrian Christian pattern.¹⁰⁵ But Longenecker has pointed out, "Paul's treatment here is in line with Palestinian allegorical exegesis, and merits the appellative that he himself gives it—i.e., 'allegorical interpretation.'"¹⁰⁶ Moreover, since Paul himself said that "these things are to be as allegories (v. 24)," Paul "means simply that they are not to be taken at face value."¹⁰⁷ Thus, Dieter Lührmann indicates that the method as such could not have seemed illegitimate to Paul's readers and his opponents, because "The basic assumption is that behind every story another meaningful and 'actual' narrative level is to be found, on which one must read the same story again, point for point."¹⁰⁸

"If, however," Longenecker posits, "we view Paul's use of the Hagar-Sarah story here as ad hominem in nature—that is, responding in kind to some treatment of the same story by his Galatian opponents—then we need not see Paul as saying that allegory was built into the biblical narrative itself but that the biblical narrative is now being treated by the interpreter

---

101. Daube, "Rabbinic Methods," 239–64.

102. Cole, *Galatians*, 178. See more detail on the surface similarities between Philo and Paul in Gal 4:21–31 in Longenecker, *Galatians*, 205; Witherington, *Grace in Galatia*, 324–25.

103. Hanson, *Allegory and Event*, 80.

104. Hays, *Echoes of Scripture*, 166.

105. Longenecker, *Galatians*, 209.

106. Ibid.

107. Hays, *Echoes of Scripture*, 116.

108. Lührmann, *Galatians*, 89.

(whether the Judaizers, or Paul, or both) in allegorical fashion."[109] In this case, Paul's readers would not have any trouble understanding Paul's allegory. Moreover, it seems that Paul would not have used allegory if he thought that his readers could not comprehend it.

However, in Gal 4:22—even though Paul used the quotation formula "it is written that . . . "—he did not directly quote from the Old Testament but instead summarized the stories about Abraham as found in several chapters of Genesis (Gen 16:15; 21:2-3, 9 [LXX]). Paul, perhaps, simply quotes the tradition. "This tradition also includes an interesting interpretation: 'Abraham had two sons, one from the slave woman, and one from the free woman.'"[110] Paul did not directly quote from Scripture for two reasons. First, as C. K. Barrett points out, here Paul was responding to the scriptural arguments of his opponents, for here "it is written" does not identify a specific text but rather "allows a genuine Old Testament foundation of the Judaizers' argument."[111]

The second reason is that "the ad hominem nature of Paul's use of Hagar and her son Ishmael vis-à-vis Sarah and her son Isaac is the fact that none of the principals are named as the story begins and thereafter in the main only descriptive epithets are used in referring to them."[112] Moreover, as Barrett observes, it "implies that the story is already before the Galatians: they will know that the slave is Hagar, the free woman, Sarah."[113]

In Gal 4:27, Paul again used a quotation from Isa 54:1, according to LXX. Although there is no direct evidence in the original text that the prophet ever applied it to the barren Sarah, this quotation from Isaiah is appropriate here for several reasons. Paul's citation of this text may be an example of his following Hillel's second hermeneutical rule. As Longenecker explains:

> According to the second of the seven *middôt* or interpretive principles ascribed to Rabbi Hillel, when the same word occurs in two separate passages, then the considerations of the one can be applied to the other (gĕzêrâ sāwâ, or interpretation by verbal analogy). Here the fact that Sarah was barren (cf. στεῖρα in Gen

---

109. Longenecker, *Galatians*, 210.
110. Betz, *Galatians*, 241.
111. Barrett, "Allegory," 9.
112. Cf. Longenecker, *Galatians*, 207.
113. Barrett, "Allegory," 9.

11:30 LXX) allows Paul to connect Sarah with Isa 54:1, which also contains *the* word "barren" (cf. στεῖρα in Isa 54:1 LXX).[114]

Paul gives another proof from Scripture in Gal 4:30. He quotes from Scripture assuming his readers will recognize its authority. Paul's quotation is slightly different from the LXX. The last two words, "of the free woman," are not found in the LXX, Paul having re-allegorized the Hagar-Sarah story from his own perspective.[115] It seems reasonable to say that Paul's use of Scripture is explicitly allegorical.[116] Moreover, we have found that Paul's use of Scripture in Gal 4:24–31 displays an ad hominem characteristic.[117]

"It seems reasonable to conclude, then," as Hanson says of this passage:

> St. Paul was quite ready to use allegory, and even to use it in order to evacuate the ordinances of the Torah of their literal meaning on occasion, but . . . he employed this allegory in a Palestinian rather than an Alexandrian tradition . . . His motives for using it were, as far as we can discover, far from being those of the Alexandrians, and especially Philo, who wanted by allegory to avoid the necessity of taking historical narrative seriously; Paul on the contrary used allegory as an aid to typology, a method of interpreting the Old Testament which, however fanciful some of its forms may be, does at least regard history as something meaningful.[118]

Who Did Paul Refer to as "Cast Out"?

The traditional view is that Paul excluded Jews from salvation according to Gal 4:21–31. Briggs identifies "Hagar the slave woman" as a very specific "other": the Jews. Briggs notes, "Paul replaced the distinction between Jew and Gentile in the Christian community with an in fact far more drastic one between Christian (Jew and Gentile) and non-Christian Jew."[119]

Kenneth S. Wuest identifies "Hagar the slave woman" and her children as the followers of legalistic Judaism, saying, "This Hagar or Sinai corresponds, Paul says, to the then existent city of Jerusalem, the center of the

---

114. Longenecker, *Galatians*, 215. See also Daube, "Rabbinic Methods," 252–53.

115. Betz, *Galatians*, 250; Longenecker, *Galatians*, 217; Witherington, *Grace in Galatia*, 338.

116. Hanson, *Allegory and Event*, 80.

117. Longenecker, *Galatians*, 210.

118. Hanson, *Allegory and Event*, 82–83.

119. Briggs, "Galatians," 225.

apostate observance of Judaism. Just as Hagar, a slave, bore children that by birth became slaves, so the followers of legalistic Judaism are in bondage of law . . . The heavenly Jerusalem which is free, therefore represents Sarah; and finally, grace, and the faith way of salvation, for it is contrasted to the earthly Jerusalem which represents legalistic Judaism."[120]

Wuest notes that Paul excludes the Jew from salvation in Gal 4:30 and concludes with Lightfoot's words[121] in verse 30:

> The law and the gospel cannot coexist. The law must disappear before the gospel. It is scarcely possible to estimate the strength of conviction and depth of prophetic insight which this declaration implies. The apostle thus confidently sounds the death-knell of Judaism at a time when one half of Christendom clung to the Mosaic law with a jealous affection little short of frenzy, and while the Judaic party seemed to be growing in influence, and was strong enough even in the Gentile churches of his own founding to undermine his influence and endanger his life. The truth which to us appears a truism, must then have been regarded as a paradox.[122]

In parallel with this line of interpretation, Hans Dieter Betz reads the two covenants in Gal 4:24 as a stark contrast between the "old covenant" and the "new covenant."[123] Betz therefore asserts that "Paul's aim is clearly to discredit the 'old covenant' as the pre-Christian condition before salvation came."[124] He also interprets that the one from Mount Sinai refers to the "Sinai covenant." Hagar is represented as the slave woman, and her children's destiny is slavery. Therefore, "Those who belong to this covenant, the Torah covenant of Judaism, are in the situation of 'slavery under the Law' (cf. Gal 3:22–25, 28; 4:1–10; 5:1; also 2:4)."[125] Furthermore, Betz notes in verse 25 that Paul "wants to create a dualistic polarity between 'Judaism' and 'Christianity,' in order to discredit his Jewish-Christian opposition."[126]

For Betz, "The opposite of the 'present Jerusalem (v 25),' i.e., the political and religious institution of Judaism, is 'the Jerusalem above.'"[127]

---

120. Wuest, *Galatians in the Greek*, 133–34.
121. Lightfoot, *Epistles of Paul*, 184.
122. Cf. Wuest, *Galatians in the Greek*, 134–35.
123. Betz, *Galatians*, 243.
124. Ibid., 244.
125. Ibid.
126. Ibid., 246.
127. Ibid.

Betz goes on to say that for Paul the "heavenly Jerusalem" is identical with the "new age," but Paul "differs from Jewish apocalypticism by the radical dualism separating the two cities as the representatives of Judaism and Christianity."[128] Betz comes to the following conclusion:

> The last two words "of the free woman" are not found in the LXX and must be regarded as Paul's own interpretation, which he includes in the quotation. This suggests that we should read Gen 21:10 in the light of Gal 4:28–29; if God has given the inheritance to the Gentile Christians (cf 3:14, 29; 4:1, 7), the Jews are excluded from it, and the Christians constitute "the Israel of God" (6:16). Hence, the term "exclude" (ἐκβάλλω) must be taken seriously; Paul does the same with the Jews as his Jewish-Christian opponents want to do with him ... In Galatians there is no room or possibility for an eschatological salvation of Judaism as in Rom 11:25–32. Romans 9–11, therefore, means that Paul had revised his ideas as compared with Galatians. According to Galatians, Judaism is excluded from salvation altogether, so that the Galatians have to choose between Paul and Judaism.[129]

According to Betz's reading, there is no room for the inclusion of Judaism in salvation in Galatians, yet he recognizes that according to Paul there is a possibility for an eschatological salvation for Judaism in Romans.

Views of the New Consensus

Excluding Both Jews and Jewish Christians

Dunn interprets Paul's "allegory" as differing from the traditional view. He notes that in Gal 4:24, Paul does not refer to two covenants as an old covenant and a new covenant; Paul is talking about only one covenant here: the covenant with Abraham and his seed promising blessing to the nations.[130] In other words, "the Abraham covenant seen in terms of freedom and promise is a fuller expression of God's electing grace and a fuller embodiment of the ongoing divine will than the Abraham covenant seen in terms of law and flesh."[131]

---

128. Ibid., 247.
129. Ibid., 250–51.
130. Dunn, *Epistle to the Galatians*, 249.
131. Ibid.

Dunn also suggests that, in verse 26, Paul's thought reflects the Jewish apocalyptic understanding of a heavenly Jerusalem.[132] Dunn, therefore, interprets Gal 4:30 as an instance of "rhetorical flourish" that speaks to the exclusion of both Jews and the law-observant missionaries. Dunn comments,

> Betz (250–1) is justified in pointing to the contrast between the commanded "Throw out" here and the criticized "shout out" of v. 17 ("Paul does the same with the Jews as his Jewish Christian opponents want to do with him"; cf. Lightfoot 184—Paul "confidently sounds the death-knell of Judaism!"). Nevertheless, it would be a mistake to read a text cited for rhetorical effect as though it were a dogmatic statement. That Paul has the other missionaries particularly in view is certainly likely (particularly Mussner 332, Longenecker 217 and Martyn, "Covenants"), but it is doubtful whether the rhetorical flourish can be so restricted.[133]

Excluding Only Jewish Christians

From Gal 4:21–31, some contemporary scholars (such as Richard B. Hays, Longenecker, Witherington, and Martyn) identify Paul's opponents as Jewish-Christian missionaries who required converts to be circumcised and obey Mosaic law. According to these scholars, the conflict between "Hagar" and "the free woman" represents an inner-church struggle between two Jewish-Christian Missions, even though such scholars have different views concerning the degree with which Torah-observant Jewish Christians were involved in a mission to Gentiles.

Hays says that when Paul addresses the story of Abraham, Sarah, and Hagar as an allegory (Gal 4:24a), "the reader, conditioned by Paul's earlier adamant identification of Abraham's seed with Christ (3:16), expects a christological reading of the patriarchal narrative."[134] Hays also notes, "But Paul's allegorical reading fails to execute the anticipated identification of Isaac—Abraham's seed who was offered up as a sacrifice—with Jesus Christ. Instead, Paul reads Isaac as a prefiguration of the church."[135] In Gal 4:24, he says, the "two covenants" are not a contrast between the old covenant

---

132. Ibid., 255.

133. Ibid., 258. Barrett also reads that "cast out" includes "Jewish Christian," "Judaizers," and "Jews as the children of Hagar" (Barrett, "Allegory," 164–65).

134. Hays, *Echoes of Scripture*, 86.

135. Ibid.

at Sinai and the new covenant in Christ. "Rather, the contrast is drawn between the old covenant at Sinai and the older covenant with Abraham, which turns out in Paul's rereading to find its true meaning in Christ."[136]

Hays notes that Paul used figurative portrayals of Abraham, Sarah, Hagar, and Ishmael to address the pastoral and theological issues. For this reason, he insists that "the voice of Scripture must be heard as a voice directed to the present moment."[137] Hays explains:

> It is no accident that Paul's only direct quotation here from Genesis 21 is Sarah's demand to Abraham: "Cast out the slave girl and her son; for the son of the slave girl shall not inherit with the son of the freewoman" . . . In quoting Gen. 21:10 (LXX), Paul effaces all hints that these are the words of Sarah. They become the words of *Graphe* (Scripture), whose second person singular imperative ("Cast out") is not directed to the reader of the letter. That is why Paul changes the wording from "shall not inherit with my son" . . . He could make his strange reading of the text appear more convincing by pointing out that it was Torah advocates who were persecuting non-Torah-observant Christians rather than the other way around.[138]

Longenecker, however, argues that in Gal 4:24, the two covenants are Torah-centered, "under which the Judaizers were attempting to subsume the faith of Galatian Christians, and the New Covenant that is Christ-centered, which Paul proclaimed."[139] In Gal 4:25–26, "Mt. Zion in the context of his [Paul's] polemic with the Galatian Judaizers would probably only have introduced an element of ambiguity" because "they seem to have thought more in historical than transcendental terms and since they undoubtedly equated Mt. Sinai (historical revelation) and Mt. Zion (eschatological redemption) in their understanding of salvation history."[140]

Longenecker indicates that in Gal 4:30, Paul was not against all Jews or Judaism in general. Nor did Paul ask for Gentile believers to expel their Jewish Christian brothers and sisters. Instead, Paul called for the expulsion of Judaizers (Jewish Christians). But, Longenecker says, "That does not

---

136. Ibid., 114–15.
137. Ibid., 116.
138. Ibid., 116–17.
139. Longenecker, *Galatians*, 211.
140. Ibid., 214.

mean that Paul saw all Jewish Christians or all Jews in the same light."[141] In other words, Paul was specifically saying that "contrary to how the Judaizers may have used Gen 21:10 against him, in an allegorical treatment of the passage its message is really to be seen as directed against the troublers of the Galatian believers, and so the Galatian believers should 'cast out' the Judaizers and their influence from the Christian congregation of Galatia."[142]

Witherington takes a different view from Dunn's regarding two covenants in Galatians 4:24. "Dunn has failed to grasp the radical character of Paul's argument when he says 'what Paul describes as two covenants for the purposes of his exegesis are in effect two ways of understanding the one covenant purpose of God through Abraham and for his seed,'" Witherington writes.[143] Moreover, "It is the argument of the agitators, not Paul, that the Mosaic covenant is an extension of the Abrahmic covenant."[144] However, Witherington emphasizes that "the Mosaic covenant is made explicit by juxtaposing the word 'covenants' with mention of Mount Sinai. It is in order to point out that 2 Cor. 3:4–18 shows that Paul quite naturally associates the giving of the ten commandments with Mount Sinai."[145]

Concerning Gal 4:24, Witherington notes that two verbs in the verse have a distinctive meaning related to producing offspring: "Γεννάω is used in the LXX to refer to the male's role in 'begetting' while τέκειν refers to the female's role."[146] Therefore, "Paul is interested in the role of other males [rather than in Abraham's role]—his own role, and that of the Judaizers. Paul is seeking to beget children unto freedom, whereas the agitators are capable of begetting only slave children."[147]

Witherington goes on to say that "Paul is here doing an allegorical interpretation contrasting the effect of his own ministry with that of the agitators."[148] Hence, Paul did not draw a contrast between Judaism and Christianity, "but between a focus or reliance on two different covenants by two different groups of Christians, covenants which produce two different

141. Ibid., 217.
142. Ibid.
143. Witherington, *Grace in Galatia*, 330.
144. Ibid.
145. Ibid.
146. Ibid., 331.
147. Ibid.
148. Ibid.

effects on Christians."¹⁴⁹ Witherington thinks the proper way to understand the scriptural discussion in Gal 4 is in light of Gal 3:6f.—rather than to read Gal 4 in the light of 2 Cor 3, where there is a clear contrast between an old and a new covenant and between two different ministries. According to Witherington, Paul had the Abrahamic covenant primarily in mind here.¹⁵⁰ He was thinking of the fulfillment of the Abrahamic covenant in the new one.¹⁵¹ Therefore, Witherington could not find here a contrast between non-Christian Judaism and Christianity: "The argument here is an in-house one involving polemics against Judaizing Christians."¹⁵² Witherington explains why, in verse 25, Paul is not speaking about Jews and the heart of Judaism being enslaved by the law:

> Especially revealing is the similar language in Gal. 2:4 contrasting freedom in Christ with slavery in the context of mentioning the false brothers in Jerusalem. But is Paul speaking about Jews and the heart of Judaism being enslaved by the Law, or is he speaking in particular about the Jerusalem church with its Jewish Christians? The previous discussion by Paul about the "guardian" that Jews were under during their spiritual minority suggests a broader reference here to all Torah-true Jews in Judea, which would include Jewish Christians of this orientation. It must be remembered that it appears that the Judaizing Christians of Jerusalem did not see themselves as a separate entity from Judaism, but rather a movement within that religious group. Their allegiance was to the present Jerusalem and their Jewish heritage, not just to the Jerusalem church. Paul does not necessarily disagree with this assessment if the Judaizers continue down a covenantally nomistic path, but his point is that this is not a viable option. It is a failure to grasp the radical implications of the Gospel, in particular of Christ's death and resurrection, and the implications of the new eschatological situation of Christians.¹⁵³

Therefore, Witherington believes that, in Gal 4:30, Paul was not referring to non-Christian Jews persecuting Christians but rather to the agitators who had made themselves a part of the Galatian Christian communities.¹⁵⁴

149. Ibid.
150. Ibid.
151. Ibid., 332.
152. Ibid.
153. Ibid., 333–34.
154. Ibid., 338.

J. Louis Martyn also explains why Paul does not make a contrast between the old and new covenants in Gal 4:24: "Paul does not draw the thought of two covenants from a literal reading of Genesis 16–21."[155] Because the "Teachers" have emphasized the term "covenant," using it in the singular to refer to the nomistic covenant of Sinai and inviting the Galatian Gentiles to enter it, Paul is indicating two covenants in the Genesis stories: one of them having to do with the circumcision of the flesh, the other representing the power of God's promise.[156] Therefore, "Paul's thought of two covenants is *novum*, introduced by the apostle himself as he composed this latter."[157] Moreover, Martyn points out that when Paul says that the Hagar covenant is from Mount Sinai, Paul "shows that he is working out his interpretation *from* present developments *to* the Genesis stories, there is no reference to Sinai in those stores, or indeed in any other part of Genesis just as there is no Hagar covenant there."[158]

Martyn notes in verse 26 that "the present Jerusalem" is referring to the Jerusalem church and that "Jerusalem that is above" refers to a heavenly church that stands in contrast with the empirical church located in the earthly city of Jerusalem, but not a heavenly city.[159] Martyn goes on to say, "In Gal 4:26, then, Paul envisions a distinctly apocalyptic contrast. On the earthly stage he sees the Jerusalem church, at present satisfied to house the False Brothers with their ungodly support of the enslaving Law-observant mission to Gentiles."[160] Therefore, the heavenly Jerusalem church is the mother of the Galatian churches but not the earthly church in Jerusalem.[161]

Martyn comes to the same conclusion in Galatians 4:30 as Hays, Longenecker, and Witherington—but for different reasons. In verse 30, Paul asks the Galatian church to exclude the Teachers who are the law-observant missionaries, but not the Jews.[162] In summarizing the difference between these three interpretations:

1. In Gal 4:30–31, Paul's opponent is the Jew; therefore, Paul excludes Judaism from salvation.

155. Martyn, *Galatians*, 436.
156. Ibid.
157. Ibid.
158. Ibid., 436–37.
159. Ibid., 440.
160. Ibid., 440–41.
161. Ibid., 441.
162. Ibid., 446.

2. According to the new consensus' view, like Dunn, Paul's opponents are not only the Jew, but also Jewish Christians and Judaizers.
3. Others see Paul's opponents as Jewish Christian, not as Jews.

Among contemporary scholars, a new understanding of Paul's allegory in Galatians 4:21–31 has emerged. These new consensus scholars identify Paul's opponents as being not the Jews but Jewish Christ followers, even though they hold different views on covenant and on earthly and heavenly Jerusalem. The new consensus does not recognize here any contrast between "old covenant" (Judaism) and "new covenant" (Christianity).[163] In other words, Paul did not exclude Jews from salvation in Gal 4:21–31.

Not Exclusion but Restoration

Susan G. Eastman adds to the new consensus' view in Gal 4:30. "Thus," she says, "although the traditional interpretation and the new consensus diverge in their understanding of the metaphorical 'characters' in the birth narratives and in their interpretation of the imperative in Gal. 4:30, they both identify the slave woman and her son in 4.30 with flesh and blood people. In both cases the dualism set up by Paul's oppositional columns remains, sharply dividing 'insiders' from 'outsiders.'"[164] Eastman's research of the verse suggests that interpretations of it need not founder on either "the Scylla of anti-Judaism or the Charybdis of exclusive apostolic power."[165] She concludes with:

> As has been argued by the new consensus, Paul's allegory in 4:21–5:1 does not concern Jews or Judaism, but rather the circumcising message and methods of Jewish Christian missionaries in Galatia. But as the investigation of Paul's use of imperatives demonstrates, it is extremely unlikely that the singular imperative embedded in his citation of Gen. 21:10 directs his loyal converts in Galatia to expel the Teachers and their followers. Rather, the command speaks directly to Abraham concerning Hagar and Ishmael; it is overheard by Paul's addressees, who are precisely those who are seeking rectification through the law. If, and only if, they persist in relying on the fleshly act of circumcision, they will share the fate of the slave woman and her son, but the simple fact that Paul

---

163. I will discuss the Mosaic covenant in 2 Cor 3:4–18 in further detail later.
164. Eastman, "Cast Out," 313.
165. Ibid., 333.

addresses his allegory to them implies that his final hope for them is not exclusion, but restoration.[166]

Conclusion

According to new consensus' interpretation, Paul did not exclude the Jews from salvation in Gal 4:21–31. Furthermore, as Eastman has pointed out, even when Paul addressed this allegory to his opponents, he wished to restore them rather than just exclude. If, as Eastman says, Paul's address of his allegory to his opponents implies that his final hope for them is restoration, not exclusion, then this suggests that Paul had the mind of a prophet, which I will discuss next. In any case, both the new consensus and Eastman show that there is no indication of Paul's exclusion of non-Christ-believing Jews.

Did Paul Curse Jews Who Opposed the Gospel?

As Alan Segal has indicated, "Paul considered himself as part of a new Jewish sect."[167] Paul believed that he was called by God in the same manner that the prophets Jeremiah, Isaiah, and Ezekiel were called. It is also possible that Paul perceives himself in parallel with Moses (Rom 9:3–4).

If Paul thought his calling was like that of the prophets, then it is worth reconsidering the character of prophets. Abraham J. Heschel describes the character of such prophets well:

> The words of the prophet are stern, sour, stinging. But behind his austerity is love and compassion for mankind. Ezekiel set forth what all other prophets imply: "Have I any pleasure in the death of the wicked, says the Lord God, and not rather that he could turn from his way and live?" Ezek. 18:23 . . . Almost every prophet brings consolation, promise, and the hope of reconciliation along with censure and castigation. He begins with *a message of doom*; he concludes with *a message of hope*.[168] A prophet's duty is to speak to the people, "whether they hear or refuse to hear." A grave responsibility rests upon the prophet (Ezek. 33:6–7; cf. 3:16–21) . . . yet being a prophet is also joy, elation, delight (Jeremiah 15:16).[169] The

---

166. Ibid.
167. Segal, *Paul the Convert*, xiv.
168. Heschel, *Prophets*, 1:12.
169. Ibid., 1:19.

prophet is not only a censurer and accuser, but also a defender and counselor. Indeed, the attitude he takes to the tension that obtains between God and the people is characterized by a dichotomy. In the presence of God he takes the part of the people. In the presence of the people he takes the part of God.[170]

When Paul—as with other prophets—spoke harsh words to his people, there was love and compassion for them behind his anger. He also thought he had a duty to speak to his people, whether they accepted his teaching or not. Furthermore, Paul not only accused his people, but also defended them. Consider 1 Thess 2:14–16, in which Paul violently criticized those Jews who opposed the gospel: "For you, brethren, became imitators of the churches of God in Christ Jesus that are in Judea, for you also endured the same suffering at the hands of your own countrymen, even as they did from the Jews, who killed the Lord Jesus and the prophets, and drove us out. They are not pleasing to God, but hostile to all men." Because such harsh language concerning Jews cannot be found in any other Pauline epistles, some scholars even doubt Paul's authorship.[171]

On the other hand, Heikki Räisänen argues that this passage is authentic precisely because of such harsh language.

"There is no reason to doubt the authenticity of 1 Thess 2:14–16 on the score that it clashes with Rom 11:25ff," Räisänen says. "Paul has here concrete hostile Jews in mind, whereas in writing Romans he—in a different mood, to be sure—considers the subject more calmly from a theological point of view."[172] He is, perhaps, right to believe this text is Pauline, yet Räisänen's reasoning is questionable. Did Paul concretely have hostile Jews in mind here? First, assuming the authenticity of 1 Thess 2:14–16, how was Paul using the words "Judean" and "the Jews" in this context? Did Paul use these words generally for the nation, or did he reject those of a specific region? Second, did he regard all Jews as Christ-killers? Third, because of Paul's harsh speech, are we to think Paul wished his people to be under the

---

170. Ibid., 1:24.

171. Bailey and Clark, "Thessalonians," 279–80. Bailey believes that so "un-Pauline is the passage that some have supposed that all or part of it was added at a later time" (ibid.). Gager also denies Paul's authorship, writing that "on virtually every ground-language, ideas, structure, presumed dates-the passage is inconsistent with the Paul of the other letters" (Gager, *Origins of Anti-Semitism*, 255). Baur thought that this passage was un-Pauline because ohe read that the punishment of Jews occurred in the destruction of Jerusalem (70 CE) (Baur, *Paul the Apostle*, 85–97).

172. Räisänen, *Paul and the Law*, 263.

wrath of God forever? Finally, can this be taken as evidence that Paul was hostile toward Judaism and Jewish people?

Paul's Use of Ἰουδαῖοι

First, Paul uses the Greek word Ἰουδαῖοι in verse 14, but major English Bible translators translate it "Jews."[173] Malcolm Lowe discusses its meaning in "Who Were the Ἰουδαῖοι?"[174] He indicates that its first meaning is "members of the tribe of Judah" (Hebrew *Y'hudah*, Greek Ἰούδα). Its second meaning is "followers of the Jewish religion," that is, Jews. Its third meaning is "people living in or originating from Judea" (Ἰουδαία). Philip F. Esler rejects the use of Jews or Jewish Christian in the first century but uses the term "Judean" to refer mostly to the inhabitants of Judea, but also to Jews in the Diaspora whom the Romans and others regarded as Judeans by birth.[175]

Since Judea's boundaries did not remain fixed, three possible regions may reasonably have been referred to in Jesus's time:

1. Judea in the strict sense, approximating the territory assigned to the tribe of Judah and not including Samaria or the Galilee.
2. The area governed by Pontius Pilate; namely, Judea as in the previously mentioned territory, plus Samaria and Idumea.
3. The kingdom of Herod the Great and the last Hasmoneans; that is, the whole of the historic land of Israel.[176]

According to Lowe's description, in this context Paul used Ἰουδαῖοι to mean citizens of the province of Judaea. Paul expressed sympathy for Thessalonians who had suffered under their countrymen just as God's congregations in Judea had suffered under their countrymen (v. 14).[177]

As Davies says, "The term he uses is 'Jew' (Ἰουδαῖοι), not 'Israelites' (Ἰσραηλεῖται) or 'Hebrews' (Ἑβραῖοι) ... Paul is thinking not of the Jewish people as a whole but of unbelieving Jews who have violently hindered the gospel ... When he wrote to the Thessalonians, Paul had not made up his

---

173. See KJV, NASB, NEB, NIV.
174. Lowe, "Who Were the Ἰουδαῖοι?," 101–30.
175. Esler, *Conflict and Identity*, 62–74.
176. Lowe, "Who Were the Ἰουδαῖοι?," 102–103.
177. Stern, *Jewish New Testament Commentary*, 617–18.

mind on the final destiny of Israel, and his later epistles reveal his further wrestling with this question."[178]

All this needs to be read in light of the fact that, in Romans, Paul dealt with the final fate of Israel—whereas he believes that God will save Israel in the end (Rom 11).

Are All Jews "Christ-Killers"?

In the English translation of Ἰουδαῖοι ("the Jews") in 1 Thess 2:14, readers are easily misled to generalize from Judean Jews to all Jews. Moreover, because of the comma between verses 14 and 15, we tend to read Paul as blaming all Jews as "Christ-killers."[179] In Greek, no comma appears between verses 14 and 15.

How did this interpretation arise? The English translation of verses 14 and 15, "τῶν Ἰουδαίων τῶν καὶ τὸν κύριον ἀποκτεινάντων Ἰησοῦν," shows a comma after "the Jews," but in Greek there is no comma—because when the New Testament was originally written, no such punctuation was used.[180] Depending on this punctuation, "the Jew" could mean either all Jews or just specific Jews. The comma makes the predicate ("who killed the Lord Jesus") apply to all Jews. But without the comma, the predicate specifies which particular Jews (or Judeans) are meant. As Abraham J. Malherbe notes, Paul here "does not speak of all Jews, but of those who acted against their fellow Jews."[181]

---

178. Davies, *Jewish and Pauline Studies*, 126–27.

179. According to Tellbe, Thessalonian non-Christians Jews accused Paul of being a false Jewish prophet (Acts 21:28; 24:5–9) (Tellbe, *Synagogue and State*, 109). However, according to Tellbe, "While the Thessalonians' opponents were primarily Gentiles (mainly Greeks, perhaps some Romans), for contextual, historical, and lexical reasons it cannot be excluded that Paul also had Jews in mind in his brief reference to the Thessalonians' opponents in 1 Thess. 2:13–16. Hence, sumfule,thj should best be rendered by 'countrymen' or 'fellow residents', i.e., the Thessalonians' townspeople. I find therefore no real reason to question Luke's portrayal of extremely zealous Thessalonian Jews as instigators of the persecution and of Gentiles who carry out this persecution. As a matter of fact, Paul's extraordinarily harsh denunciation of the Jews in 1Thess. 2:14–16 only makes sense if Paul in some way held Jews responsible for the Thessalonian conflict. Rather than taking 1 Thess. 2:14–16 as an exaggeration of history, this text appears to reflect Paul's reaction to his own experience of some zealous Jews in Thessalonica" (ibid., 115).

180. For more detail, see Gilliard, "Antisemitic Comma," 481–502.

181. Malherbe, *Letters to the Thessalonians*, 169.

Malherbe goes on to say, "the comma that is printed between vv 14 and 15 in Greek editions of the text and in modern translations is wrong."[182] The comma makes it appear that Paul charged all Jews (Ἰουδαῖοι) with killing Jesus. In other words, in verses 14 and 15 "the Jews" refers to Judeans—which indicates specific Jews, and we cannot generalize to all Jews. It is unlikely that Paul designated all Jews as Christ-killers. We must understand that when Paul addressed specific Jews with harsh language, as in this case, he was following after the pattern of the prophets.[183]

Are All Jews under God's Wrath Forever?

In verse 16, we need to determine whether Paul wished to curse Jewish people forever. First of all, in verse 16, it seems that "Paul does have a tendency to generalize (see 1:7–8; cf. Rom 12:17–18; 1 Cor 7:7; 15:19; 2 Cor 3:2; Phil 4:5) . . . He uses 'all,' not to generalize, but probably to mark the transition from his comments on Jewish hostility against Jewish Christians in Judea to Jewish hostility against the Gentiles whom he wished to save . . . Paul, however, does not dwell on the details of the opposition but proceeds to locate it in a larger framework."[184]

However, if Paul was like any other prophet, he should have controlled his emotion. Of course, Paul was a man who had emotion, but the prophets required the suppression of emotion in order to serve God.[185] We cannot simply assert that Paul "flashes out in these stern sentences of anger" as if this offers some sort of rationale.[186] Here, Paul seems to be angry at the

182. Ibid.

183. Heschel, *Prophets*, 1:16. According to Abraham Heschel, one of the characteristics of the prophets is that "the prophets remind us of the moral state of a people: few are guilty, but all are responsible. If we admit that the individual is in some measure conditioned or affected by the spirit of society, an individual's crime discloses society's corruption" (ibid.). But this does not mean that—as Abraham Heschel claims—although the prophets emphasized corporate responsibility, Paul perhaps used the same principle that while a minority of Jews are guilty of Jesus' death, nevertheless, all are responsible.

184. Malherbe, *Letters to the Thessalonians*, 176.

185. Heschel, *Prophets*, 1:25.

186. Moffatt, *Thessalonians*, 29. Moffatt saw that Paul was a very emotional man. Moffatt comments on "the wrath has come upon them" like this: "'The wrath has come upon them,' apparently a reminiscence of Test. Levi. vi. II. This curt and sharp verdict on the Jews sprang from Paul's irritation at the moment. The apostle was in no mood to be conciliatory. He was suffering at Corinth from persistent Jewish attempts to wreck the Christian propaganda, and he flashes out in these stern sentences of anger. Later on

Jews who oppose the gospel, but "Paul is not openly hostile to the people of Israel, and he remains eager for their conversion and ultimate eschatological salvation."[187]

Perhaps Paul shows some anger toward his opponents, yet he did not show concrete hostility toward the whole Jewish people. The prophet's anger is characteristically different from that of other human beings. The prophet's anger is expressed in the wish for their welfare, not for their destruction. Paul's anger is expressed in this same way.

However, "'The wrath of God' is none other than the eschatological wrath for which the whole world is destined just before Messiah's kingdom."[188] In Rom 1:18, Paul says that both Jews and Gentiles who do not believe in Jesus as the Messiah are now under the wrath of God. Paul does not say that those Jews who oppose the gospel are under the "wrath of God" forever, but εἰς τέλος. As Johannes Munck points out, in 1 Thess 2:16: "'Wrath is come upon them to the end,' this passage makes the same statement as Romans 11."[189] In other words, "The wrath remains on the Jews until the end (εἰς τέλος) but then is lifted, the 'end' coinciding with the coming of the Deliverer from Zion to turn away ungodliness from Jacob (Rom. 11:25–27)."[190] So it is certainly not forever. Paul's thought on Israel shows that no inconsistency exists between Thessalonians and Romans,

---

(Rom. ix.–xi.) he took a kinder and more hopeful view" (ibid.). Gager writes that since we cannot find the kind of hot temper Paul expresses in 1 Thess 2:13–16 in any of Paul's other writings, 1 Thess 2:13–16 must not belong to Paul's writings (Gager, *Origins of Anti-Semitism*, 255–56).

187. Beker, *Paul the Apostle*, 331.

188. Thomas, *1 and 2 Thessalonians*, 259.

189. Munck, *Christ and Israel*, 64. Munck indicates that εἰς τέλος literally means "completely" and "forever," writing, "The expression εἰς τὸ τέλος may therefore mean 'to the end,' i.e., until the last events at the end of the world. Thus mention is made of the endurance of the faithful 'to the end' in Matthew 10:22; 24:13; Mark 13:13; cf. Revelation 2:26; Hermas, Similitudes 9, 27, 3" (ibid.).

190. Bruce, *1 and 2 Thessalonians*, 49. Räisänen thinks Paul contradicts himself from 1 Thessalonians to Romans. He says, "in Rom 9 he resorts to the extreme explanation of divine hardening with takes place regardless of any of man's doing (9:6–23), whereas in the very next chapter [he] puts all emphasis on Israel's own notorious disobedience. In chapter 11, at last, Paul definitely discards his predestinarian construction and replaces it with the statement that Israel's obduracy is of a temporary nature. This runs counter to 1 Thess 2:14–16 as well. The observations made in the course of this study about Paul's self-contradictions suggest that one should hardly posit a theological development in Paul's thinking about Israel from 1Thess. to Romans" (Räisänen, *Paul and the Law*, 164).

because Paul was addressing these two epistles to two different particular situations.

Karl Paul Donfried develops this idea further in his book, claiming that there is no inconsistency between 1 Thess 2:13–16 and Romans.[191] Donfried says:

> We would suggest that the relationship between 1 Thessalonians and Romans is not one of inconsistency. In Romans, Paul does not negate what he said in his first letter but augments it; 1 Thessalonians does not contain the last word concerning Israel. Because of a specific problem in the Romans congregation, which we have described in detail elsewhere, Paul needs to deal with the issue of the relation of Jew and Gentile in connection with the question of Israel's future. Therefore, while not denying what he has said previously, he adds some new information in Rom. 11:25–32, namely, that at the end God's mercy will be extended to Israel in a mysterious way and all Israel will be saved. The negative statements about the Jews in 1 Thess. 2:13–16 are not denied in Romans ... Beker's magisterial treatment of Paul has helped us to understand the apocalyptic context of the apostle with greater precision and therefore has assisted us in the re-evaluation of the function of 1 Thess. 2:13–16 both with regard to the coherent structure of Paul's theology in general and with regard to the contingent interpretation necessary to deal with the particular situation facing Paul in Thessalonica, a situation, as we noted, quite different from the contingent situation of Romans.[192]

In this respect, there is no essential contradiction between Thessalonians and Romans. Paul thinks that all Israel will be saved in the end by God's mercy. For Paul, those Jews who oppose the gospel are under the "wrath of God"—a state that is temporary, not permanent. It seems that Paul uses severe language to call down judgment on those Jews who oppose the gospel. But "the starkness of Paul's language is like that of Jewish apocalyptic writings,"[193] and his denunciation of "those Jews who oppose the gospel" takes place within a specific situational context. Therefore, Paul's denunciation should not be generalized to apply to all universally.

---

191. See Donfried, *Paul, Thessalonica*, 195–208.
192. Ibid., 207–208.
193. Malherbe, *Letters to the Thessalonians*, 177.

Did Paul Oppose Judaism and the Jewish People?

Jacob Jervell reads 1 Thess 2:14-16 plainly in the traditional way. He seems to hold that Paul was against Jews in that particular verse, even though he does not believe Paul was against Jews overall. "Recall the attitude in 1 Thessalonians," he says, "where Israel had nothing but the wrath and judgment of God to expect from the future."[194]

A dictionary definition of "anti-Semitism" includes such terms as "prejudice against Jews; dislike or fear of Jews; discrimination against or persecution of Jews."[195] Does Paul show this kind of attitude toward Jewish people? Does he not say that he is willing to be cursed for the Jewish people's sake (Rom 9:2-3)? Does he not advise Christian Gentiles not to be arrogant toward non-believing Jewish people (Rom 11)? Paul sees the rejection of the Messiah by his own people as a temporary reality. He knows that God has not rejected his own people (Rom 11:1f.), and he envisions a time when they will be grafted back onto God's olive tree (Rom 11:17-24).

Because of Paul's harsh language in Thessalonians, we must consider whether Paul was really against Israel. If so, how about the prophets Jeremiah, Isaiah, Ezekiel and others? The prophets did not worry about political correctness—they spoke for God with harsh and stern language, requiring people to repent in their hearts and to change their behaviors. Similarly, Paul was angry with those Jews in 1 Thess 2:14-16 because he wanted them to repent from their wrong behavior, which was hindering the gospel. Paul did not accuse them out of hate but with love and compassion, as would any other prophet. In Rom 9:3 Paul expresses a great burden of sorrow over Israel. Paul was even willing to be cursed for their sake.

This burden of prayer for Israel is similar to Moses' prayer in Exod 32:30-32: "And it came about on the next day that Moses said to the people, 'You have committed a great sin. But now I will go up to the Lord; perhaps I can make atonement for your sin.' So Moses went back to the Lord and said, 'Oh, what a great sin these people have committed! They have made themselves gods of gold. But now, please forgive their sin—but if not, then blot me out of the book you have written.'"

Since Paul's calling was similar to that of the prophets, he used the language of Israel's prophets. Paul's anger comes with compassion to those

---

194. Jervell, *Unknown Paul*, 36. I am aware that Jervell does not think Paul was against the Jewish people in Romans and the Acts, but he suggests Paul had a different attitude toward Jews earlier in 1 Thess 1:14-16 and Galatians.

195. *Webster's New World Dictionary*, 1967 ed., s.v. "anti-Semitism," 26.

Jews who oppose the gospel, but he does not hate them or the rest of the Jewish people. Like Moses, Paul seeks to lead his people in the way of the Lord, and like Moses, he meets with misunderstanding and failure to hear the message. But Paul is no more against the Jews than Moses was against the people of Israel.

The Controversy over the Mosaic Covenant

Another controversial text among scholars who hold that Paul had set aside the Mosaic covenant and the law is 2 Cor 3:4–18. This is the only place in the NT where the two covenants are apparently contrasted.[196]

Even E. P. Sanders reads this text in the traditional way.[197] Although Paul mentions the new covenant in 1 Cor 11:25, here in 2 Cor 3:14 Paul also mentions the old covenant once. Victor Paul Furnish[198] and Sanders read 2 Cor 3: 4–18 to mean that Paul annulled the old covenant. Alfred Plummer argues that Paul drew a contrast between the old and new covenant, rendering the old covenant obsolete, and that he had completely broken with Jewish law. Thus, Plummer has interpreted this verse to mean that Christianity is superior to Judaism, arguing that Paul makes a strong statement against Judaism in verse 14.[199]

Ernst Käsemann follows the same line of thought as Plummer. He says that the "phenomenon of the true Jew is eschatologically realized in the Christian who has freed himself from Judaism."[200] He does not minimize the Old Testament because it is written down. The implication he draws is rather that the new covenant of which Jeremiah speaks has become a reality. Therefore, Paul had to decide between the new covenants, instead of seeing both in historical continuity in light of the concept of the renewed covenant.[201]

Campbell, on the contrary, has warned that Paul is not a systematic theologian. He points out that "nowhere do we have as a central theme in any of Paul's letters a stark contrast between Christianity and Judaism in terms of new covenant. Paul does not think so much in terms of static

---

196. Sanders, *Paul, the Law*, 137–41.
197. Ibid., 137–40.
198. Furnish, *II Corinthians*, 229.
199. Plummer, *Second Epistle*, 83–99.
200. Käsemann, *Perspectives on Paul*, 146.
201. Ibid., 154.

abrogation—of the replacement of one covenant by another—but rather, in terms of dynamic transformation."[202]

I have already noted that Davies, in his article "Paul and the People of Israel," has explained the word "new" can be used both of Jeremiah's new covenant and also of the new moon:

> The ministry of the old covenant, and by implication the old covenant itself, had its glory (2 Cor. 3:7). Moreover, just as the new covenant conceived by Jeremiah, Jubilees and the sectarians at Qumran did not unambiguously envisage a radical break with the Sinaitic covenant but a re-interpretation, so Paul's new covenant. Thus Jer. 31:33 does not look forward to a new law but to "my law", God's sure law, being given and comprehended in a new way. The adjective *"hadasah"* in Jer. 31:33, translated *"kaine"* by Paul, can be applied to the new moon, which is simply the old moon in a new light. The new covenant of Paul, as of Jeremiah, finally offers re-reinterpretation of the old.[203]

Campbell's and Davies' views on this text make more sense in the context of Paul's own Jewish background. In 2 Cor 3, Paul explains the ministry of two kinds of covenant. The Mosaic covenant was the ministry of the law; the new covenant is a ministry of the law, plus the Spirit.

As Scott Hafemann states, "'The law is common to both covenants... The Old Covenant was ministry of the Law without the empowering work of the Spirit, the New Covenant is the ministry of the Law along with the Spirit's empowerment to accomplish the Law's demands' ... The Letter/Spirit contrast is therefore not a contrast between two kinds of Covenants. But between two distinct ministries, a contrast that will become explicit in 3:7–18."[204]

In 2 Cor 3, in order that Paul might "discover the true meaning of the covenant, a new light has been thrown upon it; it is in this sense it has become new."[205] Respectively, 2 Cor 3:11 and 13 refer to the ministry of Moses and to the glory on Moses's face. Paul did not found a new religion with a new meaning, nor had Paul replaced the old covenant with the new covenant. Paul did not oppose the Mosaic covenant because he is a minister

---

202. Campbell, *Paul's Gospel*, 70. Also see ibid., *Paul and the Creation*, 134–39.
203. Davies, *Galatians Debate*, 11.
204. Hafemann, *Paul, Moses*, 172–73.
205. Davies, *Jewish and Pauline Studies*, 130.

of the new covenant. Rather, Paul had a particular understanding of the new covenant through Christ.

Paul compares two covenants: the Mosaic covenant in which God wrote his law on the tablets of stone, and the new covenant, in which God puts his law in man's heart. Paul's point here is that Jesus, the Messiah, is the one who has the real power to deliver from death (sin) and empower him (or believers) to do good works for the Lord. The law itself could not accomplish this transformation (Rom 8).

Therefore, Paul does not contrast two covenants but instead shows that Jesus, the Messiah, is the new covenant, and Jesus is the Spirit who can free from sin. The Mosaic covenant shows God's glory; the new covenant proclaims the ultimate revelation of divine glory (2 Cor 3:10–11). For Paul, the old covenant was good, yet the new covenant is better. Moreover, in 2 Cor 3:4–11, Paul uses *a fortiori* argument to compare old covenant and new covenant experiences of the presence and power of God (vv. 8, 9, 11). In other words, as David Rudolph notes, Paul "refers to something genuinely important to emphasize what is even more important."[206]

In 2 Cor 3, Paul says negatively of the law that "the letter [written code] kills." Here Paul uses the Greek word, γράμμα—"a writing"—instead of γραφή which means "document" and includes its contents or statement. As Walter C. Kaiser Jr. has said, this word selection is significant: "The Greek word here is not γραφή; it is γράμμα from which we get 'grammar,' or at least the root for it. Hence what he is talking about is the 'outward form' merely, not the spiritual import nor the content of that Law."[207]

---

206. Rudolph, "A Jew to the Jews," 34.

207. Kaiser, *Contemporary Preaching*, 50. Gaston is opposed to this view on gramma. He says, "The most prevalent interpretation in the modern period has been the realistic, which understands gramma as synonymous with nomos, giving a contrast of Law and Spirit. While this is consonant with much of modern theology, there are major exegetical problems. First, no other instance can be cited where gramma is used in this sense, and in the context of the other two passages in Paul, gramma is clearly distinguished from Law; some without the gramma keep the Law (Rom. 2:27, cf. 29), and the Law is 'holy, just, good . . . and spiritual' (Rom 7:12, 14, cf. 6). Second, the word nomos appears nowhere in 2 Cor, and there is no evidence whatsoever that the super apostles are urging the Corinthians to 'Judaize.' Third, if the Law were the topic here rather than two contrasting ministries, then it would certainly be digression unrelated to its context. The formalistic interpretation was often taken in the ancient church and is somewhat related to the popular usage of today which distinguishes between the 'literal' meaning of the text and the deeper meaning of its real intention. Stated in that general form, this interpretation cannot possibly be correct . . . Gramma can refer neither to the Law nor to Scripture but specifically here to the ministry of the rival missionaries" (Gaston, *Paul and the Torah*,

In other words, Paul's point is that the letter alone cannot produce transformed life; hence, it leaves us lifeless—whereas the Spirit enables us to follow the law so we can live in all the fullness the law intends (Rom 8:4; Ps 19:119; Deut 28, 30). In this respect, Paul says the letter kills and the works of the law are under a curse.

However, Paul did not draw a contrast in black and white terms between the new and old covenant, nor is it true that "the simplest explanation of this dual form of contrast seems to be that he came to relegate the Mosaic dispensation to a less glorious place because he found something more glorious."[208] Paul simply compared two ministries but eliminated neither one nor the other.

We need to take into account Paul's theology in general, and a consideration of the coherent structure of interpretation is necessary in order to understand the particular situation facing Paul in his letters. Though Paul contrasts the two ministries in 2 Cor 3, he does not contrast the old and new covenants as such.

Paul's understanding of the nature of the Mosaic covenant is grounded in the Abrahamic covenant. God made this covenant with Abraham, and God fulfilled his promise through Jesus the Messiah. In Gal 3:15–4:11, Paul shows his belief that the Mosaic covenant climaxed God's revelation to his people. Paul understood that the Mosaic covenant is in continuity with the earlier promise of God, the Abrahamic covenant (Exod 3:15). The covenant with Abraham is the fundamental covenant that God made with his people (Gal 3:15–4:11). Because the covenant is a promise, God will ensure that the necessary conditions are fulfilled.

In this context, Paul does not indicate that there are two different means of salvation. Nor does he see the law as contrary to the promise of God. Rather, in Gal 3:18, Paul is trying to say that his opponents' interpretation of the Mosaic covenant is fundamentally wrong because their interpretation makes the covenants contradictory. Paul denies that the Mosaic law teaches a different way of salvation. Paul's opponents incorrectly viewed the law as the source of life (Gal 3:21). For Paul, the Mosaic covenant was, in fact, a gracious one. In Gal 3:15–4:11, Paul explains the Mosaic covenant to his opponents through the lens of the Abrahamic covenant. In Gal 3:15-18, Paul also indicates that the Mosaic and Abrahamic covenants are not contradictory. In verse 17, he says the law that came into

---

156–57).

208. Sanders, *Paul, the Law*, 138.

being 430 years after the covenant with Abraham could not abolish those promises. In verse 18, he goes on to say, "for if the inheritance is based on Law, it is no longer based on promise; but God has granted it to Abraham by means of a promise" (Gal 3:18).

As John Fischer has pointed out, once made, promises are continually in effect: "verses 15–17 contain an important principle, not only God's consistency throughout the covenants, but also that a later covenant does not invalidate an earlier one. This is consistent with covenant renewal procedures in the ancient Near East."[209] In this sense, for Paul, Abraham is a true prototype. As Campbell has indicated, "If Abraham is a true prototype, then surely we must speak in terms of a renewed covenant, in terms of fulfillment and affirmation, rather than purely in terms of stark contrast."[210]

Did Paul Consider Judaism Rubbish?

"What is surpassingly valuable becomes, in Paul's mind, what is exclusively valuable," Sanders says. "In light of Christ, the law loses its glory entirely (2 Cor. 3:10), and righteousness under the law changes from 'gain' to 'loss' (Phil. 3:7). It seems to be this way of thinking that leads him to give the law a purely negative role: it kills (2 Cor. 3:6)."[211]

In other words, Paul opposes Judaism not because of any inherent errors such as "self-righteousness" or "legalism," but simply because it is not Christianity.[212] Paul said he considered as rubbish all human confidence in Judaism. In this context, Paul did not contrast one religion with another (Judaism versus Christianity) but compares value in the Messiah. As Fischer points out:

> He [Paul] nevertheless described his Jewish connections in the present tense as a current experience. The context does not indicate that Paul considers these things as "impediments"; he is merely stressing the comparative values of the two experiences—participation

---

209. Fischer, "Jewish Root" 2. This renewal procedure in the Ancient Near East was done when the relationship was changed (leadership of the ruling nation). When covenant was renewed, a new document would be prepared to bring the stipulations of the earlier ones up to date, but not to exclude the stipulations of the earlier covenant or the original. See more details on treaty in Kline, *Treaty of the Great King*, and ibid., *Structure of Biblical Authority*.

210. Campbell, *Paul's Gospel*, 73.

211. Sanders, *Paul, the Law*, 140–41.

212. Ibid., *Paul and Palestinian Judaism*, 442–7.

in Judaism and a relationship with the Messiah. When compared to any (and every) experience (verse 8), a relationship with the Messiah makes the others seem like "rubbish" in comparison . . . Philippians 3 emphasizes Paul's conviction that "knowing Jesus as his Messiah was far more valuable than any of these privileges and accomplishments." This is exactly what Paul stresses, while at the same time he does not disavow his life in Judaism.[213]

In assessing the comparative value of the two experiences, Paul does not abandon one for the other. Paul did not think that the *law* is rubbish in Phil 3—but rather stresses that his human confidence is rubbish. Paul does not blame the law or Judaism. In Rom 7, Paul confirmes the law as holy.

Watson thinks Paul left Judaism for a different reason than Sanders offers. Watson believes Paul drew a contrast between Judaism and Christianity in Philippians rather than a comparison. He reads Phil 3:2–11 "as a whole single antithesis, designed to show that any attempt to combine Judaism with the gospel is completely untenable."[214] In Phil 3:7–11, Paul "emphasizes the utter worthlessness of his Jewish past from his new perspective: it is 'loss' (vv. 7f.), 'rubbish' (v. 8)."[215] He thinks that in Phil 3 Paul wishes to separate the church from the Jewish community.[216] According to Watson, Paul considered Judaism to be worthless.

However, in Phil 3, it is unlikely that Paul *contrasted* Judaism against Christianity but instead *compared* them to each other. In the context, as David Rudolph indicates, "First, Paul acknowledges that his Jewishness resulted in 'gains' (Phil 3:7). Second, it is not only Jewishness that Paul considers 'loss' upon gaining Christ. He regards 'everything as loss' (πάντα ζημίαν εἶναι). Presumably, this included the Scriptures, the covenants, the promises, his mother and father, friendships, etc. Everything is relativised in Christ."[217]

---

213. Fischer, "Yes, We Do," 56.

214. Watson, *Paul, Judaism*, 77.

215. Ibid.

216. According to Davies, there is no indication that early Christianity separated from the Jewish community prior to 70 CE, and the term "New Israel" likely only began to be used after 70 CE (Davies, *Jewish and Pauline Studies*, 97). I will discuss whether Paul wished the church to separate from the Jewish community later.

217. Rudolph, "A Jew to the Jews," 47–48; Campbell, *Paul and the Creation*. Note, however, that Campbell now uses "eschatological re-evaluation of all things in Christ" rather than "relativized" as cited here because "relativized" may imply a negative stance toward Judaism (Campbell, *Unity and Diversity*, 203–23).

We must understand Paul in his eschatological context. For Paul, Jesus is the fulfillment of Judaism—or, rather, confirmation of the promises to the fathers (Rom 15:8). This is better than fulfillment, which suggests that all is already finished with the Jews, but this is not so. Watson's understanding of Paul from a sociological perspective, without taking full account of the historical context as well, falls short of a full understanding of Paul.[218]

In Phil 3:2–11, there is no indication that Paul left Judaism because it was worthless or because he found more value in Christ. Indeed, he did not leave the Jewish community.

Rather, Paul believed his gospel was both the completion of Judaism and the confirmation of its promises. Thus, although Paul compared value in the Messiah, he did not contrast Judaism as such against Christianity. In any case, Paul could not consciously have done so since, in Paul's lifetime, Christianity both as a term and as a separate religion did not yet exist.

Did Paul Deny the Election of Israel?

C. H. Dodd thought Rom 9–11 was arbitrarily inserted into that letter because it is different from Paul's style in Rom 1–8.[219] On the other hand,

---

218. As Campbell indicates, "Watson's sociological analysis operates on the hypothesis that a text presupposes an existing social situation and is intended to function within the situation in ways not necessarily apparent from the text itself. He is clear, however, that sociological analysis is not a satisfactory way of filling in gaps in our historical knowledge—it is not a substitute for historical evidence, but 'a way of interpreting the evidence'" (Campbell, *Paul's Gospel*, 123).

219. Dodd, *Epistle of Paul*, 148–50. Dodd wrote, "It has already been suggested that in ii. 1–iii. 20 we have a distinct echo of Paul's preaching style, but that is in no sense a complete sermon. Chaps. Ix–xi., on the other hand, have a beginning and a close appropriate to a sermon, and the preaching tone is maintained all through. It is the kind of sermon that Paul must often have had occasion to deliver, in defining his attitude to what we may call the Jewish question. It is quite possible that he kept by him a MS. of such a sermon, for use as occasion demanded, and inserted it here [Romans 9–11] . . . and it is likely that Paul already knew that he was going to use his sermon on the rejection of Israel when he briefly dismissed the difficulties raised in iii. 1–9. Moreover, there is a slight indication that Paul had already incorporated chaps. ix–xi. in the epistle before he went on to xii., in the fact that xii. starts with the idea of the mercy of God, and 'mercy' has been the key-word of discussion in ix.–xi, and particularly its conclusion, xi. 30–32; whereas the key-word of viii. is 'love.' And xv. 9 is only to be clearly understood in the light of ix.–xi. In other words, chaps. ix.–xi. do not constitute a mere interpolation; though, on the other hand, they were very likely not written *current calamo* with the rest of the epistle, but represent a somewhat earlier piece of work, incorporated here wholesale to save a busy man's time and trouble in writing on the subject afresh" (ibid., 149–50).

about twenty-seven years later, H. J. Schoeps interpreted Rom 9–11 very differently from Dodd.[220]

H. J. Schoeps took a contrary view to Dodd's in interpreting Rom 9–11 as authentically Paul's. Recently, many scholars have confirmed Schoeps's view.[221] Since this section has been confirmed as an integral part of the whole letter, it helps to see clearly what Paul's attitude toward Judaism and Jewish people was, even though so many dispute Paul's view on these points.

Nevertheless, as already noted, some scholars believe that Paul denied Israel's election and broke with Judaism. Sanders has said that even though Paul writes from the Jewish perspective, he denies the traditional Jewish doctrine of election. Sanders writes that "the second point at which the break is especially clear is his insistence that it is through faith in Christ, not by accepting the law, that one enters the people of God. Thus he denies two pillars common to all forms of Judaism: the election of Israel and faithfulness to the Mosaic law."[222] Moreover, Sanders sees that "the rules governing behavior were partly Jewish but not entirely, and thus, in this way, too, Paul's Gentile churches were a third entity."[223]

For Sanders, early Christianity involved "the simultaneous appropriation and rejection of Judaism."[224] Sanders tends in this instance to understand Paul's letter in the traditional way and, as Davies rightly pointed out, "Sanders tends to isolate Paulinism not only from Judaism but also from the tradition of the Churches . . . "[225] and "for Sanders the category of the Lordship of Christ in Paul supersedes that of Messiahship and thus makes Apocalyptic less significant for the Apostle." Moreover, Sanders "refuses to

---

220. Schoeps, *Paul*, 235–36. Schoeps explains why Rom 9–11 is not an insertion into the letter: "Hence chs. 9–11 are by no means a section arbitrarily inserted into the continuity of the letter as a whole; they are, on the contrary, closely bound up with the sequence of thought which controls the letter throughout. Already in 3:1–4 the apostle had touched upon the problem of unbelieving Israel after previously in 2:17–20 enumerating the advantages of the Jewish Diaspora by contrast with the surrounding heathen world" (ibid., 236).

221. For example, Campbell has argued that when we see chapter 3:1–8 as the structural center of the letter, it can be shown that there is coherence throughout the letter. See more details in Campbell, *Paul's Gospel*, 25–42.

222. Sanders, *Paul, the Law*, 207–208.

223. Ibid., 178.

224. Ibid., 210.

225. Davies, *Paul and Rabbinic Judaism*, 4th ed., xlviii.

consider the possibility that apocalyptic speculation has influenced Paul to any considerable degree in his interpretation of Jesus."²²⁶

According to Davies:

> That is the simple but fundamental fact that Paul himself understands the Christian dispensation to be 'according to the Scriptures' and in this he was not alone in the Early Church. Sanders does deal with Paul's use of Old Testament passages in an instructive way. But he so deals with them as to leave the impression that the Apostle is using the Old Testament for his own ends, as it were, without radical seriousness, if Paul be governed in his treatment of Scripture by the dogmatic stance that salvation is only in Christ.²²⁷

Davies's interpretation of Paul is more balanced than Sanders's because he has considered fully the possibilities of both Jewish apocalyptic and the early church's traditional context, rather than "consigning Paul to a vacuum."²²⁸

Watson agrees with Sanders and has stressed that Paul rejected the Jewish doctrine of election. For Watson, "Romans 4 and 9 in particular require of Jewish Christians a complete abandonment of the old notion of election as applying to the Jewish community as a whole."²²⁹

However, in Rom 11, "Paul adopts a different strategy in calling for the same social reorientation. Instead of opposing the Jewish view of election with his own view, he argues here that the Jewish doctrine of election is to a large extent compatible with his own view of the failure of Israel and the salvation of the Gentiles."²³⁰ Watson observes that "It is ironic that Paul's arguments for the consistency of God in Rom. 9–11 are apparently themselves inconsistent; for Rom. 11 is based on precisely the definition of Israel, the chosen people who are heirs to salvation, that Rom. 9 (as well as Rom. 4) has rejected so emphatically."²³¹ But Watson is not the only one who reads inconsistencies in Paul in Rom 9–11. Other scholars do too—but for differing reasons.²³²

---

226. Ibid., xlvii.
227. Ibid., li.
228. Ibid.
229. Watson, *Paul, Judaism*, 172.
230. Ibid.
231. Ibid., 168.
232. Dodd, *Epistle of Paul*, 148–50; Räisänen, "Paul, God and Israel," 178–206.

Campbell argues against a number of scholars who see Paul as self-contradictory.[233] He concludes, "When we follow closely the manner and sequence of Paul's argument in ch. 9, and recognize that the primary interest is in God's activity with Israel, then ch. 11 and its ending are not such a surprise after all, because the 'surprise' has already been tentatively introduced in chapter 9:22ff."[234] Campbell claims, "Watson's problem is that he misinterprets Paul's discussion in Rom 9: 6f as attacking Judaism's 'emphatic theology of grace,' and . . . It is not good exegetical procedure to deal with chapters as separate sections when chapters 9–11 are so obviously one continuous argument," and as Campbell goes on to observe:

> Watson fails to distinguish between Paul's revision of the doctrine of election and a complete rejection of its teaching. Only by involving Paul in the most blatant and immediate self-contradiction can one maintain that he completely rejects the doctrine of election . . . It is quite clear that he himself does not *self-consciously* reject the doctrine of election—"the gifts and the call of God are irrevocable" (11:29) is still his position. Therefore the most that we can claim here is that Paul reinterprets or revises the doctrine of election from his own messianic viewpoint.[235]

In contrast to Watson, Dan Cohn-Sherbok has shown in *Rabbinic Perspectives on the New Testament* that when Paul's interpretation of Scripture is seen to resemble that of rabbinic Judaism, it shows the coherence of Rom 9–11, rather than reading simply as separate chapters.[236] Paul's reasoning on the issue of Israel, which starts in chapter 9 and concludes in chapter 11, is thus "characteristic of the letter as a whole."[237] In other words, Paul does not contradict himself between chapters 9 and 11, but he is establishing his points of argument in chapter 9 and 10 in order to make his conclusion in chapter 11.

N. T. Wright does not deny the truth of the election of Israel, even though he rigorously criticized Judaism and Israel's "failure" to fulfill its calling. But for Wright, that election is purely functional since the purpose of Israel's election is to save the world.[238] Paul's "critique of Israel should

---

233. See Campbell, "Divergent Images," 187–211.
234. Ibid., 200.
235. Ibid., *Paul's Gospel*, 145.
236. Cohn-Sherbok, *Rabbinic Perspectives*, 79–80. See chapter 5 for more details.
237. Campbell, *Paul's Gospel*, 144.
238. Wright, *Paul Really Said*, 82.

not be read as a denial of the doctrine of election, a rejection of the belief that the Jewish people were chosen by the one true God to be his means of saving the world."[239] But Israel failed in that role, through which God meant to save the world. Wright also agrees with the New Perspective on Paul; namely, that Jews were not "legalists" who were trying to earn their salvation through good works. He stresses that Paul did not, as it were, abandon Judaism for something else.[240] Paul meant that the only true Judaism is in fact the "Christian" one. Wright says that Paul did not reject Judaism because Judaism was bad. Rather, Paul "was not opposed to the idea of Judaism *per se*, nor indeed could he be; he was claiming the high ground that this, indeed, was what Judaism had always been supposed to be, the historical people whose identity and destiny were now revealed in the crucified Messiah."[241]

Central to Wright's argument about Judaism in Paul is that God replaces the people of Israel with the church (or that Christ is the true Israel). In Rom 9–11, Paul focused primarily upon Israel's "failure" to fulfill its mission, its "rejection" of the gospel, and its "betrayal" of God's purpose.

On the other hand, Lloyd Gaston believes, as Campbell does, that in Rom 9, Paul does not put emphasis on the unbelief of Israel, but rather focuses on God's activity: "How is it that people can say that chapter 9 deals with the unbelief of Israel when it is never mentioned, and all human activity, whether doing or believing, whether Jewish or Gentile, is expressly excluded from consideration?"[242]

Could it be that Paul emphasized both God's action and Israel's failure? Perhaps Paul placed primary stress on God's activity in relation to Israel's failure. God's action is to save his people even though Israel failed to fulfill her calling. Wright maintains Paul's loyalty to Judaism, but he suggests that, for Paul, God replaced Israel with the church as a new Israel. Wright's view seems to be in direct contradiction to Rom 11:1–32.

Douglas Harink, in his book *Paul among the Postliberals*, criticizes Wright's supersessionist reading of Paul on Israel's election.[243] Harink challenges Wright's construal of key Old Testament texts and of Rom 9–11. He criticizes Wright for using the Old Testament to serve a primarily or

---

239. Ibid., 83–84.
240. Ibid., 39.
241. Ibid., "Caesar's Empire," 177.
242. Gaston, *Paul and the Torah*, 92.
243. See Harink, *Paul Among the Postliberals*, 151–98.

exclusively instrumental role for Israel's election and not recognizing the Old Testament's witness to God's abiding love for Israel. He also points out that Wright interprets Rom 9–11 to be primarily about Israel's rejection of the gospel rather than about the concept that God may either harden or have mercy on Israel. Harink says Wright's problem is that he thinks "Paul employs a linear 'covenant-historical' narrative in which there is a divinely driven linear movement from Israel, to Christ, to the church" rather than an "apocalyptic-way of thinking about Israel in God's purpose."[244]

However, as Campbell has indicated, perhaps Paul tried to prevent the anti-Judaism he knew to be on the rise in the Christian church in Rome by writing Rom 9–11.[245] In other words, Paul might have recognized that the Gentile Christians in Rome were about to venture in to a displacement theology. "For the problem was an understandable outgrowth of the shift of salvation history that has taken place," explains Douglas Moo:

> The Gentiles' rejoicing at being *included* with Jews in God's people would all too easily lead to boasting that they had *replaced* the Jew as the people of God . . . Paul therefore warns us, as he warned the first-century Gentile Christians in Rome: don't assume that Gentile preponderance in the church means that God has abandoned his people Israel. God has brought salvation to the Gentiles without violating any of his promises to Israel and without retracting his election of Israel as a corporate whole: an election that, like all God's gifts, is "irrevocable" (v. 29).[246]

A brief summary will serve to clarify here. In the beginning of Rom 9:6f, Paul redefines the true descendants of Abraham: "He distinguishes seed of promise from children of natural descent, but he never suggests that God does not keep his promise to Israel. Paul's thesis is that Israel's identity is determined by God alone."[247] Paul started to explain in Rom 3:1–8 that God remained faithful to Israel in spite of Israel's disobedience, and now again, in Rom 9:6f., Paul continually elaborates this thought, building his view on Israel's continued election, in order to prove God's faithfulness. Paul gives several points to demonstrate Israel's continued election in Rom 9–15.

---

244. Ibid., 161. I will discuss in detail later whether God's election of Israel had just an instrumental role in the OT or from unconditional love.
245. Campbell, *Paul's Gospel*, 75–76.
246. Moo, *Epistle to the Romans*, 685.
247. Campbell, *Paul's Gospel*, 143.

First, Paul expresses how much he was concerned about the Jewish people. Paul has, like the prophets or Moses, great sorrow and pain in his heart for them, and he wishes he could be accursed by God for his brethren's sake (Rom 9:2–3).

Second, Paul uses the prophet Hosea in Rom 9:25–26 to imply that the God of Israel promises to restore Israel's character in the future. Paul sees from Hosea that "God would graciously restore Israel to a new covenantal status as 'sons of the living God.'"[248]

Third, Paul uses the analogy of an olive tree to say that the Gentiles have not taken over the tree and the Jews have not been finally rejected. The wild olive shoot is grafted in, only to share the richness of the olive tree (Rom 11:7). An olive branch does not support the root, but the root supports the branches. Moreover, Paul does not talk about a new olive tree. He makes sure that this grafting is not a displacement of Jews by Gentiles (Rom 11:13–24). Paul does this by showing that the newly-grafted shoot is in fact borne by the stem of Abraham.

In addition, this shoot is grafted in among them (Rom 11:17).[249] He also asserts that they were grafted in to *share* the richness of the olive tree, not to take it over for their own exclusive benefit.

Fourth, for Paul, Christ has become a servant to the Jewish people (Rom 15:8), Χριστὸν διάκονον γεγενῆσθαι (perfect tense verb, implying a past act with abiding significance for the present). So too has Paul. Paul is a faithful servant of his Messiah; he is willing to continue to serve the Jewish people as his Messiah did, even unto death itself.

Fifth, Paul urges the Roman congregation to share their material blessings with Jewish people who are in Jerusalem. Because the Gentiles have been made partakers of the spiritual blessing of the Jews, they owe them (Rom 15:27).

Finally, Paul confirms that the Jewish people are still God's choice because they are beloved for the sake of the fathers even though they are enemies of Christians (and not of God, as the RSV and NRSV gratuitously propose) from the standpoint of the gospel (Rom 11:28). Therefore, for Paul, Israel's election is sure because "the gifts and the call of God are irrevocable" (Rom 11: 29).

---

248. Goodwin, *Paul*, 62.

249. Revised Version in contrast to the RSV and NRSV's "in their place."

We can therefore conclude that in Rom 9–11, Paul demonstrates that God's election has not failed. He is completely faithful to his promise. As Schoeps comments:

> This attitude on the part of Paul, however, is deeply connected with the attempt to find a new meaning in his own Judaism, for the unfolding of the true divine plan of salvation is intended to yield a new interpretation of the whole Jewish position as regards the faith. Paul is in fact convinced that he has never seceded from Judaism, since the Christian confession means for him the completion of his Jewish faith. But this position must first be demonstrated to others. "This section (Rom. 9–11) is the apostle's attempt to pursue the destiny of Israel with prophetic-apocalyptic categories of thought right into the inner shrine of God's counsels and actions" . . . From God's side the election has not been a mistake, and it would not be possible to call it a failure.[250]

Identifying "All Israel"

This leads to the question that necessarily arises from our previous chapters: Who was Paul referring to when he said "all Israel will be saved" (Rom 11:26)? There are several possible meanings: a remnant of the Jews, all Jewish and Gentile believers, every single Jew in the nation, the whole nation as a corporate entity, and so forth.

Although the early church father Origen understood "all Israel" to be ethnic Israel, in his *Commentarius in Matthaeum* he interpreted it as spiritual Israel—which indicates the remnant of Israel.[251]

In the modern period, C. H. Dodd was surprised by Paul's statement "all Israel will be saved"[252]—and found it both inconsistent and emotional. He develops his critique of Paul in the following way:

> The fact is that he has argued from the promise to Abraham on two divergent and perhaps inconsistent lines. If the promise means ultimate blessedness for "Israel," then *either* the historical nation of Israel may be regarded as the heir of the promise, and

---

250. Schoeps, *Paul*, 237.

251. Cf. Fitzmyer, *Romans*, 624. Origen interpreted "Israel" as "all Israel" of ethnic Israel in Rom 8:13, but in Matthew 17:5, he read "Israel" as "spiritual Israel." His interpretation of "Israel" in Romans differs from Matthew.

252. Dodd, *Epistle of Paul*, 182–83.

Paul is justified in saying that all Israel will be saved, or its place may be taken by the New Israel, the body of Christ in which there is neither Jew nor Greek; but in that case there is no ground for assigning any special place in the future to the Jewish nation as such. Paul tries to have it both ways. We can well understand that his emotional interest in his own people, rather than strict logic, has determined his forecast.[253]

Dodd claims that Paul emotionally wished for all Israel to be saved in the future rather than using "strict logic," thereby denying all Israel will be saved. R. C. H. Lenski argues "all Israel" is referring to all elect Jews.[254] On the other hand, F. F. Bruce, in his *Commentary on Romans*, contrasts his view with that of Aquinas.[255] "All Israel is a recurring expression in the Jewish literature," Bruce says, "where it need not mean 'every Jew without a single exception', but 'Israel as a whole.'"[256]

Unlike Origen, Lenski, or Bruce, D. E. H. Whiteley (1974)[257] has asserted that Paul was referring to spiritual Israel, which is made up of Jews and Gentiles—a usage found in Irenaeus.[258] This universal interpretation has been dominant throughout church history.

Francis Watson (1986), in his book *Paul, Judaism, and the Gentiles*, recognizes that in Rom 11:26 "all Israel" refers to "the whole nation" and explains:

> The promises to the patriarchs guarantee the salvation of the Jewish people as whole (11:28ff.) . . . It is because "as regards as election they are beloved for the sake of their forefathers," and because "the gifts and call of God are irrevocable" that Paul can be so confident that "all Israel will be saved" (v. 26), that they too will ultimately receive mercy (v. 31). In v. 16, Paul had grounded his belief in the salvation of Israel (v. 15) in the principle, "If the root is holy, so are the branches," a probable reference to the patriarchs.[259]

---

253. Ibid., 183.

254. Lenski, *Interpretation of St. Paul's Epistle*; Bengel, *Romans*, 154–55. Cf. Bruce, *Romans*, 421. Bengel also stated that "all Israel" refers to all elect Jews.

255. Aquinas, *Super Epistolas*, 170.

256. Bruce, *Romans*, 209. For a similar view, see Harrison, "Romans," 123; Moo, *Epistle to the Romans*, 713; Sanday and Headlam, *Romans*, 336.

257. Whiteley, *Theology of St. Paul*, 97. Similarly, see Calvin, *Romans*, 437.

258. Cf. Fitzmyer, *Romans*, 624.

259. Watson, *Paul, Judaism*, 169.

But Watson claims that Paul is inconsistent between Rom 11:26 and Rom 4 and 9:

> Although he acknowledges in vv. 17ff. that some of the branches have been broken off in order to make room for the Gentiles, he expresses his hope in vv. 23f. that God will graft them back in again. Admittedly, there is a note of caution in v. 23 ("if they do not persist in their unbelief"); but this is no longer evident in vv. 25ff. In Rom. 4 and 9, Paul has argued quite clearly that promise of salvation to Abraham and to his seed applies not to the Jewish people as a whole but to the Jewish and Gentile Christians whom God has called. But in Rom. 11 the promise to the patriarchs has no direct application to the Gentiles and instead forms the basis for Paul's confidence in the salvation of the Jews.[260]

However, Watson does point out that in Rom 11:26, "all Israel," refers to the whole Jewish people. Leon Morris's view, on the other hand, is more like that of Bruce. As Morris elaborates, "There is considerable agreement that all Israel does not mean 'each and every Israelite without exception,' the term refers to the nation as whole. It is used in this way in the Old Testament (1 Sam. 12:1; 2 Chron. 12:1; Dan. 9:11)."[261] In other words, Paul used the term "all Israel" as a corporate expression.

Now the question is: Which view is the most likely interpretation in the context of Romans? If Paul referred only to the remnant of Israel or elect Jews, he would not have had to write Rom 9–11 in the first place — i.e., if he was concerned with non-Jewish believers in Rom 9–11 as a possible threat to the salvation of Israel. Moreover, in the immediate context of v. 25, Paul plainly refers to Israel as a nation (i.e., it is hardened in part).

Furthermore, he uses the term "Israel" only twelve times in Rom 9–11. Why did he not use the term "the Jews" in Rom 9–11? Why, at this juncture, did he switch and use the term "Israel"? In Rom 1–8, Paul dealt with Gentiles as being equal with Jewish people before God in Christ. But the purpose of Rom 9–11 is to show that the Jews as a nation (the "hardened part") remain God's people; that is, Israel, in spite of their rejection of God,

---

260. Ibid., 170. See details on this issue in the last section, "The Election of Israel," in which I have argued why Paul was not inconsistent between Rom 11 and Rom 9. For a more detailed view of Paul's consistency between Rom 11 and Rom 4 and 9, see Campbell, "Divergent Images," 187–211.

261. Morris, *Epistle to the Romans*, 420. Also see Fitzmyer, *Romans*, 623. Similarly, see Barrett, *Romans*, 204–205; Käsemann, *Commentary on Romans*, 311–12; Cranfield, *Epistle to the Romans*, 577.

will be saved by him at the end of time, as God promised to the fathers. Therefore, it is clear that Paul was referring to "Israel," to the nation as a whole, rather than just to the elect individuals.

The second question is: Did Paul want to stress here that God's salvation is universal? Did Paul intend to indicate "all Israel" to be read as "spiritual Israel," made up of those Jews and Gentiles who are in Christ?[262]

Romans 9–11 is about Jewish people—but not Jewish people combined with Gentiles within the church, as we can see in the following passage. Paul expressed sorrow and grief for Jews who did not believe in Christ and wished for their salvation (Rom 1–3). He listed the "advantages" (cf. Rom 3:1–3) that proved God's election of Israel (Rom 9:4–5). God's word had not failed because some of Israel had rejected Jesus Christ as God's Messiah (v. 6). Paul placed emphasis on God's freedom of choice.

On the one hand, he gave the example of the story of Jacob and Esau (Gen 22:5) in which God chose Jacob rather than his twin, Esau, before their birth (Rom 9:11–15). On the other hand, Paul quoted Exod 33:19 to show that God chose to harden whom he desired (Rom 9:16–22). In other words, Paul argued that everything depended on divine initiative rather than on man's will, and God even hardened Pharaoh's heart according to the purpose of his will, for the glory of his name and his power (Rom 9:17).

Paul goes on to quote the Scripture from Hos 1:10 and Isa 11:5, 28:22, and 13:19 to show that God promised he would restore Israel in spite of their disobedience (Rom 9:18–29). Some scholars, such as Dunn, claim that when Paul said, "even us, whom he also called, not from among Jews only, but also from among Gentiles" (Rom 9:24), Paul meant that the called includes Gentiles. Dunn says, "Paul has now secured his base: when 'Israel' is defined by God's call then it should occasion no surprise when the 'not my people,' the other nations, the non-Jews, are included within 'Israel,' the vessels of mercy."[263]

The main argument of Rom 9, however, is about Israel's restoration, not about the inclusion of Gentiles, which has been already established and

---

262. Watson, *Paul, Judaism*, 169–70. Watson argues that Israel in Rom 11:28 refers to the Jewish people as whole, but that in Rom 4 and 9, "Paul has argued quite clearly that the promise of salvation of Abraham and to his seed applies not to the Jewish people as whole but to the Jewish and Gentile Christians whom God has called. But in Rom. 11 the promise to the patriarchs has no direct application to the Gentiles and instead forms the basis for Paul's confidence in the salvation of the Jews (ibid., 170).

263. Dunn, *Theology of Paul*, 514.

can be taken for granted.²⁶⁴ Nevertheless, in Rom 9:30–10:21, Paul tried to explain why Israel failed to accept Jesus as the Messiah and how the goal of the Torah is Jesus, the Messiah.

In Rom 11, Paul asks if God abandoned his people because of their disobedience. To answer that question, Paul quotes a verse from 1 Kgs 19. When Elijah was in grief because he thought he was the only one left who believed in the Lord of Israel, God comforted him by saying to Elijah, "I have kept for Myself seven thousand men who have not bowed the knee to Baal" (Rom 11:4). These "remnant" believers were as faithful as Elijah.

Paul further stated, "there has also come to be at the present time a remnant according to God's gracious choice" (Rom 11:5). In other words, as Cohn-Sherbok said, "the body of Jewish Christians, exceptions to the general unbelief of their race, form a group analogous to the seven thousand who refused to worship Baal, and it is in this sense that God has not cast off his people."²⁶⁵ Thus, Paul's answer is that God did not abandon his people, because a portion of them already believe in Christ.

Paul goes on to elaborate that the purpose of Israel's unfaithfulness is for the Gentiles' sake (Rom 11:11) and that their inclusion will in turn make Israel so jealous for their own God that they will return to him in faithfulness (Rom 11:12–27). Paul interpreted passages from Jer 11:14–17, Job 14:7–9, and Isa 6:13 that speak of the regrowth of the tree—shoots from a stump—to show how God's choice of Israel will be fulfilled once the Gentiles have become obedient to Jesus the Messiah (Rom 11:16–24).

Paul used the metaphor of the olive tree to remind Gentile believers that the root supports the branch²⁶⁶and therefore that Gentile believers

---

264. We followed Campbell's argument that "the Hosea citation applies primarily to Israel and that the three citations thus all have primarily reference to Israel's restoration but in and with the restoration, another 'non-people', the Gentiles, will also be blessed" (Campbell, "Divergent Images," 199). See more detail in ibid., 187–211. Räisänen acknowledges that the inclusion of Gentiles is not the primary emphasis of the chapter (Räisänen, "Paul, God, and Israel," 183).

265. Cohn-Sherbok, *Rabbinic Perspectives*, 79–80.

266. I do not see any hierarchical relationship here, as outlined in Buell and Hodge, "Politics of Interpretation," 249–50. Buell and Hodge state, "Paul's metaphor of an olive tree in Rom 11:17–24 illustrates this hierarchical relationship. Paul warns the Gentiles that they are a 'wild olive shoot' that has been grafted onto the tree, while Judeans are 'natural branches.' Paul arranges these two peoples asymmetrically, 'first the Judean and then the Greek' (Rom 1:16; 2:9–10) . . . In this ethnic family tree, the grafted branches have a more tenuous attachment and can be broken off easily at the will of the one who prunes the tree. While both peoples are subject to the will of this horticulturalist God, the Gentiles are less secure than the Judeans" (ibid.). In my reading, in Rom 11:17–24

should not be arrogant (Rom 11:17–18). Paul finally brought his argument to a conclusion: "I do not want you to be ignorant of this mystery, brothers, so that you may not be conceited: Israel has experienced a hardening in part until the full number of the Gentiles has come in. And so all Israel will be saved" (Rom 11:25–26). In this context, Paul did not refer to "all Israel" as the spiritual Israel that is made up of Jewish and Gentile believers, but instead referred to the Jewish people only. Thus the term "all Israel" should be taken as referring to the nation as a whole (a corporate expression).[267] Moreover, in Rom 9–11, Paul's argumentation of Israel's future salvation is more likely a Pharisaic midrash and very logical in its own way rather than just an emotional statement.

Did Paul Urge Believers to Separate?

Sanders argues that even though Paul did not deliberately set out to separate the church from Judaism, his congregations were socially distinct from the synagogue. He concludes that Paul implicitly and unintentionally paved the way for the church to emerge as a "third entity."[268]

Along with Sanders, Watson agrees that Paul advocated for Jewish believers to separate from the parent body. Watson argues that Paul's purpose in writing the letter to the Romans was to persuade Jewish Christians to separate from the synagogue.[269] Campbell, in his critique of Watson's analysis, suggests that "a major problem for Watson's interesting and challenging approach is that he has not given sufficient attention to Israel's dual status in Paul's theology. Israel is beloved of God and yet stands in opposition to Paul's gospel. Paul's *theology* does not provide a rationale for separation but on the contrary seeks a resolution of the separation in the

---

Paul was simply pointing out the Gentile believers' heritage and rooted connection. Paul encouraged a mutual relationship between Jew and Gentile in Christ.

267. Beker has noted that Rom 11:25–32 is a climax of the argument of the letter as a whole: "[T]he total sweep of the argument of Romans is held together by the theme of the peculiar interaction between Israel's particularity and the universality of the gospel for the Gentiles" (Beker "Faithfulness of God," 14). Cf. "for all who believe" and "for the Jew first" in Rom 1:16).

268. Sanders, *Paul, the Law*, 171–72. See Davies' criticism of Sanders' views on Paul's conception of Christ as Lord, which he calls "antithetically related to Judaism" in the preface to the fourth edition of Davies, *Paul and Rabbinic Judaism*, xlvi.

269. Watson, *Paul, Judaism*, 172. See also ibid., "Two Roman Congregations," 203–15.

coming eschatological triumph of God."[270] Campbell goes on to note that "when Paul writes Romans, Christianity as a separate entity has not yet fully emerged. The only possible candidate for a specifically Christian title is the word 'saint,' but this has an element of ambivalence and certainly is not intended to exclude Jews."[271]

According to Nanos's recent study, Paul wrote Galatians to address righteous Gentiles within Jewish subgroups—that is, synagogue communities.[272] Even though Nanos's theory that the Roman Christians were to be subordinate to the synagogue leaders is questionable,[273] it would still, if accurate, indicate that early Christianity had not yet emerged from the synagogue.

Most recently, Daniel Boyarin has stated in his book *Border Lines* that in the Antioch incident, Christian identity began to shed its geographically Jewish characteristics. He argues that since Christians subsequently claimed to be the true Israel, we can see some signs of the split that was yet to come:

> On the one hand there was sufficient pressure from Gentile Christianity in Asia Minor to stimulate Jewish hostility even, perhaps, to the point of cursing, but also that there was sufficient pressure on Gentile Christian identity to produce the need for clearer articulations of separation from Judaism. After the time of Justin and his promulgation of *Verus Israel*, becoming a Christian (or follower of Christ) meant something different—it no longer entailed becoming a Jew—and once becoming a Christian became identified with "entering [the true] Israel," the whole semantic/social field shifted. The boundary between Greek and Jew, the definition of Jewishness as national or ethnic identity, was breached or gravely threatened by the self-definition of Gentile Christianity as "Israel," leading to a reconfiguration of the cultural features that signal the boundary, indeed a reconfiguration of the understanding of the substance of the boundary itself from the genealogical to the religious. Hence

---

270. Campbell, *Paul's Gospel*, 129–30.

271. Ibid., 129. Brändle and Stegemann also point out that "the 'Christian' movement, as it was named in the final quarter of the first century, at the latest, to distinguish it from the Jews, was a new, self-supporting, although somewhat unstable form of reaction to the encounter between Jews and pagans" (Brändle and Stegemann, "Christian Congregations," 122). For more detail, see ibid., 117–23.

272. Nanos, *Irony of Galatians*, 6–7. See also ibid., *Mystery of Romans*, 30–31.

273. For why Nanos' theory on this issue poses a problem, see Campbell, "Rule of Faith," 275–76, reprinted in ibid., *Unity and Diversity*, 39–66.

orthodoxy/heresy came to function as a boundary marker, because the boundaries had indeed been blurred.[274]

However, Paul's letters show no trace that Paul encouraged Jew and Gentile believers to leave the synagogue—nor does the word "Christians," used only after 70 CE, give any indication that early Christianity separated from the synagogue. This lack of evidence more likely receives support from Rom 14–15,[275] where, likewise, no indication that Christianity separated from Jewish believers or Jewish synagogues can be found.

Rather, Rom 14–15 points to a certain amount of social interaction between the Jewish synagogue and Jewish and Gentile Christ-believers. We may conclude, therefore, that we have not found any indication that Paul urged Christ-believers to separate from the Jewish community.

Did Paul Encourage Abandoning Jewish Identity?

Another question arises: Did Paul encourage Jewish believers to abandon their Jewish pattern of life? Paul, in Rom 14–15, allows for the continuing existence of Jewish identity in Christian discipleship. If Paul affirmed the right of Jewish Christians to continue to live a Jewish lifestyle, he is, in fact, affirming Jewish identity in Christ and not arguing for a universal (Gentile) form of Christianity. The tendency of some scholars to negate a Jewish life pattern for the sake of proving this grand goal of uniform Christianity, rather than recognizing a plurality of different forms of Christianity, leads Pauline interpretation to become implicitly anti-Jewish.

Some scholars have sought to identify precisely who are "the weak" and who are "the strong" (Rom 14:1–2). Paul S. Minear, for example, argues that Paul indicates "'the weak'" are Jewish believers and "the strong" are Gentile believers. More specifically, he identifies "the weak" as legalists and "the strong" as antinomians, the lawless Gentile believers.[276]

Joseph Fitzmyer considers Minear's view highly speculative,[277] but seems to agree that "the weak" refers to the Jewish believers in the Roman community. He is aware that in Judaism there was no prohibition of eating meat, yet he argues that "some Jews abstained from meat and wine, espe-

---

274. Boyarin, *Border Lines*, 73.
275. I will discuss Rom 14–15 further in the next section.
276. Minear, *Obedience of Faith*, 8–17.
277. Fitzmyer, *Romans*, 688.

cially those who lived in pagan environments in the Diaspora (see Dan. 1:8, 12–16; 10:3; Jdt. 8:6; 10:5; 12:1–2; Esth. 14:17 [Vg]."[278] Fitzmyer explains why he identifies "the weak" as Jewish believers:

> Vegetarianism was sometimes practiced; 2 Sam 17:28 implies that such things as "wheat, barley, meal, parched grain, beans, lentils" would be used in such a practice; cf. 2 Macc. 5:27. Philo tells of the Therapeutai in Egypt, who so abstained (*De vita cont.* 4 S 37). The practice among Jewish Christians may stem from the fear of eating meat that was "unclean" (*koinon*) or that had been offered to idols, as in 1 Corinthians 8. Hegesippus tells of James, "the brother of the Lord, called 'the Upright,'" who abstained from wine, beer, and animal flesh (*oinon, sikera, empsychon*; Eusebius, *Historiaecclesiastica* 2. 23:5). Cf. Josephus, *Life* 2 S 14. Moreover, the use of *koinon* in the specific Jewish sense of "unclean" in 14:14 and *kathara*, "clean," in 14:20, as well as the implied contrast of Jews and Gentiles in 15:7–13, makes it highly likely that Paul understands the "weak" as Christian of Jewish background.[279]

David H. Stern, in contrast to Fitzmyer, asserts that "the weak" cannot be identified as Jewish believers. Judaism does not require Jews to be vegetarian (Rom 14:2). The large Jewish colony in Rome (Acts 29:17f.) would have had a ritual slaughterer who would know the ritually clean from unclean. Jewish believers, therefore, would not have had to worry about eating ritually unclean meat.[280] Also, "nothing in Judaism requires a Jew to refrain from wine (v. 21); the only exceptions are Nazirites during the period of their vow and cohanim on duty . . . On the contrary, wine-drinking is so much a part of Jewish ritual that it is lent an aura of sanctity which, at least until recently, made alcoholism very uncommon among Jews."[281] Moreover, Stern argues we cannot even be precise about the ethnic origin of the "weak":

> The weak are believers, either Gentile or Jewish, who have not yet grown sufficiently in their faith to have given up attachment to various ascetic practices and calendar observances. Their tie to these activities, however, is not supported by a rational though mistaken ideology, as with the legalists. Rather, it is irrational and emotional, linked to psychological needs, social pressures or

---

278. Ibid., 687.
279. Ibid., 687–88.
280. Stern, *Jewish New Testament Commentary*, 432–33.
281. Ibid., 433.

superstition, or it may simply be a matter of habit. When their activities in these areas are questioned in "arguments over opinions" (v. 1), they are not "fully convinced in their own minds" (v. 5), not "free of self-doubt" (v. 22), but rather easily "upset" or even "destroyed" (v. 15) and thus able to "fall away" or "stumble" (vv. 20–21). This is why Paul calls them "weak."[282]

Stern's interpretation of Rom 14–15 seems much more plausible than Minear's and Fitzmyer's. Nanos has recently identified "the weak" as non-Christian Jews rather than as Christians. In his view, Paul is writing to exhort the strong Christians to help support their weak Jewish brother to prevent him from stumbling and thus to encourage him toward faith in Christ. The strong must, in fact, behave like righteous Gentiles for the sake of the weak.[283] However, Nanos's view is just a general theological one rather than a Christological one, as Campbell argues. I am convinced that Paul addressed this exhortation to the community of believers rather than to nonbelieving Jews, because here Paul clearly portrays the weak as possibly consisting of both Jewish and Gentile believers—that is, Christ believers who were torn between loyalty to other groups (irrespective of whether they originated as Jews or Gentiles). Likewise, Campbell is unconvinced of Nanos's identification of the weak as non-believing Jews.

"Reluctantly, I find myself not fully convinced by some aspects of his comprehensive reworking of the letter," he states. "I am still inclined to the view that the weak are Christians—the measure of faith of 12:2 in my view implies a Christological foundation (rather than just a theological one). Further, Paul argues for the continuance and maintenance of the diversity that springs from the differing measure of faith gifted to believers. This could not be the case if the Jewish believers were not yet committed to faith in Christ."[284] Campbell insists that "the weak" refers to two groups of Christians. One group is made up of the Christians in Rome who feel obligated to a Jewish pattern of life; the other is mainly of Gentile origins:

> These despised the scruples of their "Jewish" brethren and were arrogant in their self-confidence as the new people of God. They only worshiped in their house groups and saw little reason why they should maintain any social contracts with Jews as such. Thus, we have a context in which groups of Christians were divided over

---

282. Ibid.
283. Nanos, *Mystery of Romans*, 85–165.
284. Campbell, "Rule of Faith," 275–76, reprinted in ibid., *Unity and Diversity*, 39–66.

their attitude toward (and therefore their connection with) the law and the synagogue . . . If Nanos's view is correct, then the Roman Christians were to be subordinate to the synagogue leaders, to obey the apostolic decree in keeping the Noachic commandments and to pay the temple tax. Christians subject to the discipline of the synagogue could have suffered prescribed beating for association with Gentiles (2 Cor. 11:24). Some of them could have been excluded if others refused to eat or worship with them . . . We conclude therefore that the division between "the weak" and "the strong" did not correspond to the division between Jewish and Gentile Christians, but cut across it.[285]

Stern's and Campbell's views are more appropriate readings of Romans 14–15 than the others. However, it is hard to pin down whom Paul specifically refers to as "the weak." Certainly the issue of Rom 14–15 is not about Paul urging Jewish believers to stop being Jews, nor is it about the division between Jewish and Gentile believers. Rather, Paul is, in fact, affirming Jewish identity in Christ, whether or not these Christ-followers are of Gentile origins.

Paul also elsewhere used plain language to urge Jewish believers to remain Jewish and for Gentile believers to remain Gentile (1 Cor 7:17f.). If Gentiles remain as Gentiles in Christ, then Jews also remain as Jews in Christ. In other words, ethnic identity still remains in Christ.[286]

Finally, Paul admonished "the strong" to seek mutual edification with "the weak" rather than to destroy them (Rom 14:19–20). In Rom 14–15, Paul, although opposed to the attitude of boasting in Christ, advised each to care for the other and so build up the community. If, as I have argued, Paul himself never ceased to practice a Jewish pattern of life according to his own claim in 2 Cor 11:22 and Rom 11:1, then he could not possibly encourage Jewish believers to give up their identity.

---

285. Ibid., 275–77.

286. See more about ethnic identity in Esler, *Conflict and Identity*, 339–56. Esler argues, following Campbell's view, that Paul allows Jewish identity to continue alongside Gentile identity in Christ. He explains, "My conclusion is reasonably consonant with the view ably championed by William Campbell that Paul is saying 'Gentiles must not regard observance of the Jewish law as incompatible with Christian faith, and Jews must not regard it as essential to Christian faith" (ibid., 351).

The Antioch Incident

Galatians 2:11–14 has been a problematic passage among scholars for centuries. J. A. Bengel argued that in Gal 2:11–14 Paul opposed Judaism.[287] This brings us to the question: Did Paul demand in the Antioch incident that Jewish believers should cease practicing the Jewish way?

In Acts 15, the Jerusalem Council considered whether Gentile believers should observe the law or not. Here, the issue is whether the Jewish believers should keep the dietary law. I will first demonstrate how scholars' views in Gal 2:11–14 have diverged over the years, then evaluate each of the views, and finally proceed to my conclusion regarding this text.

Scholars' Views on Galatians 2:11–14

Burton, in his 1921 commentary on Gal 2:11–14, interprets this text to mean that Paul was concerned about "the adherence of the Jews to their own ancestral custom enforced by Old Testament statute,"[288] rather than the freedom of the Gentiles. Paul was blamed for Peter's (and Barnabas's) hypocrisy. He observes, "over against this recent practice Paul forcibly sets forth Peter's inconsistency in compelling the Gentiles to follow the Jewish mode of life."[289] For Burton, the word ἰουδαΐζειν is important because it shows "What he regarded as the significance if not the deliberate intent of Peter's conduct in refusing no longer to eat with the Gentile Christians. Under the circumstances this amounted not simply to maintaining the validity of the Jewish law for Jewish Christians, but involved the forcing of Jewish practices upon the Gentile Christians."[290] In Antioch, Paul declares his independence from Jerusalem and the other apostles.

"In Antioch much more clearly than at Jerusalem, the issue was made between legalism and antilegalism," Burton notes. "It was incidental to the event of Antioch, but from the point of view from which Paul introduced

---

287. Bengel, *Galatians*, 12. Baur determined that Paul was against Judaism according to Gal 2:11–14. See a more detailed study on Baur in Tyson, *Luke, Judaism*, 12–19; also see Baur, *Paul the Apostle*, 134–51.

288. Burton, *Critical and Exegetical Commentary*, 105.

289. Ibid., 112.

290. Ibid.

the matter here, more decisively than ever before, he declared his independence of Jerusalem and her apostles."²⁹¹

According to Burton's view, Paul did not want Jewish believers to practice their observance of the law, on the one hand. On the other hand, the Jerusalem apostles insisted on keeping the law. As a result of this decision, Paul became an independent missionary. Burton's view is much like Baur's: because of the Antioch incident, Paul created a new religion—that is, Christianity.

In 1959, Munck maintained in his book *Paul and the Salvation of Mankind* that the Antioch incident took place before the Jerusalem meeting "as Peter and 'certain men who came from James' were there for the first time confronted with a mixed church."²⁹² Munck, unlike Burton, acknowledged that the Jewish believers understood the observance of the law and circumcision was not required for salvation. These things were not the essentials for their religion but were instead the national manners and customs among Christians of Jewish origin.²⁹³ According to Munck, in Antioch Paul accused Peter of breaking the fellowship between Jewish and Gentile believers for Jewish custom's sake, not necessarily as a salvation requirement.

Betz argued in 1979 that "Cephas may have concluded that given the theological presuppositions of the Jewish Christians he was expected to represent, his table fellowship was indefensible,"²⁹⁴ because in Acts 16:3 Paul allowed Timothy to be circumcised on account of the pressure of the "Jewish (=Jewish-Christian?)" constituency (cf. Gal 2:3–5). In other words, Paul had some responsibility for Cephas's action. Furthermore, Paul rebuked Peter for demanding that Gentiles observe the law both explicitly and implicitly. Betz notes:

> The present tense of ζῇς ("you are living") implies much more than an act of table fellowship with Christian Gentiles. It suggests that the table fellowship was only the external symbol of Cephas' total emancipation from Judaism. The *apodosis* presupposes Cephas' recent change of conduct as a self-contradiction: "how can you compel the Gentiles to live like Jews?" . . . Paul's evaluation was made *post factum* and assumes a number of intermediate

---

291. Ibid., 114.
292. Munck, *Paul and the Salvation*, 105.
293. Ibid., 107.
294. Betz, *Galatians*, 109.

considerations. By changing back to the observance of Jewish custom and law, the Jewish Christians have not only reversed their emancipation from Judaism. When they gave up the observance of the Torah, they also admitted that as a Christian one can be saved without the Torah . . . Therefore, Cephas had explicitly or implicitly made a demand upon the Gentiles to become partakers of the Torah covenant, in effect, Cephas had done the same as the "false brothers" at Jerusalem (2:4–5) . . . Ironically, therefore, by attempting to preserve the integrity of the Jewish Christians as Jews, Cephas destroys the integrity of the Gentile Christians as believers in Christ. Instead of welcoming them as converts to Christianity, he wants to make them into converts of Judaism. This contradicts the principles of the doctrine of justification by faith, which had been the basis of the faith thus far (see 2:15–16).[295]

In Betz's view, Peter was confused regarding observance of the law because Paul made Timothy undergo circumcision. Paul also thought Cephas's behavior was the same as the "false brothers" at Jerusalem (Gal 2:4–5); thus, Paul rebuked Peter's action in Antioch.

Sanders (1985) notes that in Gal 2:11–14; 4:10, the issue is that Gentiles are not required to keep the law in order to become people of God. Sanders asserts, "the controversy centers on the admission rite, circumcision, but includes other aspects of the law as well, such as food and days (Gal. 2:11–14; 4:10) . . . Gentiles do not need to accept the Mosaic law in order to be members of the people of God."[296] According to Sanders's view, in Gal 2:11–14, Paul accused Peter because he was compelling Gentiles to keep the law.

In contrast to Betz, Longenecker (1990) suggests that "there is no evidence that they are to be equated with the 'false brothers' of 2:4–5 or were Judaizers in the same sense as those who troubled the believers in Galatia."[297] He also emphasizes that Paul did not show hostility with Cephas but only engaged in a direct encounter.[298] Longenecker does not believe that Cephas realized what he was doing, but rather than he was simply reacting to the Jewish zealot pressures on the Jerusalem church.[299] However, Paul took Peter's reaction seriously because he was concerned with theological

---

295. Ibid., 112.
296. Sanders, *Paul, the Law*, 20.
297. Longenecker, *Galatians*, 73.
298. Ibid., 72.
299. Ibid., 75.

incorrectness: letting Gentile believers practice a Jewish pattern of life was dangerous for the Christian gospel.[300]

According to Cole (1991),[301] Peter had ordinary meals with Gentiles rather than the Lord's Supper; moreover, Peter had already been condemned by the Jerusalem extremists for eating ordinary meals with Gentiles at Caesarea (Acts 11:3). A similar incident had also happened in the gospel: "Christ had been condemned on exactly the same grounds (Mt. 9:11), for 'tax collectors and sinners' were reckoned with Gentiles, even if Jewish."[302] Cole further notes, "But in what way was he [Peter] trying to compel the Gentiles to live like Jews? Presumably, by inducing them, too, to observe the Jewish food laws as the price of full fellowship."[303] Cole argues that, in Paul's eyes, Peter was "apostate'" for the truth of gospel.[304]

Lührmann (1992), in his book *Galatians*, comments on the Antioch incident (Gal 2:11–14).[305] He believes that even though all the purity precepts of the law hindered Jewish Christians, the fellowship was practiced at that time in Antioch. Lührmann also writes, "Paul sees in Peter's behavior a basic demand that the Gentile Christians respect the law, which makes table fellowship between Jews and Gentiles impossible, although Peter himself did not hold to it earlier."[306] This decision meant that "the law is placed *de facto* above the gospel, even though there may be no quarrel about the Gentile Christians belonging to Christ. The consequence would have to be that the Gentile Christians should let themselves be circumcised and then commit themselves to the rules of purification in order to reestablish the full unity of the church."[307] For Lührmann, Paul condemned Peter's action because Peter put the law above the gospel, though Peter did not demand conformity as a condition for salvation.

Martyn's (1997) view on Gal 2:11–14 differs from others scholars'. He thinks Peter was somewhat aware of his ethnic identity.[308] When Peter and

---

300. Ibid., 80.
301. See Cole, *Galatians*.
302. Ibid., 115.
303. Ibid., 118.
304. Ibid., 117. Cole notes that in Jewish usage, the Greek *hypokrites* has usually been translated as the Hebrew *haneph*, or "apostate."
305. Lührmann, *Galatians*, 43–50.
306. Ibid., 44–45.
307. Ibid., 45.
308. See Martyn, *Galatians*.

Jewish believers ignored the food laws in table fellowship with the Gentiles in Antioch, they were—to some degree—conscious of their ethnic origin.[309] As Martyn explains, "Peter's withdrawal from table fellowship proved contagious precisely along ethnic lines; and that was an event which in Paul's view terminated the Antioch church's witness to the baptismal formula: 'in Christ there is neither Jew not Gentile' (cf. 3:28). It was thus this corporate move on the part of the Jewish members of the Antioch church that brought the thunderous explosion from Paul."[310] According to Martyn, Paul saw Peter distinguishing ethnic identity in spite of the fact that there was to be no ethnic barrier in Christ. The unity of God's church was so important for Paul, therefore, that he tried to maintain the different meal patterns among both Jews and Gentiles.

Martyn emphasizes that, in verse 14, it "seems in Paul's time to have had about it a ring that is artificial—perhaps even somewhat false—referring to Gentiles who take up wholly or in part the Jewish way of life without thorough-going conviction from the heart," and therefore, "Paul's remark to Peter is thus not an attack on Judaism. It is a statement about a specific act in the Antioch church that compelled the Gentile members to pretend to something, that was in a significant sense false."[311]

According to Witherington (1998), the chronology is the critical factor because "it makes a great deal of difference whether this event followed or preceded the meeting spoken of in Acts 15, not least because it, too, had something to do with issues of food and fellowship."[312] In Gal 2:14, Paul accused Peter of violating his own previously chosen manner of living. In other words, Peter was violating the implications of a law-free gospel to the Gentiles, which means Peter forced Gentile believers to keep the law.[313]

Recently, Dunn has put forth a different view on Gal 2:11–14.[314] Dunn believes the Gentile believers were already keeping the basic food laws. They knew how to properly prepare and slaughter animals when they had table fellowship with Jewish believers. In his view, Paul did not rebuke Peter

---

309. Ibid., 233.
310. Ibid., 243.
311. Ibid., 245.
312. Witherington, *Grace in Galatia*, 148.
313. Ibid., 153.

314. Dunn, "Incident at Antioch," 3–57; ibid., *Jesus, Paul, and the Law*, 129–74, reprinted in Nanos, *Galatians Debate*, 199–234.

for demanding Gentile believers to keep the dietary law. Rather, Paul was concerned about Peter's new level of requirements for Gentiles:

> Paul's charge against Peter, then, is most likely that by his action he had raised the ritual barriers surrounding their table-fellowship, thereby excluding the Gentile believers unless they "Judaized," that is, embraced a far more demanding discipline of ritual purity than hitherto. The reason why Peter had withdrawn from the table-fellowship in the first place was because the purity status of the Gentile believers had been called in question (Gal. 2:12; cf 2 Cor. 6:17 with its reference to Isa. 52:11) . . . The pillar apostles simply assumed that the devout Jewish believer would continue to observe the hereditary customs already surrounding the meal table (even if not all the refinements currently under debate among the Pharisees) . . . The table-fellowship at Antioch had not totally disregarded the law but probably had paid due heed to the basic dietary laws of the Torah. Peter, having already become less tied to the more elaborate scruples of the brothers in Judea (Acts 10–11), found no difficulty in joining in such table fellowship, as Barnabas, more used to Diaspora ways, was already doing . . . As a result of the Antioch incident, Paul became an independent missionary.[315]

However, Witherington has difficulty with Dunn's suggestion concerning the Antioch incident that in verse 14 "living like a Gentile" meant only that he was being less strictly observant as a Jew and that Antioch Gentiles and Jewish believers were following some, but not all, requirements of the dietary laws. Hence, Jerusalem held that they did not satisfy these requirements. Witherington gives at least two reasons for why he takes issue with Dunn's view:

> Firstly, it does not make sense of the language about Peter and Barnabas "withdrawing" or play-acting. There was something about this action that Paul saw as inconsistent with their former behavior, something that could constitute living like a Gentile. If the problem had merely been an insufficient attention to food law details, the solution would surely have been not "withdrawal" from table fellowship with Gentiles but more restriction on or more rigor in the already accepted practice of basically following Jewish dietary laws. Withdrawal is what the men from James precipitated on charges of living like a Gentile. This charge surely meant being

---

315. Dunn, "Incident at Antioch," 225, 227, 229, 232.

Jew Among Jews

non-observant of Kosher requirement, for they are not charged with merely living like a God-fearer or proselyte.[316]

Secondly:

> Dunn's view totally ignores the Cornelius episode in Peters' life. Unless one is prepared to argue there was no such episode prior to Paul's writing of Galatians, or that if there was, it had nothing to do with Peter's receiving a vision declaring all foods (and persons) clean, or at least no foods and persons ritually unclean, this tradition must be accounted for. I suspect that Paul is able publicly to accuse Peter of being inconsistent primarily because he knew Peter himself had for some time already been prepared to have table fellowship with Gentiles, in Gentile homes on their own terms. He knew Peter's own convictions on these matters because he knew about Peter's own experience with Cornelius. It wasn't just that Peter had given notional assent to Paul's Gospel of grace in Jerusalem; it was that Peter had already begun to live out such a Gospel himself, as had Barnabas and Paul, when they had fellowship with Gentiles. This is what I would suggest lies behind Paul's explosion at Antioch and his charges of inconsistency.[317]

Nanos also points out why Peter withdrew from the table fellowship with Gentiles and why Paul rebuked Peter in Gal 2:11–14. Nanos says that Peter "withdrew from these mixed meals and thereby separated himself, momentarily anyway, from the need to either abandon what he believed in or suffer the consequences threatened for continued noncompliance with the prevailing norms. And the other Christ-believing Jews followed his lead."[318] Nanos also notes:

> Peter may have considered his choice of action noble, perhaps what was necessary to preserve the integrity of this Jewish subgroup, or to enable it to continue to function unimpeded within the larger Jewish or even Syrian communities . . . For these Gentiles were now shamed for failing to properly assess who they are . . . They are exposed, marginalized for not conforming to the prevailing Jewish communal norms, for having believed that in Christ they have become already full members of the Jewish community, children of Abraham on equal standing with proselytes . . . Thus Paul objects to the withdrawal of Peter and the rest from eating

---

316. Witherington, *Grace in Galatia*, 153.
317. Ibid.
318. Nanos, "What Was at Stake," 317.

with these Gentiles on the terms dictated by the truth of the gospel of Christ. He recognizes the logical inference that has apparently escaped the thinking of Peter and the rest because they are instead reacting in fear or that, if deduced by them to some degree, has been suppressed to avoid the consequences considered by them to be more immediate. Such action Paul condemn as self-serving ... For Paul recognizes clearly that "the truth" of the gospel of Christ is symbolized in the way that these mixed meals are conducted within these Jewish subgroup.[319]

In this respect, Nanos concludes that the Antioch incident "offers a window into the *intra-* and *inter-* Jewish as well as pagan communal tensions that were provoked by the claims of these Christ-believing subgroups when still wholly identified as members of the larger local Jewish communities."[320]

In any case, which view among these is the best reading of Gal 2:11–14? Let us evaluate each of them.

Evaluation

First, if Burton's view—that Paul here declared his independence from Jerusalem and her apostles—is correct, then how could Paul possibly have collected the contribution from Macedonia and Achaia and taken it to Jerusalem (Rom 15:25–29)? Furthermore, James, Cephas, and John had told Paul to remember the poor when he was in Jerusalem (Gal 2:10). Also, we do not know what kind of relationship there was between these men and James or John. Their demanding was perhaps their own responsibility, but not James's or John's. Moreover, if the Antioch incident took place before the Jerusalem meeting, as Munck has indicated,[321] it shows that Paul and the Jerusalem apostles never separated because of this incident.

Second, if Paul rebuked Peter for changing back to Judaism's patterns intentionally, as Betz has claimed, then the question arises: Is there any possibility that Peter's action was not intentional, but simply a reaction to pressure from certain men, such as James, as Longenecker has indicated?[322]

---

319. Ibid.
320. Ibid., 318.
321. Munck, *Paul and the Salvation*, 105.
322. Longenecker, *Galatians*, 75.

But Paul was afraid that Gentile believers might have been misled by Peter's behavior into thinking that they had to practice a Jewish lifestyle.

Third, if Paul rebuked Peter because he was intentionally forcing Gentiles to keep the law, as Sanders and Witherington have indicated, then, contrary to Sanders and Witherington's views, Paul may have accused Peter for his unintentional rather than intentional behavior. Peter simply, without thinking, withdrew from that table fellowship out of fear of the men from James.

Fourth, if Paul's accusation of Peter in Antioch is that Peter distinguished ethnic identities in spite of there being no ethnic barrier in Christ (Gal 3:28), as Martyn has suggested, then does this mean Paul wanted to erase their ethnic identity? According to Gal 3:28, Jew and Gentile men and women are equal before God in Christ. But this can be taken to mean that in Christ, man and woman still remain of their own gender; likewise, Jews and Gentiles still remain of in their own ethnic origin. Therefore, Martyn's view of Paul's accusation of Peter is problematic.

Fifth, Dunn thinks that Paul did not rebuke Peter for demanding Gentile believers keep the dietary law. Peter had only raised the ritual barriers surrounding their table fellowship. Dunn's view poses a question. As Witherington has argued,[323] Paul accused Peter for living like a Gentile, not for merely living like a God-fearer or proselyte. In other words, Paul charged Peter with not observing kosher requirements. Also, if we can allow the historicity of Acts 10, then Peter, by his vision, knew that all people are clean in Christ. Paul knew of Peter's experience, and therefore Paul rebuked Peter for inconsistency rather than for ritual barriers surrounding their table fellowship.

Finally, Cole, Lührmann, Munck, and Nanos have differing views concerning Paul's accusation of Peter, and yet they all agree that the accusation did not take place over a salvation requirement.

Although all these scholars' views—Cole, Lührmann, and Munck's—have some substance, the most likely reading is Longenecker's. He notes that even though Peter's action was unintentionally a reaction to the Jerusalem church's pressure, Paul accused Peter because he was afraid that letting Gentile believers practice a Jewish pattern of life would be dangerous for the true understanding of the Christian gospel.

Moreover, if we can allow the historical reliability of Acts 10, then Paul knew from Peter's vision and the Cornelius episode that Peter understood

---

323. Witherington, *Grace in Galatia*, 153.

that Gentiles are clean in Christ and that he could therefore have shared table fellowship with Gentiles. Yet Peter reacted to the pressure by refusing table fellowship with Gentiles. In any case, Paul was afraid Peter's behavior might unintentionally lead Gentile believers to misunderstand the nature of the gospel.

Now then, what is the main point in Gal 2:11–14? I will follow John Fischer's interpretation, in which the issue is focused on table fellowship with Gentiles:

> The issue centered on table fellowship with the Gentiles. Peter freely ate with Gentile believers until certain people came from Jerusalem. At this point, for fear of the "circumcision party" he ceased. Peter's actions not only implied that it was necessary for Gentiles to live as Jews for a proper standing before God, it also led others astray as they followed his ill-advised example. In acting in such a fashion, Peter was not being straightforward about the nature of the gospel. He had demonstrated that Jews and Gentiles were united and equal by his former behavior, but then he backed off from his position by his later hypocritical actions. Paul's critique in verse 14f. is replete with irony when understood against the background of his own life. He was a practicing Pharisee until his death. Yet, as a strict practitioner of Judaism he was willing to have table fellowship with Gentiles. Peter was a Galilean fisherman and probably was considered one of the *am ha 'aretz*, one of the common people who did not follow all of the strictest expositions and detailed applications of the Torah, as practiced by the Pharisees. He would, therefore, have often been considered to be "like a Gentile" by the strictest Pharisees. Yet, Peter was now compelling Gentiles to live under the structures of a system he did not follow himself.[324]

We conclude therefore, that Paul charged Peter for his hypocritical action in not standing firmly for his belief, although his action was unintentional.

A Lesser Commandment

The question now is: Did Paul urge Jewish believers to cease their Jewish pattern of life in Gal 2:11–14? For Paul, as Stern points out, keeping dietary law became a less important commandment than preserving fellowship

---

324. Fischer, "Messianic Jewish Perspective," 2.

between Jewish and Gentile believers. For Paul, keeping dietary law became a less important commandment than the table fellowship with Gentile believers.[325] This does not mean that he abandoned the dietary law or urged Jewish believers to stop practicing their lifestyle.

In this context, we cannot find any evidence in Gal 2:11–14 that Paul himself abandoned a Jewish lifestyle or discouraged Jewish believers to cease to practice it.

Did Paul Abandon His Jewish Identity?

In the Antioch incident (Gal 2:11–14) we found that, for Paul, preserving fellowship between Jewish and Gentile believers was more important than keeping dietary law. In 1 Cor 9:19–23, Paul used the same rhetorical device as Gal 2:11–14 to convey his position in 1 Cor 9:19–23. In other words, for Paul, as a missionary, opening a table fellowship with Gentile believers was more important than keeping the Pharisaic halakhah in Christ.

However, in 1 Cor 7:18, Paul encouraged the Jew to remain a Jew and the Gentile to remain a Gentile. That is, Paul wished Jewish and Gentile believers to keep their ethnic identity. But in 1 Cor 9:19–23, Paul said that he became a Jew to the Jews and a Gentile to the Gentiles. Does this mean that Paul abandoned his Jewish identity and broke with Judaism for his missionary purposes, as the traditional view holds?

The traditional view is that in 1 Cor 9: 20, "under the law" refers to the Mosaic law. For example, Plummer argues that Paul completely left Judaism, according to 1 Cor 9:20. He indicates that "under the Law" refers to the Mosaic law as a whole and that "the parenthesis [Though I knew that I was not myself under Law] is remarkable as showing how completely St. Paul had broken with Judaism."[326]

Morris also points out that in 1 Cor 20, "under the Law" means the law of Moses—because, for Paul, "Christ is the end of the law" (Rom 10:4). Morris says, "But in approaching Jews he conformed to practices that would enable him to win those *under the law*. The sort of thing in mind is his circumcision of Timothy (Acts 16:1–3) and his joining in Jewish 'purification rites'" (Acts 21:23–6).[327]

325. Stern, *Jewish New Testament Commentary*, 529.
326. Plummer, *First Epistle*, 191.
327. Morris, *1 Corinthians*, 135–56. See discussion of the issues of Timothy's circumcision (Acts 16:3) and Jewish purification rites (Acts 21:23–26) at the beginning of this

Paul, Judaism, and Unbelieving Jews

Barrett interprets that "the law here [1 Cor. 9:20] means the law of Moses; but if this is repudiated, by an *a fortiori* argument all less important and directly divine laws are repudiated. Paul is now related to God through Jesus Christ (cf. 1, 30), and no room is left for law."[328] Then the question becomes: What is the issue here? What did Paul mean by "under the Law"? What kind of law did he refer to? And in what context did Paul say this (1 Cor 9:19–22) to Corinthians believers?

In 1 Cor 9:19–23, as we have seen above, these scholars have interpreted "under the law" as referring to the Mosaic law. But if we read 1 Cor 9:19–23 in the immediate context of 1 Cor 8–10, which refer to food sacrificed to idols, then the issue is not about the law itself but rather about Paul's table fellowship with Jewish and Gentile believers during the course of his missionary journeys.

If Paul formulates halakhah here for the Corinthian congregation, as Tomson points out, then Paul did not reject the law, but rather showed he had a positive relationship with the law. He says that "a quick reference to one passage suffices, which in our evaluation, as opposed to the traditional view, failed to qualify for this category: the idol food passage in 1 Cor. 8–10. Here Paul does not reject halakha as such but follows a well identifiable halakhic tradition based on positive relationship to the Jewish Law."[329] In this respect, Paul did not refer to the Mosaic law in verse 20, but may have referred to Pharisaic halakhah. As Rudolph points out:

> Paul may have used the term ὑπὸ νόμον in 1 Cor. 9:20—the term with its negative valence may have been shorthand for one "under the yoke of Pharisaic halakhah". Pharisees observed narrow interpretation of the Torah that restricted personal freedom and naturally imposed a heavier burden on the individual. The polemical descriptor "under the law" may have subtly expressed the nuance "under heavy burdens" [of the law], hard to bear . . . In 1 Cor. 9:20, Ἰουδαίοις is Paul's designation for ordinary Jew and ὑπὸ νόμον is Paul's designation for strict Jews, it is significant that in 1 Cor. 10:18 Paul moves from the universal to the particular, from the set of all Jews (Israelites) to the subset of strict Jews (priests) . . . If the initial restrictive clause in 1 Cor. 9:20 ("though I myself am not *under the Law*") means that Paul no longer viewed Pharisaic halakhah as a final authority, or that he no longer lived as a strict Jew,

---

chapter. See also Rudolph, "A Jew to the Jews," 28–29, 55–67.

328. Barrett, *First Epistle*, 212.

329. Tomson, *Paul and the Jewish Law*, 261.

then Paul was indifferent to certain halakhic interpretations and expansions of Mosaic law but not necessarily to the law itself.[330]

Moreover, in 1 Cor 9:21, Paul did not mean that he was a lawless person, nor that he had changed from Jewish to Gentile identity, but that he would make accommodations when he had table fellowship with Gentiles. Paul was more flexible than his contemporaries when he ate with Gentiles.

Daube points out that Jewish rabbis such as Hillel made the law no more burdensome than necessary in their endeavors to win people over to Judaism.[331] In the same manner, Paul also tried to win Gentiles to the Christ. Paul did not wish Gentiles to become Jews, but he urged Gentiles to keep their ethnic identity, as he said earlier (1 Cor 7:17f.).

If, in 1 Cor 9: 22, Paul meant what Rudolph argues he intended—that "'all things to all people' refers to Paul's open table-fellowship with Jewish and Gentile families during the course of his missionary journeys, and to adaption he exhibited by accommodating to his hosts within the limits of God's law"[332]—then in verses 19-23 we do not find any evidence that Paul abandoned his Jewish identity or the Mosaic law.

Gentile Believers' Identity

How is Paul's Jewishness related to the place of Gentiles among the people of God? Paul wanted Gentiles to relate to Israel, but he did not want them to give up being Gentiles or to become Jews.[333] According to Paul, Abraham is the father of Jews and Gentiles (Rom 4; Gal 3:29), but Jews specifically are the descendants of Jacob. Paul encouraged Gentile believers to remain as Gentiles in the same manner as he advised Jewish believers to remain as Jews (1 Cor 7:17f.).

In the analogy of the olive tree,[334] Paul also indicated some connection between Jewish believers and Gentile believers (Rom 11:17-24), but he did not mean that Gentile believers become part of Israel or alternatively

---

330. Rudolph, "A Jew to the Jews," 195, 197, 204-205.

331. Daube, *New Testament*, 336-37. Daube writes, "this attitude [1 Cor. 9:20ff.] had formed part of Jewish missionary practice long before Paul. Two Talmudic illustrations of Hillel's work are relevant" (ibid., 336).

332. Rudolph, "A Jew to the Jews," 205.

333. On the question of the relationship between identity and Christ, see Campbell, "All God's Beloved," 67-82.

334. See more detail in ibid.,, "Olive Tree," 642-44.

become fully Jews. In Gal 6:16, Paul refers to Gentile believers as God's people rather than as Israel.[335] Paul urged Gentile believers to keep their Gentile identity just as he had done for Jewish believers (1 Cor 7:18). Thus, Paul claimed that both Jewish and Gentile believers were equal in Christ in spite of their differences as ethnic groups (Gal 3:28). In other words, there is a mutual relationship between Jewish and Gentile believers in Christ, and they each have an equal right in Christ.

In Paul's view, Gentile believers are somehow related to Israel as a linked but distinct community of believers—they are still Gentiles and are not absorbed into the title of "Israel." Campbell's comments are a fitting conclusion to this discussion:

> In Paul's understanding, Abraham is the father of us all, i.e., of differing peoples such as Jews and Gentiles. If all were to become Jews or all were to give up their Jewishness, Abraham could not be the father of two different peoples. But whereas the apostle's strategy in Rom 14–15 for those with Jewish-related scruples is to allow them to follow their convictions, in his use of the analogy of the olive tree he seems to be affirming that there is no option for Gentile believers to separate completely from some form of Israelite if not Jewish identity. However, the Gentile believers still are not called Israelites, as this would mean one common, undifferentiated Jewish identity for all. On the other hand, the universalizing of Gentile Christian identity, as has tended to be the norm in the later history of Christianity, simply constitutes another kind of common, undifferentiated identity for all. The complexity of Paul's perspective on diversity, unfortunately lost so quickly in the history of the church, is that although he attaches Gentiles to the stem of Abraham this does not mean their proselytization to Judaism nor the universalizing of their Gentile Christian identity. Thus originally there was no one inclusive term to describe all believers in Christ. There were simply groups of Jewish and Gentile believers distinguished by their differing life-styles.[336]

---

335. I will discuss the controversial issue on Gal 6:16 in chapter 7.
336. Campbell, "All God's Beloved," 82.

A Faithful Jew

Was Paul hostile to Jews who did not believe in Christ? Did Paul abandon Judaism? If we allow some value for the historical reliability of Acts, then Luke's portrayal of Paul is of a faithful Jew committed to Judaism.

In light of our study of all the texts, it does not seem possible to think of Paul urging Jewish believers to stop being Jews. Paul himself, in fact, demonstrated willingness to keep his Jewish identity. Accepting Jesus as the Messiah does not require that Jewish people should give that identity up. As Campbell states, "It seems that to grow strong in faith in Paul's terms is to be able to welcome fully those who adhere to a differing way of life in Christ." And as Campbell adds:

> It is the latter that is the primary link between the groups who differ and it is the compelling force that obligates those in Christ who are different to accept one another. But unlike earlier understanding of this acceptance, it does not imply the giving up of one's particular identity in favour of a "Christian" identity in which other identities are dissolved. Thus there are differing identities in Christ but these are borne without being discriminated against because there is now no distinction amongst those who are in Christ.[337]

Therefore, it is reasonable to conclude that Paul was a faithful Jew even after his encounter with Christ.

---

337. Ibid., *Paul and the Creation*, 119–20.

7

Paul and True Judaism

DID PAUL TRULY HOLD that Christianity was the true Judaism? There are many different reasons to support the view that Paul did *not*, in fact, say God regards the church as the true Israel.

The first reason is that Paul was a Jewish theologian. As Brad H. Young has indicated, "Paul's conceptual theology is circular thought but not linear. The concepts are interactive; in circular thought the conceptual theological ideas are connected together in continuous motion."[1] Young contends that "when the contours of Pauline thought are considered in a cycle of interactive concepts rather than in a straight line where each new idea supersedes and eliminates the previous one, the apostle's conceptual approach to God is given fresh vigor. It is a Jewish way of thinking."[2]

N. T. Wright, on the other hand, interprets Paul's epistles in a systematic and highly conceptual manner. Douglas Harink has rightly objected to Wright's presentation of "creation and covenant history as a linear historical progression: creation-fall—functional covenant with Israel—Jesus Christ (at which time Israel's special 'privilege' is canceled)—the church (which replaces Israel as the people of God)—consummation."[3]

The attempt to systematize Paul's theology or make it fit into our modern Western mode of thinking is misguided. "The problem with our modern post-Enlightenment language," says W. S. Campbell, "is that we

---

1. Young, *Paul the Jewish Theologian*, 40.
2. Ibid., 42. Similarly, see Ehrensperger, *That We May Be*, 142–43.
3. Harink, *Paul Among the Postliberals*, 177.

conceptualize differently from Paul and perceive contradictions from our oppositional form of thinking which put Paul in an either/or dilemma that was quite foreign to his thought. We tend to argue either A or B but Paul's approach is more inclusive, not only A but B also. So for Paul, it is not a question of Jew or Gentile but to the Jew first and also to the Gentile."[4] Since Paul was a first-century Jew, deeply immersed in Jewish patterns of interpretation, we cannot presume his theological thinking is identical with our modern theology. "These Jewish ways of interpretation, especially midrash, are ways of relating the Scriptures and actual life in a vivid process of interaction rather than using systematic or doctrinal ways of thinking," explains Kathy Ehrensperger. "Instead of mere theory, interpretation is an activity that relates Scriptures to life and life to Scriptures. Thus, it may not be logical according to standards of Western ways of thinking, but this does not mean that it is incoherent with regard to the Scriptures and its relevance for the life of people."[5]

Although to interpret Paul in the context of Western thinking in the twenty-first century might seem both logical and creative, the final outcome does not come nearly close enough to Paul's thought because Paul's ways of thinking are so different from ours.

Love beyond Purpose

The second reason why Paul would not say that God replaces Israel with the church as the true Israel is that God had chosen Israel for love, not just to fulfill a specific purpose. If Paul was a scholar of the Torah, then it is reasonable to say that Paul knew the Old Testament and especially the Pentateuch and the Prophets, which contain the truth that God chose Israel because of his love and faithfulness and not for merit of her own. Moses said, "The Lord did not set his affection on you and choose you because you were more numerous than other peoples, for you were the fewest of all peoples. But it was because the Lord loved you and kept the oath he swore to your forefathers that he brought you out with a mighty hand and redeemed you from the land of slavery, from the power of Pharaoh king of Egypt" (Deut 7:7–8). After God chooses the Israelites, he expects them to serve as a kingdom of priests to all the other nations of the world (Exod 19:6).

---

4. Campbell, *Paul and the Creation*, 127.
5. Ehrensperger, *That We May Be*, 142–43.

Paul and True Judaism

Harink has recently pointed out that Wright's view of Israel's election as purely functional is not sound because "Israel is the very particular object of God's selective love." Harink develops this stringent critique further:

> There is no hint in either of these texts [Deut. 7:7–10; 10:14–15] of any *instrumental* reason for God's choice of Israel. Israel is God's people because of God's everlasting love. Nor even in the context of the rigorous call for obedience to the commandments which fills the pages of Deuteronomy, is there any notion that, should Israel "fail" in a supposed instrumental role, that God would "redefine" this covenant in such a way that Abraham's descendants after the flesh would simply fall out of God's covenant love for them. Even after the great disobedience which leads to God's curse upon Israel and to Israel's exile, God's abiding love remains (Deut. 3:1–5) . . . In text after text the exilic prophet affirms the great love and fidelity to his covenant which God sustains toward Israel (Isa. 43; 44:1–5, 21–22; 45:1–4; 49; 52:1–10; 55:3) . . . YHWH is bound to his people with a powerful bond of love. It is this love that drives him to seek out and redeem his people from bondage; it is this love that gives the prophet the confidence to declare comfort to God's people (40:1–2) . . . Israel's redemption in the midst of the nations, through the instrumentality of the nations, is the decisive vindication of YHWH's faithfulness to Israel and of his power as creator (Isa. 43:3–4) . . . Only as the servant of YHWH "raise[s] up the tribes of Jacob" and "restore[s] the survivors of Israel" does he become "light to the nations"; but precisely as he does so God's salvation reaches "to the end of the earth" (49:6) . . . It is difficult to see in the entire text of Isaiah 40–55 where Wright could derive the notion that Israel exists only to serve a role, purpose, function, or mission, which if it failed in it, would result in God simply abandoning his people for another.[6]

Paul, as a scholar of Torah, knew that God's everlasting love is directed toward the Israelite and requires Israel to serve him. Did Paul possibly think that God called Israel for merely a temporal instrumental purpose? The biblical evidence is against it. It would be most likely that Paul knew Israel has a special place in God's providence, and therefore, the gospel was to go to "the Jew first and also to the Greek" (Rom 1:16).

---

6. Harink, *Paul Among the Postliberals*, 164–68. Harink devotes an entire chapter of his book to a critique of Wright's views an Israel. Wright, on the one hand, adopts the New Perspective on Paul, but on the other continues to adhere to "Displacement" theology.

More Like Marriage

The third reason why Paul would not claim that Christianity is the true Judaism is because the Mosaic covenant was not like a business-world contract that can be canceled should the need arise, but more like a marriage contract that, in the Ancient Near Eastern world, establishes a permanent relationship.

The key to the relationship between YHWH and Israel is the covenant, just as in the Ketubah (כתבה: "marriage contract"). The bond and the relationship that results in covenant is characteristic of the biblical perspective on marriage from the Ancient Near East.

The Bible portrays the relationship between God and Israel as a marriage relationship. In Hos 2:2f., God represents himself as the husband of Israel. In Ezek 16:8, God explains to the prophet that he made covenant with Israel as a marriage contract. He says, "Then I passed by you and saw you, and behold, you were at the time for love; so I spread My skirt over you and covered your nakedness. I also swore to you and entered into a covenant with you so that you became mine" (Ezek 16:8).

When God wanted Israel as his bride, he offered her the formal, written marriage contract represented by the Torah. The Torah is God's instructions for the marriage agreement. This marriage contract can be found in the Pentateuch, particularly the Mosaic covenant and the book of Exodus. At Sinai, the Lord explained to Israel why he chose them as his people and asked their consent (Exod 19:3–7). He said, "'I . . . brought you to myself. Now if you obey me fully and keep My covenant, then out of all nations you will be my treasured possession. Although the whole earth is mine, you will be for me a kingdom of priests and a holy nation' . . . The people all responded together, we will do everything the Lord has said" (Exod 19:5–8).

This procedural covenant is very much like a wedding ceremony. When God asked Israel to follow his instruction, they promised God to keep his Torah. Paul is fully aware of the marriage relationship between God and Israel when he uses the analogy of Hosea in Rom 9:25–26. In Hos 2:19–23, God wants to remain married to Israel forever: "I will betroth you to me forever: I will betroth you in righteousness and justice, in love and compassion. I will betroth you in faithfulness, and you will acknowledge the Lord. . . I will plant her for myself in the land; I will show my love to the one I called 'Not my loved one.' I will say to those called 'Not my people.' 'You are my people;'[7] and they will say, 'You are my God.'"

Paul surely understands Hosea's message: despite Israel's unfaithfulness in her covenant relationship with her God, God still loves his unfaithful people. Paul could not erase this deeply bonded relationship between God and Israel. This marriage relationship is not temporal but will last forever.

Redemption Not Completed

The fourth reason Paul would not have held that God regards the church as the true Israel is that, according to Rom 8, redemption has not yet been completed. For Paul, the final redemption is not finished, so he still maintains hope for the salvation of all Israel. Harink explains:

> Wright's fully realized eschatology of the history of fleshly Israel fails to take into account that Jesus Christ is not the progressive conclusion of an historical narrative about creation and Israel. Rather, the apocalypse of Jesus Christ encloses the whole cosmos, and therefore also the church and fleshly Israel, within itself. The cross of Christ reveals that the present time of this enclosing is a time of suffering, waiting, and groaning—and for Israel a time of hardening. While the *ekklesia* already receives a foretaste of the final victory of God in its present experience of the Spirit (Rom. 8:12–16), the *ekklesia*, together with the creation, still awaits the full apocalypse of God's glory as corporeal and cosmic participation in Christ's resurrection (the redemption of the body); the church therefore receives its apocalyptic inheritance in the present primarily as a participation in Christ's crucifixion (8:17). And if the church, and all creation wait it, so also Israel along with the church and creation. Is it not possible to see Israel's present hardening as its unique (but unknowing) participation in the crucifixion of Jesus Christ, not as culpable "failure," but as its own share in suffering, waiting, and groaning with the church and the whole creation, as it too awaits the final redemption of all things?[8]

---

7. In Rom 9:25, Paul quoted from Hosea: "you are my people," which primarily refers to Israel even though it is controversial among scholars. I have already demonstrated why Paul did not primarily refer to just the northern tribes or Gentiles. See more detail in Campbell, "Divergent Images," 199.

8. Harink, *Paul Among the Postliberals*, 180.

Not only are Christ-believers waiting for the final redemption but also all Israel, even though its present state is mysterious. Paul fully understands that God's thoughts are not man's thoughts; neither are man's ways God's ways (Isa 55:8), for who has known the mind of the Lord? (Rom 11:34). Paul grieved over Israel's failure to recognize Jesus as the Messiah, and he thought that God was hardening the people's hearts until the final day for the Gentiles' sake (Rom 11:7–12). This paradoxical way of thinking is not foreign to Jewish ears. For Paul, while God's covenant reached its confirmation in Christ, that did not mean non-believing Jews were left out. While the covenant is in the process of reaching its fulfillment in Christ, believers are participating in the cross of Christ and waiting for the completion of the whole of redemption.

In other words, Paul may have believed that God's covenant was confirmed in the cross of Christ but is not yet completely consummated. The present time is a stage of fulfillment that is not completed but will continue until the final day. Therefore, in Paul's mind, when all Gentiles receive the gospel, God will save all Israel, as he promised to the forefathers (Rom 11). However we envisage this eventual outcome, according to Paul, God had not rejected—nor was he yet finished with—Israel.

The Promise of Future Restoration

The fifth reason Paul would not have held that God replaced Israel with the church as the new Israel is that the prophets held that God would restore all Israel. Many scholars, while acknowledging Israel's rejection of Christ, ignore the hope of Israel's prophets, who spoke of the restoration of Israel and God's fulfillment of his promises. In Rom 9–11, Paul depicts not only the temporary rejection of Jesus as Messiah, but also the future restoration of Israel. He says,

> For if their rejection is the reconciliation of the world, what will their acceptance be but life from the dead? . . . I do not want you to be ignorant of this mystery, brothers, so that you may not be conceited: Israel has experienced a hardening in part until the full number of the Gentiles has come in. And so all Israel will be saved, as it is written, "The deliverer will come from Zion; He will turn godlessness away from Jacob. And this is My covenant with them when I take away their sins." (Rom 11:15; 25–27)

Paul and True Judaism

Paul testifies from Isaiah's prophecy of the future restoration of Israel (Isa 59:20–21; 27:9; 2:2–3; 14:1–3). Isaiah was not the only one to prophesy about the future of Israel. The prophet Jeremiah said,

> 'The days are coming,' declares the Lord, when I will raise up to David a righteous Branch, a king who will reign wisely and do what is just and right in the land. In his days Judah will be saved and Israel will live in safety. This is the name by which he will be called: The Lord Our Righteousness . . . I will surely gather them from all the lands where I banish them in my furious anger and great wrath; I will bring them back to this place and let them live in safety. They will be my people, and I will be their God. I will give them singleness of heart and action, so that they will always fear me for their own good and the good of their children after them. I will make an everlasting covenant with them: I will never stop doing good to them, and I will inspire them to fear me, so that they will never turn away from me. I will rejoice in doing them good and will assuredly plant them in this land with all my heart and soul. This is what the Lord says: As I have brought all this great calamity on this people, so I will give them all the prosperity I have promised them. (Jer 23:5–6; 32:37–42 NIV)

Paul, like Jeremiah, understands that God is the one who will restore Israel unconditionally, without Israel's good works. Ezekiel also mentioned God's plan for future Israel:

> This is what the Sovereign Lord says: It is not for your sake, O house of Israel, that I am going to do these things, but for the sake of my holy name, which you have profaned among the nations where you have gone . . . For I will take you out of the nations; I will gather you from all the countries and bring you back into your own land. I will sprinkle clean water on you, and you will be clean; I will cleanse you from all your impurities and from all your idols. I will give you a new heart and put a new spirit in you; I will remove from you your heart of stone and give you a heart of flesh. And I will put my Spirit in you and move you to follow my decrees and be careful to keep my laws . . . When I have brought them back from the nations and have gathered them from the countries of their enemies, I will show myself holy through them in the sight of many nations. (Ezek 36:22–32; 39:27 NIV)

Other prophets have also mentioned God's plan to restore Israel as a whole for the sake of his holy name, such as Amos 9:11–15; Zeph 3:14–15; Zech 8:7–8; 8:13–15. So does Paul. As Arnold Fruchtenbaum notes, "God has [made] a covenant with Abraham's physical seed as well as his spiritual seed and he will always work through both. God does not give the Church up for Israel or Israel for the Church."[9] In other words, God does not choose *only* Israel or just the church but Israel and the church. God does not exclude one for the other.

So we can see that the prophets did not say God saves only Jewish people who are faithful to him, but *all* Israel—which means that God himself will restore Israel unconditionally. Thus, for Paul, in the present time God saves the remnant of Israel by grace. In the future (when Christ returns), the rest of Israel will be saved by grace, according to Rom 11.

Paul is not at all negative about Israel's future. As Campbell comments, a remnant in Paul's thought is not merely negative, reflecting failed plans or hardening of hearts. It is rather a forward-looking token of grace for the future—a saving remnant rather than a saved remnant. This is because, in Pauline eschatology, the future is still open.[10]

Is the Church the "Israel" of Galatians 6:16?

The last and most significant reason why Paul would not say God replaces Israel with the church as the true Israel is this: when he says in Gal 6:16, "And those who will walk by this rule, peace and mercy be upon them, and upon the Israel of God," the phrase "the Israel of God" refers to the Jewish people as a whole[11] as a synonym for "God's people." "Israel" was well known as the name of God's people.

However, this verse is highly controversial among scholars. Some understand this phrase to mean the Christian church has taken the place of the Jewish nation as "the true or spiritual Israel."[12]

Wright and N. A. Dahl hold the traditional view, in which Paul is thought to have taught that Gentile Christians replace Jews as the true Israel. Dahl comments that in Galatians Paul argues for a sectarian understanding of the people of God; in particular, he argues that the promise to Abraham is for those who are in Christ. Paul now uses the term "Israel of God" to refer to Christians.

---

9. Fruchtenbaum, *Israelology*, 862.

10. Campbell, *Paul and the Creation*, 110.

11. Davies, "Paul and the People," 4–39; Campbell, *Paul's Gospel*, 74–77.

12. Wright, *Climax of the Covenant*, 250; Witherington, *Grace in Galatia*, 452–53; Dahl, "Der Name Israel," 161–70; Sanders, *Paul, the Law*, 173–74.

Moreover, Dahl goes on to say that, elsewhere, Paul is perfectly capable of distinguishing between a true and false Israel, or an Israel according to the Spirit as opposed to an Israel according to the flesh. When Paul says quite explicitly that not all Israel is true Israel (cf. Rom 2:29; 9:6; Phil 3:2–3; 1 Cor 10:18; Gal 4:21–31), he means that those who believe in Jesus as the crucified Messiah are true Israel.[13] In other words, Paul identifies the Christian church as "the historic people [of] Israel."[14] This view is possible as an explicit identification of the church with "the Israel of God" if we read the RSV translation, "Peace and mercy be upon all who walk by this rule, upon the Israel of God" (Gal 6:16).

But the problem with the RSV translation is the translators have omitted the conjunction *kai,* ("and") in the Greek text, so the translation is flawed.[15] In this reading, Dahl's view is not plausible. Sanders's view—also a New Perspective view on Gal 6:16—is the same as the traditional view. Sanders asserts that in this verse, the phrase "Israel of God" refers to the church.

"Most scholars, however, have viewed the καὶ before 'the Israel of God' as epexegetical and thus have read the phrase as referring to 'those who walk by this rule' earlier in 6:16 and 'the new creation' in 6:15," Sanders says, "that is, the phrase refers to Christians. . . [T]here is substantial evidence that Paul considered Christians to be 'true Israel.' The discussion of Abraham in both Galatians 3 and Romans 4 means that those who have faith in Christ, not Jews as such, can, in Paul's view, claim that inheritance."[16] However, this interpretation is unlikely, as I will soon demonstrate.

R. Alan Cole has approached Gal 6:16 in yet a different way. What Paul says here is that believing Jews and believing Gentiles alike form the true "Israel of God." Cole states:

> If *kai* does not mean "even" but "and," then Paul would be allowing two separate and distinct groups side by side in the kingdom of God; first, those who *walk by this rule* (the principle enunciated in verse 15), and, secondly, God's Israel. But those of old Israel who do not have this "principle" are thereby automatically excluding

---

13. Dahl, "Der Name Israel," 161–70.
14. *Dictionary of Paul,* s.v. "Israel," 443.
15. This reading has been corrected in the NRSV to "And those who will follow this rule—Peace be upon them, and mercy, and upon the Israel of God."
16. Sanders, *Paul, the Law,* 174.

themselves from the true Israel, God's Israel. This is the inevitable deduction from Paul's reasoning.[17]

Cole attempts to interpret the passage in a theological and exegetical way in its broad context—yet his view still raises some questions. The problem is that in Paul's time, the difference between Christianity and Judaism had not yet clearly been distinguished, as Hans Dieter Betz points out.[18]

Paul's benediction in Gal 6:16 is similar to later Jewish benedictions: "bestow peace, happiness and blessing, grace and loving-kindness and mercy upon us and upon all Israel, your people." Betz says that Christianity was not clearly distinct from Judaism at this time; Paul might easily have used the expression for Jewish Christians who accepted his position concerning the Gentiles.[19] It seems clear that, as Betz remarks, Judaism and Christianity were not yet definitely distinguished in Paul's time.

Similar to Betz's view is that of Nanos, whose theory is that in Romans and Galatians, Gentile Christians still worshipped at the synagogue when Paul wrote these letters.[20] This is not surprising because the church in most regions did not completely separate from Israel until long after the First Jewish Revolt (66–73 CE) and in some instances for centuries later, as Daniel Boyarin argues.[21]

In fact, W. D. Davies says, "The term 'New Israel' does not appear until the second century, and the very idea of a primitive Christianity before 70 A.D. is probably mistaken."[22] For Paul, Jesus was the Jewish Messiah who completed Judaism. In this context, it is hard to maintain that the phrase "Israel of God" refers only to believing Jews.

Peter Richardson has also argued that the church did not identify itself with Israel before 160 CE. Not until one hundred years after Paul's letter to the Galatians did the church identify itself as "the true Israel."[23] This leads us to a further question: Why did no one use this verse to identify the church as "the New Israel" if Paul had already used it to refer to "New

---

17. Cole, *Galatians*, 236.
18. Betz, *Galatians*, 321–22.
19. Ibid., 323.
20. Nanos, *Mystery of Romans*, 6–9.
21. Boyarin, *Border Lines*, 70–73.
22. Davies, *Jewish and Pauline Studies*, 97; ibid., *Paul and Rabbinic Judaism*, 4th ed., lii.
23. Richardson, *Israel in the Apostolic Church*, ix.

Israel"? We cannot ignore this factor. In this context, there are two possible interpretations of Gal 6:16.

First, as W. S. Campbell has pointed out—in an important essay on Israel in *Dictionary of Paul and His letters*—that in Gal 6:15, Paul stated that in Christ, "'neither circumcision counts for anything nor uncircumcision, but a new creation.' By this, he sought to repudiate and to relativize the claims of those who wanted to force his Gentile converts in Galatia to accept circumcision—the major purpose of his letter."[24]

Second, in Gal 4:22f., Paul distinguishes between Abraham's two sons—one is born "according to the flesh" and the other "through promise." Paul's main purpose is to discourage Gentile Christians from accepting circumcision and the responsibility of keeping the whole law. Rather than show a contrast between the Israel of God and fleshly Israel (Ἰσραὴλ κατὰ σάρκα), "Paul asserts that Jesus became accursed so that 'in Christ Jesus' the blessing of Abraham might come upon the Gentiles (3:14). But there is no suggestion that the inclusion of Gentiles necessarily involves the exclusion of Jews."[25]

Third, while respecting the integrity and contingency of each letter, it is better to still interpret Gal 6:16 in some relation to Rom 9–11. There, Paul opposed the proud Gentile Christians by refusing to allow any absolute separation between the church and Israel.[26] Here, Paul indicates the Jewish people as a whole.

Finally, in Rom 15:8, Paul asserts that Christ has become (γεγενῆσθαι) a servant (διάκονον) to the Jewish people. Paul uses the perfect tense verb, which means that Christ has become—and still is—a servant or minister to the Jewish people.[27] In Gal 6:16, as Campbell indicates, the phrase "Israel of God" refers not only to Christian Jews or Gentile Christians, but to Israel as a whole. This interpretation is one possible plausible interpretation of the verse.

Ben Witherington notes that "Paul will wrestle with the fate of non-Christian Jews in Rom. 9–11, but they are not in view here."[28] However, we cannot isolate this verse from Paul's other epistles, since this term is used only here in the New Testament. For Paul, this is a mystery because Israel

---

24. Campbell, "Israel," 441.
25. Campbell, *Paul's Gospel*, 74–75.
26. Ibid., 77.
27. Ibid.
28. Witherington, *Grace in Galatia*, 453.

is beloved because of the fathers. They are heir of the promises, and at the same time, at enmity with the gospel (Rom 11:28). Therefore, Paul would not eliminate fleshly Israel and substitute the church as true Israel.

The olive tree connection functions to explain that the root of Christianity stems from Judaism. Also, Paul's olive tree analogy means that arrogant Gentile Christians must understand themselves as the addition of Gentiles to God's people, not vice versa.

Another likely possible interpretation in Gal 6:16 is that Paul simply uses "Israel" here as a synonym for "God's people." As David H. Stern notes, "both Jewish and Gentile Greek-speakers said Ἰουδαῖοι when referring to the Jews (or Judeans) as a geographic, ethnic, national, political or socio-religious entity. But Jews reserve the word 'Israel' to refer to themselves as God's people, the people of promise, whereas Gentiles did not use the term 'Israel' for themselves at all."[29]

Therefore, "Israel" was a Jewish designation. Paul is using the word "Israel" as a synonym for "God's people," with "the Israel being God's Israel," so to speak, in contrast perhaps with the Judaizers, who may in some sense be "Israel but are not of God," not God's Israel.[30] In this light, the Good News Bible's translation of Gal 6:16 is more appropriate than others in its inclusiveness: "As for those who follow this rule in their lives, may peace and mercy be with them—with them and with all of God's people!"

Regarding these two likely possible interpretations of Gal 6:16, it is most unlikely that Paul viewed the church as the true Judaism. Paul was not excluding Jews as a whole but was including Gentile believers (Rom 9: 6; 11:17–26); nor is there any implication that Paul encouraged the church to separate from the Jewish community.[31]

Equal in Christ

Did Paul ever refer to Gentiles as "Israel"? On the contrary, Paul encourages the Jew to remain as Jew and the Gentile to remain as Gentile in Christ (1 Cor 7:18). Paul says in Gal 3:28 that "there is neither Jew nor Greek" in Christ. Paul's intention is unity, but particular identity still remains. "There is neither male nor female" in Christ in the sense that we are equal in Christ, regardless of what our genders may be. Paul is hardly saying that there are

29. Stern, *Jewish New Testament Commentary*, 573.
30. Ibid.
31. Contra Watson, *Paul, Judaism*, 71–2.

no more genders in Christ. This identity could not be exchangeable. Likewise, Jewish identity remains in Christ, as Campbell emphasizes.[32]

If we consider all these aspects—the cumulative nature of Paul's theological arguments, i.e., God chose Israel for love and not just to be an instrument for him, the Mosaic covenant is like a marriage contract rather than a business contract, both Jewish and Gentile redemption has not yet been completed, and the prophets foretold that all Israel will be restored in the future—then it is reasonable to conclude that Paul would not maintain that Christianity is the true Judaism.

Most of all, Paul's benediction in Gal 6:16—in which Paul uses "Israel" to refer to the whole Jewish people or as a synonym for God's people—hardly makes the case that Paul displaces Judaism with Christianity as the true Judaism. Paul's thought is probably that the historical people of God is comprised of one people only: the Jewish people, with Gentile Christ-believers as related communities. If this is the case, then Gentile believers can never be termed "the New Israel," and Israel remains Israel. Instead, Gentile Christ-believers remain as a linked but distinct community in relation to Israel.

---

32. Campbell, *Paul's Gospel*, 74–77. Esler, in his *Conflict and Identity*, also argues against the popular view that Paul thought that, in Christ, believers are no longer Jews or Gentiles but a new entity. For Esler, Judean identity remains. For a more recent discussion, see Campbell, *Paul and the Creation*, 86–103.

8

Paul, a Hebrew of Hebrews

THE MAIN TASK OF this study has been to read Paul as Jewish in the light of contemporary scholarship after the advent of the New Perspective. In the first section, after I had shown how certain scholars have shown a strong tendency to view Paul mainly from his Hellenistic background, I went on to explore a number of recent scholars' views on Paul in his first-century Jewish context.

The New Perspective opposed generalizing tendencies in interpreting Paul's theology and brought fresh attention to Paul's understanding of law, covenant theology, and the center of his theology. Because of its fresh insights, we are able to understand Paul's relationship with Judaism more impartially. Yet the New Perspective has also brought complications to the current debate on Paul's theology and is not a solution to all the traditional problems associated with this theology.

Although this New Perspective is significant to the degree that it helps us to understand Paul and his theology in his Jewish social context and cultural background, some of these scholars still, in the traditional mold, believe Paul separated from Judaism, that he was biased against his people, and that he replaced Judaism by Christianity. Even though E. P. Sanders opposes the view that first-century Judaism was not legalistic, he still reads Paul's epistles in the traditional sense of a Pauline breach with Judaism.[1]

The current debate on Paul's theology is complicated and leads in divergent directions. Yet the basic question still remains: Who was the real

---

1. Sanders, *Paul, the Law*, 178–210.

historical Paul? My view is that the only way to progress in the current debate is to return to the biblical text and read it in its context. It is this context—Paul's Jewish roots—that is the vital element in understanding Paul's thought. However, as I have sought to maintain throughout this book, although Paul was a Diaspora Jew, his Jewish inheritance was of primary importance to his thought and must be emphasized.

What We Know of Paul

We will review what we can deduce about Paul from a historical and social perspective.

Paul's Way of Thinking

Paul's thought stands in direct relationship with Jewish tradition through *halakhah*,[2] and his Jewishness is evident in Romans, in which monotheism and the Shema are the basis of Paul's argument. Even though Paul was educated in Greek culture, his thought is firmly rooted in Judaism. His thought is molded by four central motifs of Jewish apocalyptic, whose imagery and concepts, however, he strongly modifies. Paul was a faithful Jew as demonstrated in his tendency to use inclusive *pesher* form of interpretation rather than misusing Scripture for his own ends.

Paul and Scripture

Paul's interpretation of Scripture was from a thoroughly Jewish perspective rather than simply using elements or aspects of Scripture to support his own ideas. Scripture is the primary source of Paul's thought, and his theology derives from it.

Paul was a Pharisee who was devoted to the study of the Scriptures and was educated in this process before his encounter with Christ. After his encounter with Christ, Paul continued to interpret and to reinterpret the Scripture from the Jewish perspectives of corporate solidarity and messianic fulfillment in the Christ event.

Rather than distorting first-century Judaism, Paul "learned from the scriptures the nature of God's purpose, and from current events he sought

---

2. See Tomson, *Paul and the Jewish Law*.

indication of the fulfillment."[3] He acknowledged the crucified and risen Jesus as the promised Messiah to whom the Scriptures bear witness.

Paul's interpretation of the Torah was in the context of the Christ, Jesus. For Paul, it is impossible to annul the Torah. Therefore, after Paul's encounter with Christ, Paul still probably remained a Pharisee who reinterpreted the Scripture to reveal a new meaning through Jesus, the Messiah, rather than creating his own ideas and just adding Scripture texts to back them up.

Paul did not break with Judaism following his Damascus road experience, and did not found a new religion. Luke's perception of Paul was that of a faithful Jew who was committed to the Jewish people and to the Torah in Acts.

In Gal 1:13–17, Paul's message is that of his own practice before his calling, wherein he fought against Gentiles needing to become Jews before being recognized as having full standing before God. Paul understood that Gentiles do not have to become Jews in order to be God's family. Here, Paul's point is that his gospel to the Gentiles is rooted in divine revelation and divine calling. Paul can hardly be said to have left Judaism, but he possibly "considered himself as part of a new Jewish sect."[4]

Paul's use of Scripture in Galatians is explicitly allegorical. Moreover, according to the new consensus interpretation, Paul did not exclude the Jews from salvation. Even when Paul addressed this allegory to his opponents, he wished to restore them rather than just exclude.

Paul and Covenant

Even though Paul spoke in harsh language to those Jews who opposed the gospel, he was fulfilling his call as a prophet and was therefore using the censorious language of Israel's prophets. Paul did not generalize Ἰουδαῖοι as a nation in 1 Thess 2:14 but rather used it to indicate a specific region meaning citizens of the province of Judea—referring to certain Judeans rather than all Jews.

Paul did not annul or oppose the Mosaic covenant. He did not found a new religion with a new meaning, nor did Paul replace the old covenant with the new covenant because he was a minister of the new covenant. In 2 Cor 3:4–18, Paul *compares* two covenants rather than *contrasts* them. He does

---

3. Ellis, *Paul's Use*, 135.
4. Segal, *Paul the Convert*, xiv.

not think so much in terms of static abrogation—of the replacement of one covenant by another—but rather in terms of "dynamic transformation."[5]

In Phil 3:2–11, Paul did not draw a contrast between Judaism and Christianity, nor did Paul wish to separate the church from the Jewish community. In context, Paul does not contrast one religion against another, but he compares the value of both in the light of Messiah, Jesus—though that does not mean Paul abandons one in order to embrace the other.[6] We must understand Paul in an eschatological context. For him, Jesus is the fulfillment or confirmation of the promises of Judaism.

Paul demonstrates God's faithfulness to his promise of Israel's election, not a breach with Judaism. He uses the analogy of an olive tree to illustrate that the Gentiles have not taken over the tree, and neither have the Jews been finally broken off. The wild olive shoot is grafted in, and an olive branch does not support the root, but the root supports the branches. Paul does not tell of a new olive tree. Instead, Paul confirms that the Jewish people are still God's choice because they are beloved for the sake of the fathers even though they are enemies to Christians from the standpoint of the gospel (Rom 11:28) and wished to save "all Israel" as a whole nation in Rom 11:26.

Paul and Jewishness

There is no indication that early Christianity had already separated from Jewish believers or the Jewish synagogue. In fact, Rom 14–15 points to a certain amount of social interaction between the Jewish synagogue and Gentile believers.

Paul encouraged Jewish believers to keep their Jewish identity rather than discouraging such behavior. There is no evidence that Paul discouraged Jewish believers from ceasing to practice their pattern of life. Paul, himself, demonstrated maintenance of his Jewish identity, and he urged Jewish believers to remain as Jews and Gentile believers to remain as Gentiles (1 Cor 7:17f.).

Paul would not claim that Christianity is the true Judaism, or that God replaced the church as the true Israel.[7] He never referred to Gentiles as "Israel."

5. Campbell, *Paul's Gospel*, 70.
6. Contra Sanders, *Paul and Palestinian Judaism*, 442–47.
7. Contra Wright, *Paul Really Said*, 39, 82–84.

Paul, Defined

In summary, there is no evidence that Paul left his Jewish heritage or turned against it. Rather, he remained consistent with his Jewishness—not aiming to separate Christianity from first-century Judaism.

Paul's letters can be better understood if we would re-evaluate each of Paul's letters, both in relation to the coherent structure of Paul's theology in general and with regard to the contingent interpretation necessary to account for the particular situation facing Paul in each local church. Moreover, Paul must be primarily understood within the context of first-century Judaism.

Since Paul was transformed by the Christ event, his theology is one of transformation. The old is transformed into the renewed rather than abandoned or displaced. Paul's thought probably is that the historical people of God comprises the Jewish people, with Gentile Christ-believers as related communities. If this is the case, then Gentile Christ-followers can never be termed "New Israel," and Israel remains Israel.[8] For Paul, as Douglas Harink says, "Israel's election is not only not cancelled or replaced, but in fact sustained and preserved in the apocalypse of Jesus Christ."[9]

Moreover, Paul was a Jewish reformer—viewing the world in Jewish perspective—and also the apostle for Gentiles in an eschatological context. But he did not found a new religion, nor was he against those Jewish people who did not believe in Jesus as the Messiah. For Paul, the One God of Israel was also the One God of the nations, as Mark Nanos indicates.[10] Therefore, I have argued that Jesus the Messiah was for Paul both the completion of Judaism and the confirmation of the promises, but not its displacement.

Paul has been misunderstood because of his form of argument, including his use of Scripture and his view of Jews and Gentiles in Christ, but especially of those Jews who were not convinced that Jesus was the Messiah.

Even after the advent of the New Perspective, there is still a need for Paul to be interpreted from the perspective of his Jewish context. In dialogue with contemporary New Testament scholarship, we should view Paul as a Jew living in continuity with his own traditions, albeit interpreted in the light of Christ.

---

8. Ibid., iv–v.
9. Harink, *Paul Among the Postliberals*, 24.
10. Nanos, *Mystery of Romans*, 179–201.

Bibliography

Alford, Henry. *The Greek Testament*. 4 vols. 1845–1860. Reprint, Chicago: Moody, 1958.
Anderson, R. Dean, Jr. *Ancient Rhetorical Theory and Paul*. Rev. ed. Leuven, Belgium: Peeters, 1999.
Aquinas, Thomas. *Super Epistolas S. Pauli Lectura*. Edited by R. Cai. Turin, Italy: Marietti, 1953.
Augustine. *Augustine on Romans: Propositions from the Epistle to the Romans and Unfinished Commentary on the Epistle to the Romans*. Chico, CA: Scholars, 1982.
Badenas, Robert. *Christ: The End of the Law: Romans 10:4 in Pauline Perspective*. Sheffield, UK: JSOT, 1985.
Bahnsen, Greg L., et al. *Five Views on Law and Gospel*. Grand Rapids: Zondervan, 1996.
Bailey, J. W. *The First and Second Epistles to the Thessalonians*. Interpreter's Bible XI. Nashville: Abingdon, 1955.
Bailey, John, and James Clark. "I and II Thessalonians." *IB* 2 (1955) 279–80.
Baird, William. *From Deism to Tübingen*. Vol. 1 of *History of New Testament Research*. Minneapolis: Fortress, 1992.
Baker, David L. *Two Testament One Bible: A Study of the Theological Relationship between the Old and New Testaments*. Downers Grove: InterVarsity, 1991.
Barclay, J. M. G. *Jews in the Mediterranean Diaspora: From Alexander to Trajan (323 BCE–117 CE)*. Berkeley: University of California Press, 1996.
———. *Obeying the Truth*. Edinburgh: T. & T. Clark, 1988.
Barrett, C. K. *Acts*. 2 vols. London: T. & T. Clark, 1994.
———. "The Allegory of Abraham, Sarah, and Hagar in the Argument of Galatians." In *Rechtfertigung: Festschrif Für Ernst Käsemann zum 70. Geburtstag*, edited by J. Friedrich et al., 1–16. Tübingen, Germany: Mohr-Siebeck, 1976.
———. *Epistle to the Romans*. Black's New Testament Commentary. Peabody: Hendrickson, 1991.
———. *First Epistle to the Corinthians*. Black's New Testament Commentary. Peabody: Hendrickson, 1968.
———. *Second Epistle to the Corinthians*. Black's New Testament Commentary. Peabody: Hendrickson, 1973.

Bibliography

Barth, Karl. *The Epistle to the Philippians*. Translated by J. W. Leitch. Richmond: John Knox, 1962.

———. *The Epistle to the Romans*. Translated by Edwyn C. Hoskyns. Oxford: Oxford University Press, 1968.

Bassler, Jouette M., ed. *Thessalonians, Philippians, Galatians, Philemon*. Vol. 1 of *Pauline Theology*. Minneapolis: Fortress, 1991.

Baur, F. C. *The Church History of the First Three Centuries*. Translated by Allan Menzies. London: Williams & Norgate, 1878.

———. *Paul the Apostle of Jesus Christ: His Life and Works, His Epistles and Teachings*. 2 vols. Peabody: Hendrickson, 2003.

Bean, E. William. *New Treasures: A Perspective of New Testament Teachings through Hebraic Eyes*. Oak Greek: Cornerstone, 1995.

Beare, F. W. *A Commentary on the Epistle to the Philippians*. Peabody: Hendrickson, 1959.

Beasley-Murray, G. R. *2 Corinthians*. Broadman Bible Commentary 11. Nashville: Broadman, 1975.

Becker, Jurgen. *Paul, Apostle to the Gentiles*. Translated by O. C. Dean Jr. Louisville: Westminster John Knox, 1993.

Beet, J. A. *II Corinthians*. London: Hodder & Stoughton, 1882.

Beker, J. Christiaan. "The Faithfulness of God and the Priority of Israel in Paul's Letter to the Romans." *Reformed Theological Review* 79 (1986).

———. "The Faithfulness of God and the Priority of Israel in Paul's Letter to the Romans." In *Christians Among Jews and Gentiles: Essay in Honor of Krister Stendahl on His Sixty-fifth Birthday*, edited by G. W. E. Nickelsburg and G. W. Macrae, 10–16. Philadelphia: Fortress, 1980.

———. *Paul the Apostle: The Triumph of God in Life and Thought*. Philadelphia: Fortress, 1980.

———. "Recasting Pauline Theology." In vol. 1 of *Pauline Theology*, edited by Jouette M. Bassier, 15–24. Minneapolis: Fortress, 1991.

———. *The Triumph of God: The Essence of Paul's Thought*. Translated by Loren T. Stuckenbruck. Minneapolis: Fortress, 1990.

Bengel, J. A. *Gnomon of the New Testament on Galatians*. Translated by James Bryce. Edinburgh: T. & T. Clark, 1860.

———. *Gnomon of the New Testament on Romans*. Translated by James Bryce. Edinburgh: T. & T. Clark, 1752.

Bernard, J. H. *The Second Epistle to the Corinthians*. Expositor's Greek Testament. Grand Rapids: Eerdmans, 1990.

Best, Ernest. *The First and Second Epistles to the Thessalonians*. Peabody: Hendrickson, 1986.

———. *The Letter of Paul to the Romans*. Cambridge Bible Commentary. Cambridge: Cambridge University, 1967.

Betz, Hans Dieter. *Galatians: A Commentary on Paul's Letter to the Churches in Galatia*. Philadelphia: Fortress, 1979.

———. "Transferring a Ritual: Paul's Interpretation of Baptism in Romans 6." In *Paul in His Hellenistic Context*, edited by Troels Engberg-Pedersen, 84–118. Minneapolis: Fortress, 1995.

Blass, F., and A. Debrunner. *A Greek Grammar of the New Testament*. Translated and revised by R. Runk. Chicago: Chicago University Press, 1961.

Bibliography

Boccaccini, Gabriele. *Middle Judaism: Jewish Thought 300 BCE to 200 CE*. Minneapolis: Fortress, 1991.

Bockmuehl, Markus N. A. "'The Noachide Commandments' and New Testament Ethics: With Special Reference to Acts 15 and Pauline Halakah." *RB* 102 (1995) 72–102.

———. *Revelation and Mystery in Ancient Judaism and Pauline Christianity*. Grand Rapids: Eerdmans, 1997.

Boers, Hendrikus. *The Justification of the Gentiles: Paul's Letters to the Galatians and Romans*. Peabody: Hendrickson, 1994.

———. "We Who Are by Inheritance Jews, Not from Gentiles, Sinners." *JBL* 111 (1992) 273–91.

Boman, Thorlief. *Hebrew Thought Compared with Greek*. New York: Norton, 1970.

Borgen, Peder, and Soren Giversen, eds. *The New Testament and Hellenistic Judaism*. Peabody: Hendrickson, 1995.

Bornkamm, Gunther. *Paul*. Translated by D. M. G. Stalker. Minneapolis: Fortress, 1971.

Boyarin, Daniel. *Border Lines: The Partition of Judaeo-Christianity*. Philadelphia: University of Pennsylvania Press, 2004.

———. *A Radical Jew: Paul and the Politics of Identity*. Berkeley: University of California Press, 1994.

Brändle, Rudolf, and Ekkehard W. Stegemann. "The Formation of the First 'Christian Congregations' in Rome in the Context of the Jewish Congregations." In *Judaism and Christianity in First-Century Rome*, edited by Kal P. Donfried and Peter Richardson, 117–27. Grand Rapids: Eerdmans, 1998.

Brauch, Manfred T. *Hard Sayings of Paul*. Downers Grove: InterVarsity, 1989.

Bray, Gerald. *Biblical Interpretation: Past and Present*. Downers Grove: InterVarsity, 1996.

Briggs, S. "Galatians." In vol. 2 of *Searching the Scriptures II*, edited by E. Schüssler Fiorenza, 218–36. New York: Crossroad, 1994.

Bring, R. *Commentary on Galatians*. Philadelphia: Muhlenberg, 1961.

Brown, Colin, ed. *The New International Dictionary of New Testament Theology*. 4 vols. Grand Rapids: Zondervan, 1971.

Brown, F. *The New Brown-Driver-Briggs-Gesenius Hebrew and English Lexicon*. Peabody: Hendrickson, 1979.

Bruce, F. F. *1 and 2 Corinthians*. Grand Rapids: Eerdmans. London: Marshall, Morgan, & Scott, 1971.

———. *1 and 2 Thessalonians*. Word Biblical Commentary. Waco, TX: Word, 1982.

———. *The Book of the Acts*. Rev. ed. Grand Rapids: Eerdmans, 1988.

———. *The Epistle of Paul to the Galatians: A Commentary on the Greek Text*. New International Greek Testament Commentary. Grand Rapids: Eerdmans, 1982.

———. *The Epistle of Paul to the Romans*. Tyndale New Testament Commentaries 6. Downers Grove: InterVarsity, 1963.

———. *Israel and the Nations: The History of Israel from the Exodus to the Fall of the Second Temple*. Revised by David F. Payne. Downers Grove: InterVarsity, 1997.

———. *New Testament History*. New York: Doubleday, 1971.

———. *Paul: Apostle of the Heart Set Free*. Grand Rapids: Eerdmans, 1977.

Brunner, Emil. *The Letter of Paul to the Romans*. Philadelphia: Westminster, 1959.

Byrne, Brendan. *Romans*. Sacra Pagina 6. Collegeville, MN: Liturgical, 1996.

Buell, Denise Kimber, and Caroline Johnson Hodge. "The Politics of Interpretation: The Rhetoric of Race and Ethnicity in Paul." *JBL* 123 (2004) 235–51.

Bultmann, Rudolf. *History of the Synoptic Tradition*. Peabody: Hendrickson, 1963.

Bibliography

———. *Theology of the New Testament.* 2 vols. Translated by Kendrick Grobel. New York: Scribner's, 1951–55.

Burton, Ernest De Witt. *A Critical and Exegetical Commentary on the Epistle to the Galatians.* 1921. Reprint, Edinburgh: T. & T. Clark, 1988.

———. *Syntax of the Moods and Tenses in New Testament Greek.* Edinburgh: T. & T. Clark, 1898.

Byrne, Brendan. *Romans.* Sacra Pagina 6. Collegeville, MN: Liturgical, 1996.

Cadbury, H. J., and K. Lake. *The Beginnings of Christianity.* 5 vols. London: Macmillan, 1933.

Calvin, John. *Commentaries on the Epistles of Paul the Apostle to the Corinthians.* Vol. 20. Translated by the Rev. John Pringle. Grand Rapids: Baker, 1989.

———. *Commentaries on the Epistles of Paul the Apostle to the Galatians and Ephesians.* Vol. 21. Translated by the Rev. William Pringle. Grand Rapids: Baker, 1989.

———. *Commentaries on the Epistle of Paul the Apostle to the Romans.* Vol. 19. Translated and edited by the Rev. John Owen. Grand Rapids: Baker, 1989.

Campbell, William S. "All God's Beloved in Rome: Jewish Roots and Christian Identity." In *Celebrating Romans: Template for Pauline Theology,* edited by Sheila E. McGinn, 67–82. Grand Rapids: Eerdmans, 2004.

———. "Beyond the New Perspective: Reflection on the Contemporary Evaluation of Sanders and Dunn." Paper presented at the British New Testament Conference, Manchester, UK, 2001.

———. "The Contribution of Traditions to Paul's Theology." In *1 and 2 Corinthians,* vol. 2 of *Pauline Theology,* edited by David M. Hay, 234–54. Minneapolis: Fortress, 1993.

———. "Divergent Images of Paul and His Mission." In *Reading Israel in Romans: Legitimacy and Plausibility of Divergent Interpretation,* edited by Cristina Grenholm and Daniel Patte, 187–211. Romans through History and Cultures Series. Harrisburg, PA: Trinity, 2000.

———. "The Interpretation of Paul: Beyond the New Perspective." Presentation given at the New Testament Postgraduate Seminar, Oxford University, 2001.

———. "Israel." In *Dictionary of Paul and His Letters,* edited by Gerald F. Hawthorn et al., 441–46. IVP Bible Dictionary Series 7. Downers Grove: InterVarsity, 1993.

———. "Martin Luther and Paul's Epistle to the Romans." In *the Bible as Book: The Reformation,* edited by Orlaith O'Sullivan, 103–14. London: British Library, 2000.

———. "Olive Tree." In *Dictionary of Paul and His Letters,* edited by Gerald F. Hawthorn et al., 642–44. IVP Bible Dictionary Series 7. Downers Grove: InterVarsity, 1993.

———. *Paul and the Creation of Christian Identity.* London: T. & T. Clark, 2006.

———. *Paul's Gospel in an Intercultural Context: Jew and Gentile in the Letter to the Romans.* Frankfurt: Lang, 1991.

———. "Perceptions of Compatibility between Christianity and Judaism in Pauline Interpretation." *BibInt* 13 (2003) 298–316.

———. Review of *Paul in the Greco-Roman World,* by J. Paul Sampley. *Theology* 110 (2006) 294.

———. "The Rule of Faith in Romans 12:1–15:13: The Obligation of Humble Obedience as the Only Adequate Response to the Mercies of God." In *Pauline Theology III, Romans,* edited by David M. Hay and E. Elizabeth Johnson, 256–86. Minneapolis: Fortress, 1995.

———. *Unity and Diversity in Christ: Interpreting Paul in Context; Collected Essays.* Eugene, OR: Cascade, 2013.

Bibliography

Catchpole, D. R. "Paul, James and the Apostolic Decree." *NTS* 23 (1977) 428-44.
Chepey, Stuart D. "Nazirites in Late Second Temple Judaism." PhD diss., University Oxford, 2002.
Chilton, Bruce. *Rabbi Paul*. New York: Doubleday, 2004.
Chilton, Bruce, and Jacob Neusner. *Judaism in the New Testament: Practice and Beliefs*. New York: Routledge, 1995.
Cohen, Shaye J. D. *From the Maccabees to the Mishnah*. Philadelphia: Westminster, 1989.
———. *The Beginnings of Jewishness: Boundaries, Varieties*. Los Angeles: University of California Press, 1999.
Cohn-Sherbok, Dan. *Rabbinic Perspectives on the New Testament*. Studies in the Bible and Early Christianity 28. Lewiston, NY: Mellen, 1990.
Cole, R. Alan. *Galatians*. Tyndale New Testament Commentaries. Grand Rapids: Eerdmans, 1991.
Conybeare, W. J., and J. S. Howson. *The Life and Epistles of St. Paul*. Grand Rapids: Eerdmans, 1989.
Conzelmann, Hans. *Gentiles - Jews - Christians*. Translated by M. Eugene Boring. Minneapolis: Fortress, 1992.
Cosgrove, C. H. "The Law and the Spirit: An Investigation into the Theology of Galatians." PhD diss., Princeton Theological Seminary, 1984.
———. "The Mosaic Covenant Teaches Faith: A Study in Galatians 3." *Westminster Theological Journal* 41 (1978) 146-64.
Cousar, Charles B. *Galatians*. Interpretation: A Bible Commentary for Teaching and Preaching. Louisville: John Knox, 1982.
Cranfield, C. E. B. *A Critical and Exegetical Commentary on the Epistle to the Romans*. 2 vols. ICC on the Holy Scriptures of the Old and New Testaments 28. Edinburgh: T. & T. Clark, 1975-1979.
———. *On Romans and Other New Testament Essays*. Edinburgh: T. & T. Clark, 1998.
———. "'The Works of the Law' in the Epistle to the Romans." *JSNT* 43 (1991) 89-101.
Dahl, Nils Akstrup. "Der Name Israel: Zur Auslegung von Gal. 6:16." *Judaica* 6 (1950) 161-70.
———. *Studies in Paul: Theology for the Early Christian Mission*. Minneapolis: Augsburg, 1977.
———. Review of *Paul and Palestinian Judaism*, E. P. Sanders. *RSR* 4 (1978) 153-58.
Das, Andrew A. *Paul, the Law, and the Covenant*. Peabody: Hendrickson, 2001.
Daube, David. *The New Testament and Rabbinic Judaism*. London: Athlone, 1956.
———. "Rabbinic Methods of Interpretation and Hellenistic Rhetoric." *HUCA* 22 (1949) 239-62.
Davies, W. D. *Jewish and Pauline Studies*. Philadelphia: Fortress, 1984.
———. *Paul and Rabbinic Judaism: Some Rabbinic Elements in Pauline Theology*. London: SPCK, 1955.
———. *Paul and Rabbinic Judaism*. 4th ed. Philadelphia: Fortress, 1980.
———. "Paul and the People of Israel." *NTS* 24 (1977) 4-39.
Dean, William. "Hebrew Law and Postmodern Historicism." Address given at Iliff School of Theology, unpublished manuscript, 1987.
Deidun, T. J. *New Covenant Morality in Paul*. AnBib 89. Rome: Pontifical Biblical Institute, 1981.
Deming, Will. "Paul and Indifferent Things." In *Paul in the Greco-Roman World*, edited by Paul Sampley, 384-403. Harrisburg, PA: Trinity, 2003.

Bibliography

Denney, James. *The Epistles to the Thessalonians.* Expositor's Bible. London: Hodder & Stoughton, 1892.

———. *The Second Epistle to the Corinthians.* Expositor's Bible. London: Hodder & Stoughton, 1894.

Dodd, C. H. *According to the Scriptures: The Sub-Structure of New Testament Theology.* London: Nisbet, 1957.

———. *The Epistle of Paul to the Romans.* London: Hodder & Stoughton, 1949.

———. *The Mind of Paul: Change and Development.* Manchester: Rylands Library, 1934.

Donaldson, Terence L. "The 'Curse of the Law' and the Inclusion of the Gentiles, Galatians 3:13–14." NTS 32 (1986) 94–112.

———. *Paul and the Gentiles: Remapping the Apostle's Convictional World.* Minneapolis: Fortress, 1997.

Donfried, Karl P. *Paul, Thessalonica, and Early Christianity.* Grand Rapids: Eerdmans, 2002.

———, ed. *The Romans Debate.* Rev. ed. Peabody: Hendrickson, 1991.

Donfried, Karl P., and Johannes Beutler, eds. *The Thessalonians Debate: Methodological Discord or Methodological Synthesis.* Grand Rapids: Eerdmans, 2000.

Donfried, Karl P., and Peter Richardson, eds. *Judaism and Christianity in First-century Rome.* Grand Rapids: Eerdmans, 1998.

Dunn, James D. G. *The Epistle to the Galatians.* Black's New Testament Commentary. Peabody: Hendrickson, 1993.

———. "The Incident at Antioch (Gal 2:11–18)." JSNT 18 (1983) 3–57.

———. *Jesus, Paul and the Law: Studies in Mark and Galatians.* Louisville: Westminster John Knox, 1990.

———. *The Partings of the Ways between Christianity and Judaism and Their Significance for the Character of Christianity.* Philadelphia: Trinity, 1991.

———. "The Relationship between Paul and Jerusalem According to Galatians 1 and 2." NTS 28 (1982) 461–78.

———. *Romans.* 2 vols. Word Biblical Commentary 38. Dallas, TX: Word, 1988.

———. *The Theology of Paul the Apostle.* Grand Rapids: Eerdmans, 1998.

———. "Who Did Paul Think He Was? A Study of Jewish-Christian Identity." NTS 45 (1999) 174–93.

———, ed. *Jews and Christians: The Parting of the Ways A.D. 70 to 135.* Grand Rapids: Eerdmans, 1999.

Du Toit, Andre. "A Tale of Two Cities: 'Tarsus or Jerusalem?' Revisited." NTS 46 (2000) 375–402.

Eastman, Susan G. "'Cast Out the Slave Woman and Her Son': The Dynamic of Exclusion and Inclusion in Galatians 4:30." JSNT 3 (2006) 309–36.

Edersheim, Alfred. *The Life and Times of Jesus the Messiah.* Peabody: Hendrickson, 1886.

Ehrensperger, Kathy. "Paul's Identity: 'A Hebrew of Hebrews' or a Hellenistic Confluence of Ideas?" Review of *Paul Beyond the Judaism/Hellenism Divide*, edited by Troels Engberg-Pedersen. JBV 24 (2003) 249–54.

———. *Paul and the Dynamics of Power: Communication and Interaction in the Early Christ-Movement.* London: T. & T. Clark, 2007.

———. *Paul at the Crossroads of Culture: Theologizing in the Space Between.* London: T. & T. Clark, 2013.

———. "Scriptural Reasoning: The Dynamic That Informed Paul's Theologizing." IBS 26 (2004) 32–52.

———. *That We May Be Mutually Encouraged: Feminism and the New Perspective in Pauline Studies*. New York: T. & T. Clark, 2004.

Elliott, Neil. *Liberating Paul: The Justice of God and the Politics of the Apostle*. Maryknoll, NY: Orbis, 2000.

———. "Paul and Politics of the Empire." In *Paul and Politics: Ekklesia, Israel, Imperium, Interpretation, Essays in Honor of Krister Stendahl*, edited by Richard Horsley, 17–39. Harrisburg, PA: Trinity, 2000.

———. *The Rhetoric of Romans: Argumentative Constraint and Strategy and Paul's Dialogue with Judaism*. Sheffield: Sheffield Academic, 1990.

Ellis, E. Earle. *Paul's Use of the Old Testament*. Grand Rapids: Eerdmans, 1957.

Elwell, Walter A., and Robert W. Yarbrough, eds. *Readings from the First-Century World: Primary Sources for New Testament Study*. Grand Rapid: Baker, 1998.

Engberg-Pedersen, Troels. *Paul and the Stoics*. Louisville: Westminster John Knox, 2000.

———. ed. *Paul in His Hellenistic Context*. Minneapolis: Fortress, 1995.

———. ed. *Paul Beyond the Judaism/Hellenism Divide*. Louisville: Westminster John Knox, 2001.

Epstein, Isidore. *Judaism: A Historical Presentation*. London: Penguin, 1959.

Esler, Philip F. *Conflict and Identity in Romans: The Social Setting of Paul's Letter*. Minneapolis: Fortress, 2003.

———. *The First Christians in Their Social Worlds: Social-Scientific Approaches to New Testament Interpretation*. London. New York: Routledge, 1994.

———. "Social Identity, the Virtues, and the Good Life: A New Approach to Romans 12:1–15:13." *BTB* 33 (2003) 51–63.

Evans, Craig A., ed. *The Interpretation of Scripture in Early Judaism and Christianity: Studies in Language and Tradition*. Journal for the Study of the Pseudepigrapha Supplement Series 33. Sheffield: Sheffield Academic, 2000.

Evans, Craig A., and James A. Sanders, eds. *Paul and the Scriptures of Israel*. Studies in Scripture in Early Judaism and Christianity 1; Journal for the Study of the New Testament Supplement Series 83. Sheffield: JSOT, 1993.

Evans, E. *The Epistles of Paul the Apostle to the Corinthians*. Clarendon Bible 13. Oxford: Clarendon, 1930.

Fallon, F. T. *2 Corinthians*. New Testament Message 11. Dublin: Veritas, 1980.

Finegan, Jack. *The Archeology of the New Testament*. Boulder, CO: Westview, 1981.

Fischer, John. "Galatians from a Messianic Jewish Perspective." In *Messianic Outreach* 9 (1989) 1–5.

———. "The Jewish Root of Bible and Christianity." Lecture given at Saint Petersburg Theological Seminary, 1991.

———. "Messianic Congregations Should Exists and Should Be Very Jewish." In *How Jewish Is Christianity?*, edited by Stanley N. Gundry and Louis Goldberg, 129–39. Grand Rapids: Zondervan, 2003.

———. "Yes, We Do Need Messianic Congregations!" In *How Jewish Is Christianity?*, edited by Stanley N. Gundry and Louis Goldberg, 50–64. Grand Rapids: Zondervan, 2003.

Fitzmyer, Joseph A. "Glory Reflected on the Face of Christ (2 Cor 3:7–4:6) and a Palestinian Jewish Motif." *TS* 42 (1981) 630–44.

———. *Romans: A New Translation with Introduction and Commentary*. Anchor Bible 33. New York: Doubleday, 1992.

———. *The Semitic Background of the New Testament*. Grand Rapids: Eerdmans, 1997.

Bibliography

Flusser, David. *Jewish Sources in Early Christianity*. New York: Adama, 1987.
Frame, James Everett. *A Critical and Exegetical Commentary on Epistles of St. Paul to the Thessalonians*. Edinburgh: T. & T. Clark, 1988.
Fruchtenbaum, Arnold G. "A Danger of Throwing out the Baby with the Bath Water." In *How Jewish Is Christianity?*, edited by Louis Goldberg and Stanley N. Gundry, 66–78. Grand Rapids: Zondervan, 2003.
———. *Israelology: The Missing Link in Systematic Theology*. Tustin, CA: Ariel Ministries, 2001.
———. "Messianic Congregations May Exist within the Body of Messiah, as Long as They Don't Function Contrary to the New Testament." In *How Jewish Is Christianity?*, edited by Stanley N. Gundry and Louis Goldberg, 111–28. Grand Rapids: Zondervan, 2003.
Fuller, Daniel P. *Gospel and Law: Contrast or Continuum?* Grand Rapids: Eerdmans, 1980.
———. "Paul and the Works of the Law." *WTJ* 38 (1975–1976) 28–42.
Furnish, Victor Paul. *II Corinthians: A New Translation with Introduction and Commentary*. Anchor Bible Commentary 32A. Garden City, NY: Doubleday, 1984.
Gager, John G. *The Origins of Anti-Semitism: Attitudes toward Judaism in Pagan and Christian Antiquity*. Oxford: Oxford University Press, 1985.
———. *Reinventing Paul*. Oxford: Oxford University Press, 2000.
Garive, Alfred E. *Romans*. Century Bible. London: Caxton, n.d.
Garlington, D. "The New Perspective on Paul: An Appraisal Two Decades Later." *CTR* 2 (2005) 17–38.
Gasque, W. Ward. *History of the Interpretation of the Acts of the Apostles*. Peabody: Hendrickson, 1980.
Gaston, Lloyd. "Faith in Romans 12 in the Light of the Common Life of the Roman Church." In *Common Life in the Early Church Essays Honoring Graydon F. Snyder*, edited by Julian V. Hills, 258–64. Harrisburg, PA: Trinity, 1998.
———. *Paul and the Torah*. Vancouver: University of British Columbia Press, 1987.
Gaventa, Beverly Roberts. *From Darkness to Light: Aspects of Conversion in the New Testament*. Overtures to Biblical Theology. Philadelphia: Fortress, 1986.
Gilliard, Frank D. "The Problem of the Antisemitic Comma between 1 Thessalonians 2:14–15." *NTS* 35 (1989) 481–502.
Godet, Frederic Louis. *Commentary on Romans*. Grand Rapids: Kregel, 1997.
Goodwin, Mark J. *Paul: Apostle of the Living God*. Harrisburg, PA: Trinity, 2001.
Goudge, H. L. *The Second Epistle to the Corinthians*. London: Methuen, 1927.
Grabbe, Lester L. *An Introduction to First Century Judaism*. Edinburgh: T. & T. Clark, 1996.
Gruen, Erich S. *Heritage and Hellenism: The Reinvention of Jewish Tradition*. Berkeley: University of California Press, 1998.
Gundry, Robert H. "Grace, Works and Staying Saved in Paul." *Bib* 66 (1985) 1–38.
———. *A Survey of the New Testament*. 3rd ed. Grand Rapids: Zondervan, 1994.
Guthrie, Donald. *Galatians*. Edited by Ronald E. Clements and Matthew Black. New Century Bible Commentary. Grand Rapids: Eerdmans, 1973.
Hafemann, Scott J. *Paul, Moses, and the History of Israel*. Peabody: Hendrickson, 1996.
Haldane, Robert. *Exposition of the Epistle to the Romans*. 1839. Reprint, London: Banner of Truth, 1958.
Hansen, G. W. *Galatians*. Downers Grove: InterVarsity, 1994.

Bibliography

Hanson, Anthony T. "The Midrash in II Corinthians 3: A Reconsideration." *JSNT* 9 (1980) 2–28.

———. *Studies in Paul's Technique and Theology.* Grand Rapids: Eerdmans, 1974.

Hanson, R. P. C. *Allegory and Event: A Study of the Sources and Significance of Origin's Interpretation of Scripture.* London: John Knox, 1959.

———. *2 Corinthians.* Torch Bible Commentaries. London: SCM, 1967.

Harink, Douglas. *Paul Among the Postliberals: Pauline Theology beyond Christendom and Modernity.* Grand Rapids: Brazos, 2003.

———. "Paul and Israel: An Apocalyptic Reading." Paper presented at the Pauline Soteriological Group at the SBL Annual Meeting, Philadelphia, PA, 2005.

Harrison, Everett F. "Romans." Edited by Frank E. Gaebelein et al. Expositor's Bible Commentary 10. Grand Rapids: Zondervan, 1976.

Harvey, Graham. *The True Israel: Use of the Names Jew, Hebrew and Israel in Ancient Jewish and Early Christian Literature.* AGJU 35. Leiden Brill, 1996

Hatch, Edwin. *The Influence of Greek Ideas and Usages.* Edited by Fairbairn, A. M. Peabody: Hendrickson, 1995.

Hawthorn, Gerald F. *Philippians.* Word Biblical Commentary 43. Waco, TX: Word, 1983.

Hawthorn, Gerald F., et al., eds. *Dictionary of Paul and His Letters.* Downers Grove: InterVarsity, 1993.

Hay, David M., ed. *Pauline Theology* II. Minneapolis: Fortress, 1993.

Hay, David M., and Elizabeth E. Johnson, eds. *Looking Back, Pressing On.* Vol. 4 of *Pauline Theology.* Atlanta: Scholars, 1997.

———. *Romans.* Vol. 3 of *Pauline Theology.* Minneapolis: Fortress, 1995.

Hays, Richard B. *Echoes of Scripture in the Letters of Paul.* New Haven: Yale University Press, 1989.

———. "The Role of Scripture in Paul's Ethics." In *Theology and Ethics in Paul and His Interpreters: Essays in Honour of Victor Paul Furnish,* edited by E. H. Lovering and J. S. Summney, 30–48. Nashville: Abingdon, 1996.

Hendrickson, William. *Exposition of Paul's Epistle to the Romans.* 2 vols. Grand Rapids: Baker, 1980.

———. *Philippians.* Grand Rapid: Baker, 1962.

Hengel, Martin. *Acts and the History of Earliest Christianity.* Eugene, OR: Wipf & Stock, 2003.

———. *Judaism and Hellenism: Studies in Their Encounter in Palestine During the Early Hellenistic Period.* Eugene, OR: Wipf & Stock, 2003.

———. *The Pre-Christian Paul.* Philadelphia: Trinity, 1991.

Heschel, Abraham J. *The Prophets.* 2 vols. New York: Harper & Row, 1962.

Hester, J. D. "The Rhetorical Structure of Galatians 1:11–2:14." *JBL* 103 (1984) 223–33.

Hill, C. *Hebrews and Hellenists.* Minnesota: Fortress, 1992.

Hilton, Michael, and G. Marshall. *The Gospel and Rabbinic Judaism.* Hoboken, NJ: KTAV, 1988.

Hock, Ronald F. "Paul and Greco-Roman Education." In *Paul in the Greco-Roman World,* edited by J. Paul Sampley, 209. Harrisburg, PA: Trinity, 2003.

Hodge, Charles. *Commentary on the Epistle to the Romans.* Grand Rapids: Eerdmans, 1994.

———. *An Exposition of the Second Epistle to the Corinthians.* New York: Armstrong, 1891. Reprint, Edinburgh: Banner of Truth, 1959.

Holmberg, Bengt. "Jewish versus Christian Identity in the Church." *RB* (1998) 397–425.

Bibliography

———. "The Methods of Historical Reconstruction in the Scholarly 'Recovery' of Corinthian Christianity." In *Christianity at Corinth: The Quest for the Pauline Church*, edited by E. Adams and D. Horrel, 255–71. Louisville: Westminster John Knox, 2004.

———. *Paul and the Power: The Structure of Authority in the Primitive Church as Reflected in the Pauline Epistles*. Philadelphia: Fortress, 1978.

Holtz, Barry W., ed. *Back to the Sources*. Summit, 1986.

Horsley, Richard A. *Paul and Empire: Religion and Power in Roman Imperial Society*. Harrisburg, PA: Trinity, 1997.

———. "Rhetoric and Empire—and 1 Corinthians." In *Paul and Politics: Ekklesia, Israel, Imperium Interpretation*, edited by Richard A. Horsley, 72–102. Harrisburg, PA: Trinity, 2000.

———. ed. *Paul and Politics: Ekklesia, Israel, Imperium, Interpretation*. Harrisburg, PA: Trinity, 2000.

Hort, F. J. A. *Judaistic Christianity*. New York: Macmillan, 1898.

Howie, Carl G. *The Creative Era: Between the Testament*. Richmond, VA: John Knox, 1964.

Hübner, Hans. *Law in Paul's Thought*. Translated by James C. G. Greig. Edinburgh: T. & T. Clark, 1984.

———. "Pauli Theologiae Proprium." *NTS* 26 (1979–1980) 445–73.

Hughes, P. E. *Paul's Second Epistle to the Corinthians*. New International Commentary on the New Testament 47. Grand Rapids: Eerdmans, 1962.

Jeffers, James S. *The Greco-Roman World of the New Testament Era: Exploring the Background of Early Christianity*. Downers Grove: InterVarsity, 1999.

Jervell, Jacob. "The Letter to Jerusalem." In *The Romans Debate*, edited by K. Donfried, 53–64. Peabody: Hendrickson, 1991.

———. *Luke and the People of God: A New Look at Luke-Acts*. Minneapolis: Augsburg, 1972.

———. *The Unknown Paul: Wssays on Luke-Acts and Early Christian History*. Minneapolis: Augsburg, 1984.

Jewett, Robert. *Christian Tolerance: Paul's Message to the Modern Church*. Philadelphia: Westminster, 1982.

———. "The Law and the Co-Existence of Jews and Gentiles in Romans." *Interpretation* 39 (1985) 341–56.

Johnson, Alan F. *Romans: The Freedom Letter*. Everyman's Bible Commentary. 2 vols. Chicago: Moody, 1984, 1985.

Juster, Dan. *Jewish Roots: A Foundation of Biblical Theology*. Shippensburg, PA: Destiny Image, 1995.

Kadushin, Max. *Organic Thinking: A Study in Rabbinic Thought*. Philadelphia: Bloch, 1938.

———. *The Rabbinic Mind*. Philadelphia: Bloch, 1972.

Kaiser, Walter C., Jr. *The Old Testament in Contemporary Preaching*. Grand Rapids: Baker, 1973.

———. *The Messiah in the Old Testament*. Grand Rapids: Zondervan, 1995.

Kaiser, Walter C., Jr., et al., eds. *Hard Sayings of the Bible*. Downers Grove: InterVarsity, 1992.

Käsemann, Ernst. *Commentary on Romans*. Translated edited by Geoffrey W. Bromiley. Grand Rapids: Eerdmans, 1980.

———. "Justification and Salvation History in the Epistle to the Romans." In *New Testament Questions for Today*, 60–78. London: SCM, 1971.

Bibliography

———. "Paul and Israel." In *New Testament Questions of Today*, 183-87. London: SCM, 1969.

———. *Perspectives on Paul*. London: SCM, 1971.

———. "The Righteousness of God in Paul." In *New Testament Questions for Today*, 168-82. London: SCM, 1969.

Kaylor, R. David. *Paul's Covenant Community: Jew and Gentile in Romans*. Atlanta: John Knox, 1978.

Keck, Leander E. *The Letter of Paul to the Philippians*. The Interpreter's One-Volume Commentary on the Bible. Edited by C. M. Laymon. New York: Abingdon, 1971.

———. *Paul and His Letters*. Philadelphia: Fortress, 1988.

Kee, Howard Clark. *Knowing the Truth: A Sociological Approach to New Testament Interpretation*. Minneapolis: Fortress, 1989.

Kelley, Shawn. *Racializing Jesus: Race, Ideology and the Formation of Modern Biblical Scholarship*. London: Routledge, 2004.

Kennedy, H. A. A. *The Epistle to the Philippians*. Expositor's Greek Testament. Edited by W. R. Nicoll. Grand Rapids: Eerdmans, 1976.

Kim, Seyoon. *Paul and the New Perspective*. Grand Rapids: Eerdmans, 2002.

Kirk, K. E. *The Epistle to the Romans*. Claredon Bible. Oxford: Clarendon, 1937.

Kline, Meredith G. *The Treaty of the Great King*. Grand Rapids: Eerdmans, 1963.

Knox, John. *The Epistle to the Romans*. Interpreter's Bible. Nashville: Abingdon, 1951.

Knox, W. L. *The Acts of the Apostles*. Cambridge: Cambridge University Press, 1948.

Koptak, Paul E. "Rhetorical Identification in Paul's Autobiographical Narrative 1:13-2:14." In *The Galatians Debate: Contemporary Issues in Rhetorical and Historical Interpretation*, edited by Mark D. Nanos, 157-68. Peabody: Hendrickson, 2002.

Kruse, Colin G. *Paul, the Law, and Justification*. Peabody: Hendrickson, 1997.

———. *Second Epistle of Paul to the Corinthians: An Introduction and Commentary*. Tyndale New Testament Commentaries. Leicester, UK: InterVarsity, 1987.

Laato, Timo. *Paul and Judaism: Anthropological Approach*. Translated by T. McElwain. South Florida Studies in the History of Judaism 115. Atlanta: Scholars, 1995.

Lapide, Pinchas, and Peter Stuhlmacher. *Paul: Rabbi and Apostle*. Minneapolis: Augsburg, 1984.

Lee, Bernard J. *The Galilean Jewishness of Jesus*. New York: Paulist, 1988.

Leenhardt, Franz J. *The Epistle to the Romans*. London: Lutterworth, 1961.

Lenski, R. C. H. *The Interpretation of St. Paul's Epistle to the Romans*. Minneapolis: Augsburg. 1936.

Levinskaya, Irina. *The Book of Acts in Its First-century Setting: Diaspora Setting 5*. Grand Rapids: Eerdmans, 1996.

Lietzmann, Hans. *An die Roimer*. HNT. Tübingen, Germany: Mohr, 1933.

Lieu, Judith M. *Image and Reality: The Jews in the World of the Christians in the Second Century*. Edinburgh: T. & T. Clark, 1996.

———. "'Impregnable Ramparts and Walls of Iron': Boundary and Identity in Early 'Judaism' and 'Christianity.'" *NTS* 48 (2002) 297-31.

Lightfoot, John. *A Commentary on the New Testament from the Talmud and Hebraica*. 4 vols. Peabody: Hendrickson, 1995.

Lightfoot, J. B. *Notes on the Epistles of Paul*. J.B. Lightfoot's Commentary on the Epistles of St. Paul. Peabody: Hendrickson, 1995.

Longenecker, Richard N. *Biblical Exegesis in the Apostolic Period*. Grand Rapids: Eerdmans, 1975.

Bibliography

———. *The Christology of Early Jewish Christianity*. Naperville, IL: Allenson, 1970.

———. *Galatians*. Word Biblical Commentary. Dallas, TX: Word, 1990.

———. *Luke-Acts*. Edited by Tremper Longman and David E. Garland. Expositor's Bible Commentary 10. Rev. ed. Grand Rapids: Zondervan, 2007.

———. *Paul, Apostle of Liberty*. New York: Harper & Row, 1964.

———. ed. *The Road from Damascus*. Grand Rapids: Eerdmans, 1997.

Lowe, Malcolm. "Who Were the Ἰουδαῖοι?" *Novum Testamentum* 18 (1976) 101–30.

Lüdemann, Gerd. *Opposition to Paul in Jewish Christianity*. Translated by M. Eugene Boring. Minneapolis: Fortress, 1989.

Lührmann, Dieter. *A Continental Commentary on Galatians*. Translated by O. C. Dean Jr. Minneapolis: Fortress, 1992.

Luther, Martin. *Commentary on Romans*. Translated by J. Theodore Mueller. Grand Rapids: Kregel, 1976.

———. *Lectures on Galatians Chapters 1–4*. Vol. 26 of *Luther's Works*. Edited by Jaroslav Pelikan and Walter A. Hansen. Saint Louis: Concordia, 1963.

———. *Career of the Reformer IV*. Vol. 34 of *Luther's Works*. Edited by Helmut T. Lehmann. Philadelphia: Muhlenberg, 1960.

———. *Lectures on Romans*. Vol. 25 of *Luther's Works*. Edited by Hilton C. Oswald. Saint Louis: Concordia, 1972.

Lyons, George. *Pauline Autobiography: Toward a New Understanding*. Atlanta: Scholars, 1985.

Machen, J. Gresham. *The Origin of Paul's Religion*. Grand Rapids: Eerdmans, 1925.

Malherbe, Abraham J. *The Letters to the Thessalonians: A New Translation with Introduction and Commentary*. Anchor Bible Commentary 32B. New York: Doubleday, 2000.

———. "Determinism and Free Will in Paul: The Argument of 1 Corinthians 8–9." In *Paul in His Hellenistic Context*, edited by Troels Engberg-Pedersen, 231–55. Minneapolis: Fortress, 1995.

Marguerat, Daniel. *The First Christian Historian: Writing the 'Acts of the Apostles.'* Cambridge: Cambridge University Press, 2002.

Marshall, I. Howard. *1 and 2 Thessalonians*. New Century Bible: London, 1983.

Martin, Ralph P. *Philippians*. Tyndale New Testament Commentary. Grand Rapids: Eerdmans, 1987.

Martyn, J. Louis. *Galatians: A New Translation with Introduction and Commentary*. Anchor Bible 33. New York: Doubleday, 1997.

———. *Theological Issues in the Letters of Paul*. Nashville: Abingdon, 1997.

Matlock, R. Barry. *Unveiling the Apocalyptic Paul: Paul's Interpreters and the Rhetoric of Criticism*. Sheffield: Sheffield Academic, 1996.

McGinn, Sheila E. *Celebrating Romans: Template for Pauline Theology*. Grand Rapids: Eerdmans, 2004.

McKnight, S. *Galatians: The NIV Application Bible Commentary*. Grand Rapids: Zondervan, 1995.

Meeks, Wayne, ed. *The First Urban Christians: The Social World of the Apostle Paul*. New Haven: Yale University Press, 1983.

———. "Judgment and the Brother: Romans 14:1–15:13." In *Tradition and Interpretation in the New Testament: Essays in Honor of E. Earle Ellis*, edited by G .G. Hawthorne and O. Edtz, 290–300. Grand Rapids: Eerdmans, 1987.

Bibliography

―――. "Judaism, Hellenism, and the Birth of Christianity." In *Paul Beyond the Judaism/Hellenism Divide*, edited by T. Engberg-Pedersen, 17–28. Louisville: Westminster John Knox, 2001.

―――. *The Writings of St. Paul*. New York: Norton, 1972.

Metzger, Bruce M. *A Textual Commentary on the Greek New Testament*. New York: United Bible Societies, 1971.

Meyer, H. A. W. *Epistle to the Corinthians*. 6th ed. Meyer's Commentary on the New Testament. Revised and edited by William P. Dickson. Winona Lake, IN: Alpha, 1980.

―――. *The Epistle to the Romans*. 6th ed. Meyer's Commentary on the New Testament. Revised and edited by William P. Dickson. Winona Lake, IN: Winona Lake: Alpha, 1980.

―――. *The Epistle to the Galatians*. 5th ed. Translated by G. H. Venables and Henry E. Jacob. New York: Funk & Wagnalls, 1884.

Michael, J. H. *The Epistle to the Philippians*. London: Hodder & Stoughton, 1928.

Minear, Paul S. *The Obedience of Faith: The Purposes of Paul in the Epistle to the Romans*. London: SCM, 1971.

Moffatt, James. *The First and Second Epistles to the Thessalonians*. Expositor's Greek Testament. Edited by W. Robertson Nicoll. Grand Rapids: Eerdmans, 1990.

Moo, Douglas J. *A Commentary on the Epistle to the Romans*. The New International Commentary. Grand Rapids: Eerdmans, 1996.

Moore, George F. *Judaism: In the First Centuries of the Christian Era*. 2 vols. Peabody: Hendrickson, 1997.

Morris, Leon. *1 and 2 Thessalonians*. Rev. ed. Tyndale New Testament Commentaries. Grand Rapids: Eerdmans, 1984.

―――. *1 Corinthians: An Introduction and Commentary*. Tyndale New Testament Commentaries 7. Leicester, UK: InterVarsity, 1990.

―――. *The Apostolic Preaching of the Cross*. Grand Rapids: Eerdmans, 1965.

―――. *The Epistle to the Romans*. Grand Rapids: Eerdmans, 1988.

―――. *Galatians: Paul's Charter of Christian Freedom*. Downers Grove: InterVarsity, 1996.

―――. *New Testament Theology*. Grand Rapids: Zondervan, 1986.

Moule, H. C. G. *The Epistle to the Romans*. Cambridge Bible for Schools and Colleges. Cambridge: Cambridge University, 1887.

Moulton, James Hope. *Prolegomena. A Grammar of New Testament Greek 1*. Edinburgh: T. & T. Clark, 1908.

Munck, Johannes. *Christ and Israel: An Interpretation of Romans 9–11*. Philadelphia: Fortress, 1967.

―――. *Paul and the Salvation of Mankind*. Atlanta: John Knox, 1959.

Murphy-O'Connor, Jerome. *Paul: A Critical Life*. Oxford: Clarendon, 1996.

Murphy-O'Connor, Jerome, and James G. Charlesworth, eds. *Paul and the Dead Sea Scrolls*. New York: Crossroad, 1990.

Murray, John. *Epistle to the Romans*. New International Commentary on the New Testament. Grand Rapids: Eerdmans, 1925.

Nanos, Mark D. "Challenging the Limits That Continue to Define Paul's Perspective on Jews and Judaism." In *Reading Israel in Romans*, edited by Cristina Grenholm and Daniel Patte, 212–24. Harrisburg, PA: Trinity, 2000.

Bibliography

———. "How Inter-Christian Approaches to Paul's Rhetoric Can Perpetuate Negative Valuations of Jewishness—Although Proposing to Avoid That Outcome." *BibInt* 3 (2005) 255–67.

———. "Introduction." In *The Galatians Debate: Contemporary Issues in Rhetorical and Historical Interpretation*, edited by Mark D. Nanos, xi–xlii. Peabody: Hendrickson, 2002.

———. "The Inter- and Intra-Jewish Political Context of Paul's Letter to the Galatians." In *Paul and Politics: Ekklesia, Israel, Imperium, Interpretation*, edited by Richard Horsley, 146–59. Harrisburg, PA: Trinity, 2000.

———. *The Irony of Galatians: Paul's Letter in First-Century Context*. Minneapolis: Fortress, 2002.

———. "The Jewish Context of the Gentile Audience Addressed in Paul's Letter to the Romans." *Catholic Biblical Quarterly* 61 (1999) 283–304.

———. *The Mystery of Romans*. Minneapolis: Fortress, 1996.

———. "What Was at Stake in Peter's 'Eating with Gentiles' at Antioch?" In *The Galatians Debate: Contemporary Issues in Rhetorical and Historical Interpretation*, edited by Mark D. Nanos, 282–318. Peabody: Hendrickson, 2002.

———, ed. *The Galatians Debate: Contemporary Issues in Rhetorical and Historical Interpretation*. Peabody: Hendrickson, 2002.

Neusner, Jacob. *Introduction to Rabbinic Literature*. New York: Doubleday, 1994.

———. *The Midrash an Introduction*. London: Aronson, 1994.

———. *Studying Classical Judaism a Primer*. Westminster: John Knox, 1991.

Nickelsburg, George W. E. and Stone, Michael E. *Ancient Judaism and Christian Origins: Diversity, Continuity and Transformation*. Minneapolis: Fortress, 2003.

———. *Faith and Piety in Early Judaism: Texts and Documents*. Valley Forge, PA: Trinity, 1991.

Nygren, Anders. *Commentary on Romans*. 1944. Reprinted by Philadelphia: Fortress, 1949.

O'Neill, J. C. *Paul's Letters to the Romans*. Pelican New Testament Commentaries. Baltimore: Penguin, 1979.

Overman, J. Andrew. "Kata nomon Pharisaios: A Short History of Paul's Pharisaism." In *Pauline Conversations in Context: Essays in Honor of Calvin J. Roetzel*, edited by J. C. Anderson, P. Sellow, and C. Setzet, 180–93. Sheffield: Sheffield Academic, 2002.

Pearson, B. A. "1 Thessalonians 2:13:16; A Deutero-Pauline Interpolation." *Harvard Theological Review* 64 (1971) 79–94.

Perelmuter, Hayim G. *Siblings. Rabbinic Judaism and Early Christianity at Their Beginnings*. New York: Paulist, 1989.

Perkins, Pheme. *Abraham's Divided Children: Galatians and the Politics of Faith*. Harrisburg, PA: Trinity, 2001.

Plummer, Alfred. *A Commentary on St. Paul's First Epistle to the Thessalonians*. London: Scott, 1918.

———. *First Epistle of St. Paul to the Corinthians*. ICC. Edinburgh: T. & T. Clark, 1994.

———. *Second Epistle of St. Paul to the Corinthians*. ICC. Edinburgh: T. & T. Clark, 1985.

Pritchard, James B., ed. *The Ancient Near East: An Anthology of Texts and Pictures*. 2 vols. Princeton: Princeton University Press, 1958.

Räisänen, Heikki. "Galatians 2:16 and Paul's Break with Judaism." *NTS* 31 (1985) 543–53.

———. *Jesus, Paul, and Torah*. Translated by David E. Orton. Sheffield: JSOT, 1992.

Bibliography

———. "Legalism and Salvation by the Law." In *Die Paulinische Literatur und Theologi*, edited by S. Pedersen, 63–83. Aarhus, Denmark: Forlaet Aros, 1980.

———. *Paul and the Law*. Philadelphia: Fortress, 1983.

———. "Paul, God, and Israel: Romans 9–11 in Recent Research." In *The Social World of Formative Christianity and Judaism: Essays in Tribute to Howard Clark Kee*, edited by J. Neusner et al., 178–206. Philadelphia: Fortress, 1988.

———. "Paul's Theological Difficulties with the Law." In *Studia Biblica*, edited by E. Livingstone, 301–20. Sheffield: JSOT, 1980.

Ramsey, William M. *A Historical Commentary on St. Paul's Epistle to the Galatians*. Grand Rapids: Baker, 1979.

———. *Paul and the Law*. Philadelphia: Fortress, 1983.

Reicke, Bo. *Re-examining Paul's Letters: The History of the Pauline Correspondence*. Harrisburg, PA: Trinity, 2001.

Rendall, Frederic. *The Epistle to the Galatians*. Expositor's Greek Testament. Grand Rapids: Eerdmans, 1990.

Richardson, Peter. "An Architectural Case for Synagogue as Associations." In *The Ancient Synagogue: From its Origins until 200 CE*, edited by Olsseon B. and M. Zetterholm, 90–117. Stockholm: Almqvist & Wiksell, 2003.

———. *Israel in the Apostolic Church*. Cambridge: Cambridge University Press, 1969.

Robertson, Archibald, and Alfred Plummer. *The First Epistle of St Paul to the Corinthians*. Edinburgh: T. & T. Clark, 1994.

Robertson, A. T. *A Grammar of the Greek New Testament in the Light of Historical Research*. Nashville: Broadman, 1934.

Robinson, John A. T. *Wrestling with Romans*. Philadelphia: Westminster, 1979.

Roetzel, Calvin J. *Paul: The Man and the Myth*. Minneapolis: Fortress, 1999.

———. *The Letters of Paul*. Westminster: John Knox, 1998.

Rosenblatt, Marie-Eloise. *Paul the Accused: His Portrait in the Acts of the Apostles*. Collegeville, MN: Liturgical, 1995.

Rosner, Brian S. *Paul, Scripture, and Ethics: A Study of 1 Corinthians 5–7*. Grand Rapids: Baker, 1994.

Rothschild, Fritz A., ed. *Jewish Perspectives on Christianity*. New York: Continuum, 1996.

Rudolph, David J. "A Jew to the Jews: Jewish Contours of Pauline Flexibility in 1 Corinthians 9:19–23." PhD diss. University of Oxford, 2002.

Russell, D. S. *Between the Testaments*. Philadelphia: Fortress, 1960.

Safrai, Samuel. *The Jewish People in the First Century*. Vol. 2 of Compendium Rerum Iudaicarum ad Novum Testamentum. Philadelphia: Fortress, 1976.

———. "Talmudic Literature as an Historical Source for Second Temple Period." *Mishkan* 2–1 (1992–1993) 121–35.

Saldarini, Anthony J. *Pharisees Scribes and Sadducees in Palestinian Society*. Edinburgh: T. & T. Clark, 1988.

Sampley, J. Paul. "The Week and the Strong: Paul's Careful and Crafty Rhetorical Strategy in Romans 14:1–15:13." In *The Social World of the First Urban Christians: Studies on Honour of Wayne A. Meeks*, edited by White L. M. and Yarbrough, 40–52. Minneapolis: Fortress, 1994.

———. ed. *Paul in the Greco-Roman World: A Handbook*. Harrisburg, PA: Trinity, 2003.

Sanday, William, and Arthur C. Headlam. *A Critical and Exegetical Commentary on the Epistle to the Romans*. New York: Scribner's, 1926.

Bibliography

Sanders, E. P. Foreword to *Paul and Rabbinic Judaism: Some Rabbinic Elements in Pauline Theology*, by W. D. Davies, vii–xvii. 50th anniv. ed. Mifflintown, PA: Sigler, 1998.

———. *Paul*. Past Masters. Oxford: Oxford University Press, 1991.

———. *Paul and Palestinian Judaism*. Philadelphia: Fortress, 1977.

———. *Paul, the Law, and the Jewish People*. Minneapolis: Fortress, 1983.

Sandmel, Samuel. *The Genius of Paul*. New York: Schocken, 1970.

———. *Judaism and Christian Beginnings*. New York: Oxford University Press, 1978.

Schiffmann, L. H. *Who Was A Jew? Rabbinic and Halakhic Perspectives on the Jewish-Christian Schism*. Hoboken, NJ: Ktav, 1985.

Schlatter, Adolf. *Romans: The Righteousness of God*. Translated by Siegfried S. Schatzmann. Peabody: Hendrickson, 1995.

Schoeps, H. J. *Paul: The Theology of the Apostle in the Light of Jewish Religious History*. Translated by Harold Knight. Philadelphia: Westminster, 1961.

Scholem, Gershom. *The Messianic Idea in Judaism*. New York: Shocken, 1971.

Schreiner, Thomas. *Romans*. Baker Exegetical Commentary on the New Testament 6. Grand Rapids: Baker, 1998.

Schultz, Samuel. *The Gospel of Moses*. Chicago: Moody, 1974.

Schürer, Emil. *The History of the Jewish People in the Age of Jesus Christ*. 4 vols. Edinburgh: T. & T. Clark, 1991.

Schweitzer, Albert. *The Mysticism of Paul the Apostle*. 3rd ed. Translated by William Montgomery. Baltimore: John Hopkins University Press, 1998.

———. *Paul and His Interpreters: A Critical History*. New York: Macmillan, 1951.

Scott, J. Julius, Jr. *Customs and Controversies*. Grand Rapids: Baker, 1995.

Segal, Alan F. "Paul's Experience and Romans 9–11." *Princeton Seminary Bulletin Supplementary Issue: The Church and Israel: Romans 9–11* 1 (1995) 56–70.

———. *Paul the Convert*. New Haven: Yale University Press, 1990.

Shanks, Hershel. *Christianity and Rabbinic Judaism*. Washington, DC: Biblical Archaeology Society, 1992.

Shires, Henry M. *The Eschatology of Paul in the Light of Modern Scholarship*. Philadelphia: Westminster, 1966.

Shulam, Joseph. *A Commentary on the Jewish Roots of Romans*. Baltimore: Messianic Jewish, 1997.

Shum, Shiu-Lun. *Paul's Use of Isaiah in Romans: A Comparative Study of Paul's Letter to the Romans and the Sibylline and Qumran Sectarian Texts*. Wissenschaftliche Untersuchungen Zum Neuen Testament 156. Tübingen, Germany: Mohr-Siebeck, 2002.

Sloyan, Gerard S. *Is Christ the End of the Law?* Philadelphia: Westminster, 1978.

Smart, James. *Doorway to a New Age: A Study of Paul's Letter to the Romans*. Philadelphia: Westminster, 1972.

Spicq, Ceslas. *Theological Lexicon of the New Testament*. 3 vols. Translated and edited by Ernest. Peabody: Hendrickson, 1994.

Stanley, Christopher D. *Arguing with Scripture: The Rhetoric of Quotations in the Letters of Paul*. New York: T. & T. Clark, 2004.

———. *Paul and the Language of Scripture: Citation Technique in the Pauline Epistles and Contemporary Literature*. Society for New Testament Studies Monograph Series 69. Cambridge: Cambridge University Press, 1992.

Stendahl, Krister. *Final Account: Paul's Letter to the Romans*. Minneapolis: Fortress, 1995.

———. *Paul Among Jews and Gentiles*. Philadelphia: Fortress, 1976.

Bibliography

Stern, David H. *Jewish New Testament Commentary.* Clarksville, MD: Jewish New Testament, 1992.

———. *Restoring the Jewishness of the Gospel.* Clarksville, MD: Jewish New Testament, 1998.

Stirewalt, M. Luther. *Paul, the Letter Writer.* Grand Rapids: Eerdmans, 2003.

Stott, John. *Romans: God's Good News for the World.* Downers Grove: InterVarsity, 1994.

Stowers, Stanley K. *A Rereading of Romans.* New Haven: Yale University Press, 1994.

———. "Romans 7. 7-25 as Speech-in-Character (προσωποποιία)." In *Paul in His Hellenistic Context,* edited by Troels Engberg-Pedersen, 180-202. Minneapolis: Fortress, 1995.

Stuhlmacher, Peter. *Paul's Letter to the Romans.* Translated by Scott J. Hafemann. Louisville: Westminster John Knox, 1994.

———. *Reconciliation, Law, and Righteousness: Essays in Biblical Theology.* Philadelphia: Fortress, 1986.

———. *Revisiting Paul's Doctrine of Justification: With an Essay by Donald A. Hagner.* Downers Grove: InterVarsity, 2001.

———. "The Theme of Romans." *Australian Biblical Review* 361 (1988) 31-44.

Sumney, Jerry L. *Identifying Paul's Opponents: The Question of Method in 2 Corinthians.* Sheffield: Sheffield Academic, 1990.

Tannehill, Robert C. "Rejection by Jews and Turning to Gentiles: The Pattern of Paul's Mission in Acts." In *Luke-Acts and the Jewish People: Eight Critical Perspectives,* edited by Joseph B. Tyson, 83-101. Minneapolis: Augsburg, 1988.

Tasker, R. V. G. *The First and Second Letter of Paul to the Corinthians.* Tyndale New Testament Commentaries 8. Grand Rapids: Eerdmans, 1958.

Tellbe, Mikael. *Paul between Synagogue and State: Christians, Jews, and Civic Authorities in 1 Thessalonians, Romans, and Philippians.* Coniectanea Biblica New Testament Series 34. Stockholm: Almqvist & Wiksell, 2001.

Tenny, Merrill C. *New Testament Survey.* Revised by Walter M. Dunnett. Grand Rapids: Eerdmans, 1985.

Thackeray, Henry St. J. *The Relation of St. Paul to Contemporary Jewish Thought.* New York: Macmillan, 1900.

Thielman, Frank. "From Plight to Solution: A Jewish Framework for Understanding Paul's View of the Law in Galatians and Romans." VT Supp. 61. Leiden: Brill, 1989.

———. *Paul and the Law: A Contextual Approach.* Downers Grove: InterVarsity, 1994.

Thomas, Robert L. *1 and 2 Thessalonians.* Edited by Frank E. Gaebelein et al. Expositor's Bible Commentary 11. Grand Rapids: Zondervan, 1978.

Thorsteinsson, Runar M. *Paul's Interlocutor in Romans 2: Function and Identity in the Context Ancient Epistolography.* Stockholm: Almqvist & Wiksell, 2003.

Thrall, M. E. *The First and Second Letter of Paul to the Corinthians.* Cambridge Bible Commentary. Cambridge: Cambridge University Press, 1965.

Thuren, Lauri. *Derhetorizing Paul: Dynamic Perspective on Pauline Theology and the Law.* Harrisburg, PA: Trinity, 2000.

Tomson, Peter J. *'If This Be from Heaven . . .': Jesus and the New Testament Authors in Their Relationship to Judaism.* Sheffield: Sheffield Academic, 2001.

———. *The Image of the Judeo-Christians in Ancient Jewish and Christian Literature.* WUNT 158. Tübingen, Germany: Mohr Siebeck, 2003.

———. *Paul and the Jewish Law: Halakha in the Letters of the Apostle to the Gentiles.* Minneapolis: Fortress, 1990.

———. "Paul's Jewish Background in View of His Law-Teaching in 1 Corinthians 7." In *Paul and the Mosaic Law: The Third Durham-Tübingen Research Symposium on Earliest Christianity and Judaism*, edited by J. D. G. Dunn, 251–70. Tübingen, Germany: Mohr Siebeck, 1996.

Tyson, Joseph B. *Luke, Judaism, and the Scholars: Critical Approaches to Luke-Acts*. Columbia: University of South Carolina Press, 1999.

———. ed. *Luke-Acts and the Jewish People: Eight Critical Perspectives*. Minneapolis: Augsburg, 1988.

van Buren, Paul. *According to the Scripture: The Origins of the Church's Old Testament*. Grand Rapids: Eerdmans, 1998.

———. *The New Testament and Mythology and Other Basic Writings*. Edited by Schubert M. Ogden. Philadelphia: Fortress, 1984.

van Unnik, W. C. *Tarsus or Jerusalem: The City of Paul's Youth*. Translated by George Ogg. London: Epworth, 1962.

Vermes, Geza. *The Dead Sea Scrolls in English*. 3rd ed. London: Penguin, 1987.

———. *The Dead Sea Scrolls: Qumran in Perspective*. Philadelphia: Fortress, 1977.

———. *Jesus the Jew*. Philadelphia: Fortress, 1981.

Watson, Francis B. *Paul, Judaism, and the Gentiles: A Sociological Approach*. Cambridge: Cambridge University Press, 1986.

———. "The Two Roman Congregations: Romans 14:1–15:13." In *The Romans Debate*, edited by Karl P. Donfried, 203–15. Peabody: Hendrickson, 1991.

Wedderburn, A. G. M. *The Reasons for Romans*. Edinburgh: T. & T. Clark, 1988.

Wenham, David. *Paul: Follower of Jesus or Founder of Christianity?* Grand Rapids: Eerdmans, 1995.

Westcott, Frederick Brooke. *St. Paul and Justification, Being an Exposition of the Teaching in the Epistles to Rome and Galatia*. London: Macmillan, 1913.

Westerholm, Stephen. *Israel's Law and the Church's Faith: Paul and His Recent Interpreters*. Eugene, OR: Wipf & Stock, 1998.

———. *Preface to the Study of Paul*. 2nd ed. Grand Rapids: Eerdmans, 1997.

Whiteley, D. E. H. *The Theology of St. Paul*. 2nd ed. Oxford: Blackwell, 1974.

Wilson, G. B. *2 Corinthians*. A Digest of Reformed Comment. Edinburgh: Banner of Truth, 1979.

Wilson, Marvin R. *Our Father Abraham: Jewish Root of the Christian Faith*. Grand Rapids: Eerdmans, 1789.

Wilson, S. G. *Luke and the Law*. Cambridge: Cambridge University Press, 1983.

Witherington, Ben, III. *Grace in Galatia: A Paul's Letter to the Galatians*. Grand Rapids: Eerdmans, 1998.

———. *The Acts of the Apostles*. Grand Rapids: Eerdmans, 1998.

Witherup, Ronals D. *Paul*. New York: Paulist, 2003.

Wrede, William. *Paulus*. 2nd ed. Tübingen, Germany: Mohr, 1907.

Wright, N. T. *The Climax of the Covenant: Christ and the Law in Pauline Theology*. Philadelphia: Fortress, 1992.

———. *The New Testament and the People of God I: Christian Origins and the Question of God*. Minneapolis: Fortress, 1992.

———. "Paul's Gospel and Caesar's Empire." In *Paul and Politics: Ekklesia, Israel, Imperium, Interpretation: Essays in Honour of Krister Stendahl*, edited by Richard Horsley, 160–83. Harrisburg, PA: Trinity, 2000.

Bibliography

———. "Romans and Theology Paul." In Romans, vol. 3 of *Pauline Theology*, edited by David M. Hay and E. Elizabeth Johnson, 30–67. Minneapolis: Fortress, 1995.

———. *What Saint Paul Really Said: Was Paul of Tarsus the Real Founder of Christianity?* Grand Rapids: Eerdmans, 1997.

Wuest, Kenneth S. *Galatians in the Greek New Testament for the English Reader.* Grand Rapids: Eerdmans, 1994.

Young, Brad H. *Paul the Jewish Theologian: A Pharisee Among Christians, Jews, and Gentiles.* Peabody: Hendrickson, 1997.

Zetterholm, Magnus. *The Formation of Christianity at Antioch: A Social-Scientific Approach to the Separation between Judaism and Christianity.* New York: Routledge, 2002.

Ziesler, John. *The Epistle to the Galatians.* London: Epworth, 1992.

———. *Paul's Letter to the Romans.* Philadelphia: Trinity, 1989.

Author Index

Anderson, R. D., 42
Aquinas, Thomas, 144

Bailey, John, 123n171
Barclay, John M. G., 13–14, 16, 22
Barrett, C. K., 76n58, 79, 92, 112, 165
Barth, Karl, 76n58
Baur, Ferdinand Christian, 6–9, 10, 11, 23, 24, 29, 87n7, 123n171, 155
Beker, J. Christiaan, 29–34, 51–53, 60, 128
Bengel, J. A., 154
Betz, Hans Dieter, 12, 98, 109, 114–15, 116, 155–56, 161, 178
Boyarin, Daniel, 9–10, 11, 23, 149–50, 178
Bray, Gerald, 67n21, 73
Briggs, S., 113
Bruce, F. F., 49n45, 76n58, 79, 87, 91n15, 144
Buell, Denise Kimber, 147–48n266
Bultmann, Rudolf, 32n50, 44, 60, 76n57
Burton, Ernest De Witt, 95–96, 97, 102, 103–4, 108, 154–55, 161
Byrne, Brendan, 82

Campbell, William S., 15, 28, 69, 63–65, 67, 76n58, 77–78, 80–81, 105, 106–7n85, 109, 130–31, 134, 136n218, 139, 141, 148–49, 152–53, 167, 168, 169–70, 176, 179, 181
Chrysostom, John, 53
Clark, John, 123n171
Cohen, 105, 107n86
Cohen, Shaye J. D., 102–3
Cohn-Sherbok, Dan, 67–68, 70, 72, 139, 147
Cole, R. Alan, 98, 102, 111, 157, 162, 177–78
Cousar, Charles B., 107n
Cranfield, Charles E. B., 44, 45, 76n58, 79

Dahl, N. A., 176–77
Daube, David, 20, 110–11, 166
Davies, W. D., 9, 22, 23–24, 25, 45–48, 59–60, 105, 106, 107n, 109, 124–25, 131, 137–38, 178
Dean, William, 65
Deming, Will, 15
Dodd, C. H., 24–25, 44, 45, 76n57, 79, 136–37, 143–44
Donaldson, Terence, 64
Donfried, Karl Paul, 128
Dunn, James D. G., 4, 26, 29, 48–50, 51, 54, 60, 69n28, 76–77n58, 99, 102, 106, 115–16, 118, 158–60, 162

Author Index

Eastman, Susan G., 110, 121–22
Ehrensperger, Kathy, 18–19, 29–30, 41–43, 69, 75 170
Elliott, Neil, 28–29, 60
Ellis, E. E., 72–73, 84–85
Engberg-Pedersen, Troels, 11, 19
Esler, Philip F., 69, 124, 153n286
Eusebius, 151

Finnegan, Jack, 87
Fischer, John, 134–35, 163
Fitzmer, Joseph A., 74, 79, 150–52
Fruchtenbaum, Arnold, 108, 175–76
Fuller, Daniel P., 56
Furnish, Victor Paul, 130

Gager, John G., 53–54, 123n171, 127n
Gaston, Lloyd, 53, 54, 132n207, 140
Gaventa, Beverly Roberts, 96–97, 102
Gruen, Erich S., 21
Guthrie, Donald, 96, 98, 102, 103

Hafemann, Scott, 131
Hanson, Anthony T., 77, 81
Hanson, R. P. C., 111, 113
Harink, Douglas, 140–41, 169, 171, 173, 186
Hays, Richard B., 73n45, 82, 116–17, 120
Headlam, Arthur C., 76n57
Hegel, G. W. F., 8
Hegesippus, 151
Hengel, Martin, 20–21, 86–87, 93–94, 103, 107–8n87
Herder, J. G. von, 8
Heschel, Abraham J., 122–23, 126n183
Hillel, 20, 71, 93, 110, 112, 166
Hock, Ronald F., 16–17
Hodge, Charles, 147–48n266
Hübner, Hans, 49n45, 55, 61

Irenaeus, 144
Ismael ben Elisha, 71

Jervell, Jacob, 129

Kaiser, Walter C., Jr., 132
Käsemann, Ernst, 44, 60, 76n57, 77, 130

Kelley, Shawn, 8
Knox, W. L., 91n15

Laato, Timo, 56
Lapide, Pinchas, 65–66
Lenski, R. C. H., 144
Longenecker, Richard N., 17, 66, 68, 90nn12–13, 91–92, 97–98, 102, 111–13, 116, 117–18, 120, 156, 161, 162
Lüdemann, Gerd, 93
Lührmann, Dieter, 111, 157, 162
Luther, Martin, 44, 55, 58, 61
Lyons, 96, 102, 103

Malherbe, Abraham J., 11–12, 125–26
Marcion, 2
Marguerat, Daniel, 88n8
Martyn, J. Louis, 99–100, 102, 104, 105n77, 116, 120, 157–58, 162
Merkabah, 27
Minear, Paul S., 150, 152
Moffatt, James, 126–27n186
Moo, Douglas, 141
Morris, Leon, 108–9, 145, 164
Munck, Johannes, 24, 26, 127, 155, 161, 162

Nahman b. Issaac, 78
Nanos, Mark D., 10, 29–30, 38–41, 56–57, 66, 69, 89, 101–2, 104, 105n77, 149, 152, 153, 160–61, 162, 178, 186

Origen, 143, 144
Overman, J. Andrew, 5

Philo, 22, 111, 113, 151
Plummer, Alfred, 130, 164

Räisänen, Heikki, 3, 4, 47n29, 49n45, 50–51, 53, 63, 123, 127n190
Richardson, Peter, 178
Rosner, Brian, 70
Rudolph, David J., 91–93, 132, 135, 165, 166

Author Index

Sample, J. Paul, 14
Sanday, William, 76n57
Sanders, E. P., 4, 9, 23, 25–26, 29, 46–48, 49n45, 50–55, 57–58, 60, 85, 130, 134, 137–38, 148, 156, 162, 182
Schoeps, H. J., 137, 143
Schreiner, Thomas, 49n45, 82
Schürer, Emil, 46
Schweitzer, Albert, 30, 31–32, 59, 60
Segal, Alan F., 24n4, 26–28, 29, 60, 99, 109, 122
Shulam, Joseph, 77
Stanley, Christopher D., 83, 84n89
Stendahl, Krister, 25, 26, 54n67, 59, 60
Stern, David H., 151–53
Stowers, Stanley K., 12–13
Stuhlmacher, Peter, 49n45, 60

Tannehill, Robert C., 88n8
Tellbe, Mikael, 125n179
Thackeray, Henry St. J., 80n73, 83
Thielman, Frank, 56

Thorsteinsson, Runar M., 81–82, 83
Tomson, Peter J., 21, 25, 29–30, 34–38, 42, 65, 165

Van Buren, 22n84
Van Unnik, W. C., 17

Watson, Francis, 4, 79, 135, 136, 138–39, 144–45, 146n262, 148
Westerholm, Stephen, 49n45, 55–56
Wette, Wilhelm Martin Leberecht de, 87n7
Whiteley, D. E. H., 144
Witherington, Ben, III, 88n8, 90nn13–14, 100–101, 102, 105, 110, 116, 118–19, 120, 158, 159–60, 162, 179
Wrede, William, 58–59
Wright, N. T., 4, 139–41, 169, 171
Wuest, Kenneth S., 113–14

Young, Brad, 61

Ancient Document Index

OLD TESTAMENT

Genesis

2:24	70n33
11:30	112–13
12:3	49
15:1–21	3
16–21	120
16:15	112
18:8	49
21	70, 117
21:2–3	112
21:9	112
21:10	115, 117, 118, 121
22:5	72, 146

Exodus

3:15	133
17:11	72
19	3
19:3–7	172
19:5–8	172
19:6	170
20:12–17	70n33
32:30–32	129
33:19	146

Leviticus

18:5	74, 77
27	3

Numbers

6:1–21	88
21:8	72
25:1–5	98
25:6–15	98

Deuteronomy

3:1–5	171
4:12	39
6:4	10, 39, 40, 41
7:7–8	170
7:7–10	171
10:14–15	171
18:15–19	78
19:15	70n33
28	133
30	133
30:11–14	77, 78

ANCIENT DOCUMENT INDEX

1 Samuel

12:1	145

2 Samuel

7:5–16	3
17:28	151

1 Kings

9	72, 147

2 Chronicles

12:1	145

Esther

14:17	151

Job

14:7–9	147

Psalms

19:119	133
69:9	74
89:1–37	3
143:11–12a	32

Isaiah

1–6	83
2:2–3	175
6:13	147
8:14	74
11:5	146
13:19	146
14:1–3	175
27:9	74, 175
28:16	74, 77
28:22	146
39	83
40–55	171
40–66	83
40:1–2	171
43	171
43:3–4	171
44:1–5	171
44:21–22	171
45:1–4	171
49	171
49:6	171
52	83. 84
52:1–10	171
52:5	81, 82–83, 84
52:7	74
52:11	159
54:1	112, 113
55:3	171
55:8	174
59:20f.	74
59:20–21	175

Jeremiah

1:5	109
11:14–17	147
15:16	122
23:5–6	175
31:33	131
32:37–42	175

Ezekiel

1:28	27
3:16–21	122
16	69
16:8	172
18:23	122
33:6–7	122
36:20f.	83
36:22–23	32
36:22–32	175
39:7	32
39:21	32
39:25	32

Ancient Document Index

39:27	175	**Amos**	
		9:11–15	175
Daniel			
1:8	151	**Habakkuk**	
1:12–16	151		
7:9–13	27	2:4	78
9:11	145		
10:3	151	**Zephaniah**	
Hosea		3:14–15	175
1:10	146	**Zechariah**	
2:2f.	172		
2:19–23	172–73	8:7–8	175
		8:13–15	175
Joel			
2:32	77		

New Testament

Matthew		9:1–30	87n7
		9:20f.	89
5:17	77	10	162–63
9:11	157	10–11	159
10:22	127n189	11:3	157
17:5	143n251	11:27–30	90n12
24:13	127n189	11:30	89, 90
		13:2	17n58
Mark		13:4	89
		13:14	89
13:13	127n189	13:15	88
		13:21–26	87n7
Luke		13:39	7, 87n7
		14:1	89
4:16–21	64	15	8, 87n7, 89, 90, 91n15, 154, 158
		15:1–35	87n7
Acts		15:2	89
		15:2–3	89
2:5–6	88	16:1	91
2:16	88	16:1–3	90, 91, 92, 94, 164
9:1–2	30	16:3	88n8, 91, 155, 164n327

Acts (continued)

16:13	89
17:1–2	89
17:2–3	88
17:8	87
17:10	89
17:17	89
18:4	88, 89
18:5–6	99
18:18	88
19:8	88, 89
21	93
21:17–26	90, 92, 94
21:20–26	88n8
21:20–28	88
21:23–24	93
21:23–26	90n13, 164
21:23–27	92
21:23–27a	93
21:28	125n179
22:3	17, 22, 72, 87, 88n8, 93, 94
22:17	88
23	88n8
23:6	88
23:21–26	88
24:5–9	125n179
24:14	88n8
24:18	92
25:8	88
26:4–5	17
26:5	88
28:17	88, 89
28:23	88
29:17f.	151

Romans

1–3	146
1–5	52
1–8	136, 145
1:1–2	105
1:1–14:23	69n28
1:2–3	69
1:16	3, 94, 110, 147n266, 148n267, 171
1:16–17	58
1:17	78
1:18	127
1:18–32	69
2	47
2–3	84
2–4	40
2:9–10	147n266
2:17	82
2:17–23	84
2:17–29	137n220
2:21–23	83
2:23–29	105
2:24	81–84
2:27	132n207
2:28	132n207
2:29	177
3:1–3	146
3:1–4	137n220
3:1–8	137n221, 141
3:1–9	136n219
3:4	76n57
3:10–18	71
3:21	46, 70, 76n58
3:21–31	54
3:29	18
3:29–31	39
3:29–4:35	10n19
3:31	3
4	138, 145, 146n262, 166, 177
4:1–12	72
4:10	72
4:17–18	70n33
5–8	40
5:9–10	71
5:12–19	33
5:15–12	71
6	12, 40
7	13, 52
7:2f.	36
7:6	132n107
7:7	70n33
7:7–25	12
7:12	132n207
7:14	132n207
8	132, 173

Ancient Document Index

8:4	133	11	79, 80–81, 84, 125, 127, 129, 138, 139, 145, 147, 174, 176
8:12–16	173		
8:13	143n251		
8:17	173	11:1	22, 65, 109, 153
8:21	79	11:1f.	79, 129
9	100, 127n190, 138, 139, 140, 145, 146–47	11:1–10	79
		11:1–32	140
9–11	20, 40, 54, 73, 74, 84, 115, 127n, 136–43, 145–48, 174, 179	11:2	72
		11:4	72, 147
		11:5	72, 147
9–15	141	11:7	142
9:2–3	129, 142	11:7–12	174
9:3	129	11:11	147
9:3–4	122	11:12	71
9:4–5	146	11:12–27	147
9:6	146, 177, 180	11:13–24	142
9:6f.	141	11:14	94
9:6ff.	80	11:15	144, 174
9:6–9	70	11:16	144
9:6–23	127n190	11:16–24	147
9:7	70	11:17	142
9:11–15	146	11:17ff.	145
9:12–19	71	11:17–18	148
9:14	72	11:17–24	129, 147–48n266, 166
9:16–22	146	11:17–25	3
9:17	146	11:17–26	180
9:18	72	11:23	145
9:18–29	146	11:23f.	145
9:22ff.	81, 139	11:24	71
9:24	18, 146	11:25	145
9:25	78–79, 80, 173n7	11:25ff.	123, 145
9:25–26	81, 142, 172	11:25–26	148
9:26	79	11:25–27	127, 174
9:33	73–74	11:25–32	115, 128, 148n267
10	139	11:26	74, 143, 144, 145, 185
10:4	2, 46, 48, 50, 52, 76, 103, 105, 164	11:28	142, 180, 185
		11:28ff.	144
10:5	75, 77, 78	11:29	139, 142
10:5f.	74	11:30–32	136n219
10:5–6	77	11:31	144
10:5–8	74–81	11:34	174
10:6	75, 77	12:1–14:4	40
10:6–8	78	12:2	152
10:12–13	10n19	12:17–18	126
10:15	74	13:8–10	2, 72
10:18–21	71	14f.	37

215

Romans (continued)

14–15	37, 150, 151–53, 167, 185
14:1	152
14:1–2	150
14:2	151
14:5	152
14:14	151
14:15	152
14:19–20	153
14:20	151
14:20–21	152
14:21	151
14:22	152
15	37, 73
15:3	74
15:4	69
15:7–13	151
15:8	136, 142, 179
15:9	136n219
15:19	94
15:25–29	161
15:27	142
16:24–27	69n28
16:25–27	69n28
16:26	69
19:6–8	77

1 Corinthians

1:23	18
5–7	70
5:1	36
6:16	70n33
7	15–16n51
7:2:38	15
7:7	126
7:8	89
7:10f.	36
7:17f.	166, 153, 185
7:18	164, 167, 180
7:19	90n14
7:20–23	15
7:39	36
8	151
8–9	11–12
8–10	37, 165
9	92
9:9–11	22n82
9:9–12	71
9:14	36
9:19ff.	19, 43
9:19–22	165
9:19–23	92, 164, 165, 166
9:20	92, 94, 164, 165–66
9:20ff.	166n331
9:21	166
9:22	166
10:1–4	74
10:11	70
10:18	177
10:25–27	36, 37
11:2–16	36
11:23–25	36
11:25	130
14:16	36
14:34	36
15:3–4	66
15:19	126
15:26	33
16:8	36
20	164

2 Corinthians

3	119, 131–32, 133
3:2	126
3:4–11	132
3:4–18	105, 118, 130, 184
3:6	134
3:7	131
3:7–8	71
3:8	132, 135
3:9	132
3:10	134
3:10–11	132
3:11	131, 132
3:13	131
3:14	130
3:17–18	131
4:4	60
6:17	159

11:22	22, 65, 95, 153	2:11–14	7, 37, 87n7, 91n15, 154–64
11:24	90n13, 109, 153	2:11–21	57
12	27	2:12	159
13:1	70n33	2:14	102, 158, 159
		2:14f.	163
		2:15	100, 106

Galatians

		2:15–16	156
1:1	107	2:21	45
1:6	96	3	55n73, 177
1:6f.	107	3:3	99
1:7	106	3:6f.	119
1:10–2:21	103	3:8	49, 70n33
1:11–13	101	3:10–13	71
1:11–17	97	3:10–29	51
1:11–2:21	101	3:11–12	51–52
1:12	99	3:13	45, 99
1:13	96, 97–98, 99, 100, 103, 104–5	3:13–14	64
		3:14	115, 179
1:13–14	95, 96, 97, 98, 99, 103, 104–5, 107–8, 109	3:15–17	134
		3:15–18	133–34
1:13–17	94, 95–102, 97, 104, 109–10, 184	3:15–4:11	133
		3:16	16, 70n33, 116
1:13–2:21	87n7	3:17	133–34
1:14	18, 22, 41, 42, 94, 95–96, 97, 98, 100, 106	3:18	133, 134
		3:19	45
1:15	68, 96, 99–100, 101, 104	3:21	133
		3:22–25	114
1:15–16	100, 108–9, 110	3:24	98, 104
1:15–16a	98	3:28	114, 158, 162, 167, 180
1:15–17	97, 108	3:29	115, 166
1:16f.	89	4	119
1:18	101	4:1	115
2	89, 91	4:1–10	114
2:1–2	101	4:7	115
2:1–10	90n12, 91n15	4:10	156
2:2	90n12	4:17	116
2:3	35, 90	4:21–31	22n82, 71, 76n57, 110–13, 116, 121, 122, 177
2:3–5	155		
2:4	76n57, 114, 119		
2:4–5	156	4:21–5:1	121
2:5	101	4:22	112
2:7	108	4:22f.	179
2:7–9	101	4:24	111, 114, 115, 116–17, 118, 120
2:9–9	18		
2:10	91n15, 161	4:24–31	113
		4:24a	116

Galatians (continued)

4:25	114, 119
4:25–26	117
4:26	120
4:27	112
4:28–29	115
4:30	110, 113, 114, 116, 117, 119, 120, 121
4:30–31	120
5:1	76n57, 114
5:2	3
5:3	36, 37, 107
5:12	45
5:13	76n57
6:15	177
6:16	106, 115, 167, 176–81
13–17	99
13:17	106
15:11	45

Philippians

1:20–26	15
3	135
3:2–3	177
3:2–11	135, 136, 185
3:4–11	108
3:5	35, 41
3:6	94
3:7	134, 135
3:7f.	135
3:7–11	135
3:8	135
4:5	126

1 Thessalonians

1:7–8	126
1:14–16	86n3, 129n194
2:13–16	125n179, 128
2:14	124–26, 184
2:14–16	123, 125n179, 127n190, 129
2:15	125–26
2:16	126, 127
2:23–16	127n
4:3	36
4:13–5:10	13

2 Timothy

1:5	91
3:15	91

Revelation

2:25	127n189

Apocryphya and Septuagint

Judith

8:6	151
10:5	151
12:1–2	151

1 Maccabees

2:23–28	98
2:42–48	98

2 Maccabees

5:27	151

Old Testament Pseudepigrapha

Testament of Levi

6.2	126n186

Philo

De vita contemplativa

4 S 37	151

Josephus

Life

2 S 14	151

Mishnah, Talmud, and Related Literature

b. Batba Batra

10a	98

b. Sanhedrin

97b–98a	98

BQ (*Baba Qamma*)

83a	21

Soṭah

49b	21

Ḥagiga

13a–15b	27

b. Yoma

86b	98

m. Nazir

3:6	88
5:4	88

Greek and Latin Works

Eusebius
Historia ecclesiastica

2.23:5	151

Hermas
Similitudes

9.27.3	127n189

www.ingramcontent.com/pod-product-compliance
Lightning Source LLC
Chambersburg PA
CBHW070250230426
43664CB00014B/2479